OVERCOME DEPRESSION AND DESPAIR AND FIND FREEDOM IN A LIFE OF HARMONY WITH YOURSELF

A decision you made early in life now rules your every waking and sleeping moment. That decision can lead to depression, suicide, drug addiction, alcoholism and great unhappiness. Or it may merely cause you to feel powerless over your life course, unable to have a loving relationship with another human being.

These decisions are called your "life script." You wrote it when you were still young, under pressure from your parents and the other grownups around you.

Now, Claude M. Steiner has written **Scripts People Live** to send you an important message: **It's not too late to decide what kind of script you want for your life—if any at all.**

SCRIPTS PEOPLE LIVE

shows you how to recognize your own life script, how to break free of its control, how to avoid passing harmful scripts on to your children.

AWARENESS: EXPLORING, EXPERIMENTING,
    EXPERIENCING by John O. Stevens
BEYOND FREEDOM AND DIGNITY by B. F. Skinner
THE DISOWNED SELF by Nathaniel Branden
DR. RUBIN, PLEASE MAKE ME HAPPY
    by Theodore I. Rubin, M.D.
THE FIFTY-MINUTE HOUR by Robert Lindner
THE GESTALT THERAPY BOOK by Joel Latner
GESTALT THERAPY VERBATIM
    by Frederick S. Perls, M.D.
IN AND OUT THE GARBAGE PAIL
    by Frederick S. Perls, M.D.
THE PSYCHOLOGY OF SELF-ESTEEM
    by Nathaniel Branden
SCRIPTS PEOPLE LIVE by Claude M. Steiner
THE SECRET STRENGTH OF DEPRESSION
    by Frederic F. Flach, M.D.

SCRIPTS
PEOPLE
LIVE

Transactional Analysis of Life Scripts

CLAUDE M. STEINER

BANTAM BOOKS · TORONTO · NEW YORK · LONDON

SCRIPTS PEOPLE LIVE

*A Bantam Book / published by arrangement with
Grove Press, Inc.*

PRINTING HISTORY

*Grove Press edition published September 1974
2nd printing .... October 1974
3rd printing .... January 1975*

*Psychology Today Book Club edition published November 1974
2nd printing .... January 1975*

Bantam edition / October 1975

*Bantam Books are published by Bantam Books, Inc. Its trade-
mark, consisting of the words "Bantam Books" and the portrayal of a bantam, is registered in the United States Patent
Office and in other countries. Marca Registrada. Bantam
Books, Inc., 666 Fifth Avenue, New York, New York 10019.*

PRINTED IN THE UNITED STATES OF AMERICA

I dedicate this book to Eric Berne
teacher
friend
father
brother

CONTENTS

TABLE OF FIGURES

Preface and
Acknowledgments

When I began writing this book, I intended it to be a revision of my previous book, *Games Alcoholics Play*, updated with respect to the therapy of alcoholics and expanded with respect to script theory. As the work proceeded, it quickly lost its intended character and became, instead, a whole new book on the Transactional Analysis of Life Scripts. I have reused some sections of *Games Alcoholics Play*, but this book is mostly an extensive and concise statement of recent developments in script theory. Where I have used sections of *Games Alcoholics Play*, I have carefully weeded out two words which I no longer feel the necessity to use. The two words that I've taken out and which occurred hundreds of times in that previous book were the words "cure" and "patient," both of which are, in my opinion, inextricably tied in with medical practice which, as I take pains to explain later, has nothing to do with the practice of psychotherapy, and the use of which perpetuates the notion that medicine and psychotherapy are in some way legitimately tied together when they are, in fact, not.

I have preserved the use of the word "diagnosis" against the objections of Joy Marcus who feels that "diagnosis" should have gone out with "cure" and "patient." I have done so because I feel that diagnosis is not necessarily connected with medical practice, and is a word which I wish to claim for use in the detection and therapy of scripts.

I hope I make it clear in this book that Eric Berne was the spring whence the major ideas of script analysis originated and that, without his encouragement and support, I would never have come to write this book. I also extensively credit Hogie Wyckoff for her contributions to my political awareness, particularly in relation to sex role scripting. Her insights into women's and men's scripts were the beginning of the study of banal scripts, which led to further joint developments concerning power, competition, and cooperation.

I wish to thank Carmen Kerr for her careful reading and criticism of Section 1; she helped me find and express with clarity and honesty the depths of my feelings for Eric Berne.

Robert Schwebel was the first to bring to my awareness the importance of cooperation when he introduced "cooperative games" to our work and the Radical Psychiatry Center. Thanks are due also to Richard Lichtman for his criticism of Section 1.

I also wish to thank Joy Marcus for her intensive reading of and suggestions about Section 3 and for her continuing input into my life and thinking during the last five years.

I want further to thank the members of the "body group" in which the understanding of the scripts for joylessness and the investigation of therapies regarding this script are slowly developing. Wyoming, Laura, Rick, Olivia, and Hogie, by openly offering their naked selves and willingly and openly regarding mine, have done much to help me understand the banal scripts which prevent us from fully enjoying and taking power over our bodies.

I wish also to thank the many people whom I worked with at the Radical Psychiatry Center from 1969 to 1972 and with whom I struggled and learned to understand power and its abuses, and with whose help I developed my ideas on cooperation.

Thanks are due to Marion Weisberg for suggesting the title *Scripts People Live*.

It is difficult to fairly acknowledge the contribution made by Susan Tatum, which could be easily stereotyped by saying she typed the various sections of this book. True, she did type and retype my writings, but to state her contribution in this way would be untrue and unreal; her thinking, her understanding, and her contributions are present throughout the pages of the book, and it is difficult to credit and value them completely. I also wish to thank Karen Parlette for her help in typing and putting together the last stages of the manuscript.

I also want to thank Fred Jordan, a kind and gentle man, whose occasional but well-timed reassurance and support made the anxious work of writing a large book easier, and whose eventual, thorough reading of it put it in its final present form.

—*Claude Steiner*
1974

Introduction

The Basic Assumptions of Transactional Analysis

Eric Berne, known to millions for having written the book *Games People Play,* is nevertheless not commonly known for what I consider the most important fact of his existence. Namely, that he was a far-reaching pioneer, a radical scientist in the field of psychiatry.

What I mean when I assert that Eric Berne was a radical is that he re-examined the basic assumptions held by psychiatry, and the investigations that he made resulted in ideas which were diametrically opposed to what was accepted as fact, in his day. Trained professionals, especially psychoanalytically trained ones, cannot accept his concepts without having to change, at the root—which is to say radically—what they have learned about what makes people tick, what makes them unhappy or causes dysfunction, and what it is that can bring about a change for them.

Before I go into details I want to briefly state the three concepts which together set transactional analysis apart from the mainstream of psychiatry today:

1. *People are born O.K.* Taking the position "I'm O.K., You're O.K." is the minimum requirement for good psychiatry and lasting emotional and social well-being.

2. *People in emotional difficulties are nevertheless full, intelligent human beings.* They are capable of

understanding their troubles and the process which
liberates people from them. They must be involved in
the healing process if they are to solve their difficulties.

3. *All emotional difficulties are curable, given adequate knowledge and the proper approach.* The difficulty psychiatrists are having with so-called schizophrenia, alcoholism, depressive psychosis, and so on is
the result of psychiatric ineptness or ignorance rather
than incurability.

PEOPLE ARE O.K.

The first and most important concept, in my belief,
which Berne introduced to psychiatry is embodied in
his aphorism: "People are born princes and princesses,
until their parents turn them into frogs." Eric Berne
presented many of his most radical ideas in the form
of aphorisms which were veiled statements that disguised the implications of his thoughts from the minds
of those who heard them in order to soften the blow of
their meaning. Stated in this oblique way, the notion
that people are born O.K. and that the seeds of emotional disturbance, unhappiness, and madness are not
in them but in their parents who pass it on to them is
made palatable to those who, faced with the full
meaning of that assertion, would almost surely reject
it.

Stemming from "faith in human nature," the conviction that people are at birth and by nature O.K.,
Berne developed the existential positions which have
been recently popularized by the writings of Amy and
Thomas Harris.[1] Existential positions are feelings
about oneself and others. The first position is: "I'm
O.K., You're O.K." When people, due to circumstances
of their lives, shift from the central position to the
other three positions—namely, "I'm O.K., You're not
O.K.," or "I'm not O.K., You're O.K.," and "I'm not
O.K., You're not O.K."—they also become increasingly

[1]Harris, Thomas A. *I'm OK—You're OK.* New York: Harper &
Row, 1969.

dysfunctional, disturbed, unhappy, and less able to function adequately in a social grouping.

The "I'm O.K., You're O.K." life position is the position people need to have in order to achieve their fullest potential. It is not intended to promote the notion that all of people's actions are acceptable. The existential position "I'm O.K., You're O.K." is a point of view about people apart from their actions and power, a point of view required in intimate, close relationships in order for emotional and social well-being to be possible. Berne implies that this attitude is not only a good point of view to hold but a true one as well.

When a psychiatrist regards people from that position (I'm O.K., You're O.K.—and so are your mother, your father, your sister, your brother, and your neighbor), he immediately places himself completely apart from most other psychiatrists and from his training. He no longer looks within the "patient" for a neurotic conflict, a psychosis, a character disorder, or some other diagnostic category of psychopathology, all of which were considered to be insulting by Berne; but he looks instead for what it is that this person is exposed to in the way of social interaction and pressures which make his behavior and feelings quite adequately explainable. Instead of seeing people seeking psychiatric help, no matter how disturbed, as not O.K. he thinks, "there but for the grace of God go I," which implies a belief that it is external circumstances and not internal weakness that makes people into psychiatric "patients." This approach is not new in psychiatry, since it was anticipated by Wilhelm Reich and Carl Rogers, and is the approach of Ronald Laing. It is, however, simply very much in disrepute and without support in psychiatric circles. The stance "I'm O.K., You're O.K." in psychiatry is quite extraordinary since most psychiatrists follow the medical model of illness in which the very first thing the physician does when confronted with a patient is to arrive at a diagnosis by looking at, speaking with, and examining exclusively the person to find what is wrong with him or her ("You're not O.K., we need only figure out how").

The consequence of his belief in the basic sound-
ness of people, is that transactional analysis shifts attention away from what goes on inside of people and
instead devotes its attention to what goes on between
people which is very often not O.K., that is, destructive and oppressive.

Let me restate, in my own words, this first of the
three basic assumptions of transactional analysis as
follows:

1. *Human beings are, by nature, inclined to and
capable of living in harmony with themselves, each
other, and nature.*

If left alone (given adequate nurturing), people
have a natural tendency to live, to take care of themselves, to be healthy and happy, to learn to get along
with each other, and to respect other forms of life.

If people are unhealthy, unhappy, uninterested in
learning, uncooperative, selfish, or disrespectful of life,
it is the result of external oppressive influences, which
overpower the more basic positive life tendency that
is built-in to them. Even when overpowered, this tendency remains dormant, so that it is always ready to
express itself when oppression lifts. Even if it is not
given a chance to be expressed in a person's lifetime
this human life tendency is passed on to each succeeding generation of newborns.

COMMUNICATION AND CONTRACTS

The second radical point of view advanced by
Berne has to do with the way he related to the
people he worked for. His views in that area were not
veiled by aphorisms and jokes. Berne was vigorous
in pursuing relationships with his clients in which he
treated them as equals with equal responsibility
(though, at times, different tasks) toward the common goal of psychotherapy and with equal intelligence and potential to contribute to the process.

The language and mode of communication which
he began to use when he introduced his methods was
so unusual and unorthodox that it brought him into
almost immediate conflict with other practitioners in

the field. Specifically, he assumed that his patients could understand what he was thinking about them and that he could speak to them without speaking *down* to them. He rejected the usual psychiatric practice of using one language in speaking with people and another in speaking with psychiatric colleagues. As he developed the new concepts of his theory, he used, in every instance, words which were immediately understandable to most people. For example, when he observed that people act in three very distinct ways, he called those three modes the Parent, the Adult, and the Child, instead of calling them some other, more "scientific" name such as the exteropsyche, neopsyche, and archaeopsyche. When he began to speak about human communication and recognition he did not name the unit of interaction an "interpersonal communication unit," but he called it a stroke. He did not call the troubles that people repeatedly have with each other "social dysfunction patterns," but he called them games. He did not call the way in which people live out their lives based on early decisions a "lifetime repetition compulsion," but he called it a script.

In doing this he made a very clear-cut choice to appeal not to his fellow professionals, who were in fact almost universally repelled by his new terminology and concepts, but to appeal to the people he worked with by providing them with a channel of communication in which he and they could all work together. This point of view was based on the belief that everyone, including people called "patients," has at her or his[1] disposal a functioning Adult ego state which only needs to be activated, and encouraged.

The logical consequence of this point of view was that, for instance, he was willing to invite his clients to any discussion or conference that he had with another professional about them. He instituted the stunning practice of having inmates in a mental hospital

---

[1]In order to avoid the sexist connotations implicit in the use of solely masculine pronouns such as "he" and "his," I have throughout this book deliberately included "she" and "her" as well.

observe the staff and trainees as they discussed their group therapy sessions.[1] These discussions, in which the staff was under the close scrutiny of the patients just as the patients had been under close scrutiny by the staff, was based on another aphorism of Berne's: "Anything that's not worth saying in front of a patient is not worth saying at all."

It's not surprising that many professionals who were subjected to this "fish bowl" approach to psychiatry found themselves extraordinarily uncomfortable. It forced them to face how much of what they said at staff conferences was mystified and glibly one-up to the people they were supposedly serving.

A further extension of this approach was the all-important therapeutic contract (see Chapter 20). The therapeutic contract is simply an agreement between a person and her or his therapist which places responsibility on both parties involved. The client asks for help and gives full consent and cooperation to the process of psychotherapy, and the therapist accepts the responsibility for helping to effect the desired changes and for staying within the bounds of the contract. Without this agreement, according to transactional analysis, psychotherapy cannot properly occur. This excludes from the realm of psychotherapy those activities which are basically policing operations in which psychiatrists or mental health workers force people, whom they call "patients," into weekly or daily brainwashing or sensory deprivation sessions without their approval or participation.

It also excludes the many vague forms of "therapeutic" activities in which nothing in particular is offered and nothing in particular is expected—least of all an actual cure or remedy to the clients' difficulties. Further, this approach implies that unlike medical knowledge, which is (correctly and incorrectly) seen as so complex that it cannot be understood by laymen, psychiatric knowledge can and should be made available and comprehensible to all parties involved.

[1]Berne, Eric. "Staff-Patient Staff Conferences." *American Journal of Psychiatry* 125 (1968): 286–293.

CURABILITY

Berne believed that people with psychiatric difficulties can be cured. This means that not just the
mildly neurotic, but the drug abuser, the severely depressed, the "schizophrenic," everyone with a functional psychiatric disorder (that is, a disorder which is
not based on an identifiable physical disease or gross,
detectable chemical imbalance) was seen as curable.
By curing patients Berne did not mean, as he often
remarked, "turning schizophrenics into brave schizophrenics" or changing alcoholics into arrested alcoholics, but to help them, as he also often said, "to get
back their membership in the human race."

The notion that psychiatrists could in fact "cure"
the severe emotional disturbances of the people they
work with was as radical and stunning a notion as has
ever been introduced recently into psychiatry. Nevertheless, Eric Berne was adamant on this point. For
transactional analysts whom he trained he gave the
following rule: "A transactional analyst will try to cure
his patient in the first session. If he does not succeed
he will spend the next week thinking about it and
then will try to cure him in the second session, and so
on until he succeeds or admits failure." The fact that
psychiatrists have had no success with alcoholism,
schizophrenia, and depression did not mean to Berne
that those disturbances were incurable, as had been
the psychiatric profession's inclination to think; it simply meant that psychiatrists had not yet developed an
approach which was effective with them. The usual
cop-out of psychiatric professionals with respect to
people that they cannot help (which is to ascribe
them incurable or unmotivated status) was unacceptable to Eric Berne.

I quote Berne from his last public address:[1]

---

[1]The title of this speech delivered on June 20, 1970, just three
weeks before he died, was "Away from the Impact of Interpersonal
Interaction or Non-Verbal Participation" and the full text appeared
in the Eric Berne Memorial Issue of the *Transactional Analysis
Journal* I:1, January 1971, pp. 6–13, which can be obtained from
the International Transactional Analysis Association, 3155 College
Avenue, Berkeley, Ca. 94705.

Another way that we (psychotherapists) get out of doing anything is the fallacy of the whole personality. 'Since the whole personality is involved,' (we ask) 'how can you expect to cure anybody, particularly in less than five years?' O.K. Here's how. If a man gets an infected toe from a splinter, he starts to limp a little, and his leg muscles tighten up. In order to compensate for his tight leg muscles his back muscles have to tighten up. And then his neck muscles tighten up; then his skull muscles; and pretty soon he's got a headache. He gets a fever from the infection; his pulse goes up. In other words, everything is involved—his whole personality, including his head that's hurting, and he's even mad at the splinter or whoever put the splinter there, so he may spend a lot of time going to a lawyer. It involves his whole personality. So he calls up this surgeon. He comes in and looks at the guy and says: 'Well, this is a very serious thing. It involves the whole personality as you can see. Your whole body's involved. You've got a fever; you're breathing fast; your pulse is up; and all these muscles are tight. I think about three or four years—but I can't guarantee results—in our profession we don't make any guarantees about doing anything—but I think in about three or four years—of course a lot of it is going to be up to you—we'll be able to cure this condition.' The patient says, 'Well, uh, O.K. I'll let you know tomorrow.' And he goes to see another surgeon. And the other surgeon says, 'Oh, you've got an infected toe from this splinter.' And he takes a pair of tweezers and pulls out the splinter, and the fever goes down, the pulse goes down, then the head muscles relax, and then the back muscles relax, and then the feet muscles relax. And the guy's back to normal within forty-eight hours, maybe less. So that's the way to practice psychotherapy. Like you find a splinter and you pull it out. That's going to make a lot of people mad, and they'll prove that the patient was not completely analyzed. And it's not cricket to say, 'Okay doctor, how many patients have you completely analyzed?' Because the answer to that is: 'Are you aware how hostile you are?' So every-

*body's writing papers. And there's only one paper to
write, which is called* How to Cure Patients—*that's
the only paper that's really worth writing if you're
really going to do your job.*

In this statement Berne, again in his usual veiled
manner, makes a most startling analogy. Does he
mean that psychiatry could be as simple a matter as
pulling a splinter, given that we understood emotional disturbance as well as we understand infections? Did he mean that speedy cures can be effected
of disturbances that involve the "whole personality"?
Did he imply that psychiatrists are mystifying their
patients and evading their responsibilities?

I believe that he did, and his faith in this point of
view has spurred me on to write this book.

The above three basic principles are deeply imbedded in the fiber of transactional analysis. I have
highlighted them because they are, to me, the most
fundamental aspects of the theory. Of course, transactional analysis includes a great deal more than what
I have said above, much of which I will discuss in the
pages of this book. But the above three points are, to
me, principles of transactional analysis that cannot be
dispensed with without uprooting and disemboweling
it.

I'm O.K. You're O.K. what's your game give me a stroke Cha Cha Cha

I am fearful that transactional analysis, which was
originally created as a psychiatric theory and practice,
will become, because of its popular appeal and features, a consumer item, sold at every counter, plasti-
cized, merchandized, and made more and more palatable to larger and larger crowds of consumers. It is
in danger of slowly losing its fundamental distinguishing features and reverting to the more easily acceptable notions in which people are assumed to be born
with defective personalities, in which psychiatrists
treat people as if they were invalids, and in which

people with emotional difficulties are seen as ill and
often incurable.

I observe that transactional analysis is in the process of being homogenized, reinterpreted, and thus
destroyed by the mass market which is using it so as
to make the largest amount of profit without regard
for its scientific integrity. I expect, a bit facetiously
perhaps, that soon there will be, across the country,
transactional analysis gymnasia, churches, and hamburger stands, just as there are already transactional
analysis do-it-yourself home therapy kits, record sets,
Hawaii tours, and quickie workshops to improve business productivity. Not that gymnasia, hamburger
stands, or do-it-yourself kits are to be disapproved of
in themselves; but the ones I see so far have more to
do with how to make a quick buck and add to the
gross national product, than with Eric Berne's transactional analysis.

An example (of the changes being made in transactional analysis) appears in *I'm OK—You're OK,* where
Amy and Tom Harris introduce a subtle but fundamental shift. They list the unhealthy position "I'm not
O.K., You're O.K." as being the first and "universal position" from which all people need to extricate themselves. With calm disregard for Berne's firm stance on
this point, the Harrises reverse one of Eric Berne's
fundamental points about people and re-establish the
notion that people begin life not O.K., needing to rid
themselves of their original sin.

In an interview in *The New York Times Magazine,*
November 22, 1972, this point of view is made clear.
The interviewer writes: "The first position (I'm Not
O.K., You're O.K.) Harris maintains, in the face of
much criticism, is the universal position occupied by
the child, who is small, dirty, and clumsy in a world
controlled by tall, clean, and deft adults. (Or so it
seems to the child.) Here lies a critical theoretical
difference between Harris and Eric Berne; for as Harris described it to me, Berne believed that we are
born princes and the civilizing process turns us into
frogs, while he himself believes that we are all born
frogs."

Harris, whether he means to or not, retreats to the commonplace and demeaning notion that people are by nature tainted and therefore incapable of living life adequately without a large measure of authoritative, civilizing "help."

Transactional analysis is being used by banks and airlines and race tracks as a device taught to their employees to better deal with their customers. There might be nothing wrong with this if what was taught was, in fact, transactional analysis. But the fact is that transactional analysis is being corrupted and transformed to serve the needs of the banks, airlines, and race tracks, not only in subtle ways which strip it of its basic principles, but even in the very crudest ways.

For example, in an article called "OTB Placating Losers with an EGO Triple," again in *The New York Times* (March 21, 1973), we read:

The T.A.C.T. system (Transactional Analysis for Customer Treatment) was purchased by OTB (Off-Track Betting) from American Airlines, which developed it from the theories found in I'm OK— You're OK. *According to the author, Dr. Thomas A. Harris, everyone's personality is divided into three ego states: parent, adult and child.*

In the OTB training course, sellers and cashiers are taught to recognize which state a horseplayer may be in—and to react with the proper ego state of their own.

For example, a customer who yells and threatens to punch the employee or stick a hand through the window would be in a child ego state. A customer behaving like a "parent" would be authoritative and demanding, likely to make sweeping statements. In the adult ego state, the decision-making part of the triad, the person would be calm and rational.

"We try to swing the behavior on to an adult level," said Erika Van Acker, director of training at OTB. *"But sometimes you have to play a different role. If an angry customer is coming from a heavy child ego state, the clerk might want to go into a heavy parent ego state.*

"He might say something like, 'This kind of behavior isn't tolerated here.'"

The terms "stroke" and "stroking" are very big in T.A.C.T. "Usually," says Miss Van Acker, "all an irate customer needs is a stroke. Just be nice to them, and they calm down."

The reader might ask what is wrong with the above use of transactional analysis. Briefly, transactional analysis was invented for use as a contractual therapeutic technique. Berne was very suspicious and antagonistic to one-sided situations where one person held all the cards. Perhaps it was because of this that he enjoyed the game of poker where everyone starts with an even chance. In any case, transactional analysis was designed as a two-way, cooperative, contractual process; its one-sided use as a tool for behavior control is an abuse of its potency, similar to slipping a customer a sedative in a coke so that he'll buy a used car.

I am afraid that within five years transactional analysis is going to be completely discredited because of such misuse and that its value will be discarded by any serious-minded person. It is one of my purposes to present a clear, sober, understandable exposition of transactional analysis which is true to the principles that Eric Berne postulated.[1] The profound and radical are being taken out of transactional analysis. In this book I want to put them back in.

Eric Berne

Eric Berne was forty-six years old, a physician and a psychiatrist when he abandoned his training as a psychoanalyst after fifteen years of pursuing the title of psychoanalyst.

---

[1] I believe that the International TA Association is failing to protect the educational and scientific status of TA by taking a completely laissez-faire stance with respect to its members' exploitation-for-gain of the system. (See Steiner, Claude M. "Inside TA." *Issues in Radical Therapy* I,2 (1973): 3–4.)

He parted, as he said, "on good terms" when his 1956 application for membership as a psychoanalyst was rejected by the San Francisco Psychoanalytic Institute. The rejection was probably quite painful to him but it spurred him to intensify his long-standing ambition to add something new to psychoanalytic theory.

He never spoke about why he was rejected, probably because he was angry about it. I suspect that he was not submissive enough to psychoanalytic concepts (he certainly wasn't when I met him two years later). His main bone of contention with psychoanalysis at that time was that he felt that an effective therapist had to be more active in his pursuit of his patients' cures than psychoanalysts were allowed to be.

For about ten years, he had been doing research on intuition. His interest in the subject started when, as an army psychiatrist, as he processed thousands of army discharges daily, he began to play a little game to entertain himself. The game consisted of an attempt to guess the profession of a dischargee after hearing the answer to these two questions: "Are you nervous?" and "Have you ever been to see a psychiatrist?"

He found that he was able to guess the profession of the men, especially if they were mechanics or farmers, with remarkable accuracy.

These findings led to the writing of a series of articles on intuition (see Dusay[1] for a review of these articles) which culminated in the development of transactional analysis.

As a physician he had been trained to diagnose "psychopathology" and to apply to his patients psychiatric views of what they were and to feel free to impose upon them what they "ought" to be. Thus, it was unusual for him to be "open-minded" to information detected by his intuition and to use it without prejudgment.

This is when, as he often said, he put aside all the

[1]Dusay, John M. "Eric Berne's Studies in Intuition." *Transactional Analysis Journal* I,1 (1971): 34–45.

"jazz" he had learned and "began to listen to what the patients were saying."

Thus, Berne began to use his findings about intuition in his therapeutic work. Instead of using the notions and categories learned by him as a psychiatrist, instead of deciding that a person was, for instance, a "severe latent homosexual" or a "paranoid schizophrenic," he "tuned in" to the person and gathered information by using his intuition.

For instance, a man whom he would have diagnosed as a "severe latent homosexual" was seen by Berne's intuition as a man who felt "as though he were a very young child standing naked and sexually excited before a group of his elders, blushing furiously and writhing with almost unbearable embarrassment." He called this latter description of the man an "ego image"; that is, the therapist's intuitive image of the person which in some way describes his ego.[1] It is important to note here that the crucial difference between the ego image and the "severe latent homosexual" diagnosis is that the information about the ego image came mostly from his client, whereas the information about the "latent homosexual" diagnosis would have come mostly from Eric Berne and his psychoanalytic teachers.

Berne continued to use ego images in his therapeutic hour, and found that relating to a person in terms of what he intuited about their feelings and experiences was much more effective in helping them than was relating to them in terms of the diagnosis that he would have made as a psychiatrist.

He began to see in every patient an ego image which related to the person's childhood, so that he gradually incorporated in every one of his psychiatric cases an understanding of the person's childhood feelings as manifested throughout the interviews. One woman's childhood ego image was "a little blond girl standing in a fenced garden full of daisies"; another

[1]Berne, Eric. *Intuition v. the Ego Image.* Reprinted from the *Psychiatric Quarterly*, Vol. 31, October 1957, pp. 611–27. Utica, New York: State Hospitals Press.

ego image was "a boy scared riding in the passenger
seat of a car while his angry father drives at top
speed."

Eventually he saw that childhood ego images existed in every person, and he named them ego states.
He saw then that the Child ego state was distinct
from another "grownup" ego state which was the one
that the person presented to the world and which
was most obvious to everyone. Later he saw that there
were two "grownup" ego states, one rational which
he called the Adult and the other not necessarily rational, which he called the Parent, because it seemed
to be copied from the person's parents.

He continued to observe his patients, and to disregard information learned in his training. He discovered the importance of strokes, and time structuring.
He observed transactions, games, pastimes, and eventually scripts. By the end of the sixties his theory was
almost completely developed.

He eventually abandoned the use of psychiatric
diagnoses. He often told a joke about the way that
people are diagnosed: the person who has less initia-
tive than the therapist is called passive-dependent
and the person who has more is called a sociopath.

He always maintained theoretical ties with psychoanalysis but these became increasingly less important in his thinking over the years and almost completely absent from his group work.

At first he postulated that transactional analysis was
useful in bringing about "social control," that is, control over "acting out" while psychoanalysis did the
real therapeutic job. Slowly he began to see transactional analysis doing the main job of "curing" the patients and psychoanalytic technique being used in the
obscure work of script analysis. Later, even script
analysis became non-psychoanalytic, and then psychoanalytic thinking only became manifest in an occasional case presentation.[1]

---

[1] I have edited tape recordings of such presentations by Berne at
his weekly Seminar into an eight-hour tape called *Eric Berne: Out
of His Later Years* that can be obtained from: TA/Simple, Box
5155, Berkeley, Ca. 94705.

Scripts

In the early years of transactional analysis Eric Berne was still a psychoanalyst by method; that is to say, he still practiced one-to-one, on-the-couch psychotherapy with intensive personal analysis and scrutiny. The work he did during these individual sessions included script analysis. The theory of scripts was part of the transactional analysis theory from the very beginning. In his very first book on transactional analysis[1] he said,

> Games appear to be segments of larger, more complex sets of transactions called scripts ... A script is a complex set of transactions, by nature recurrent, but not necessarily recurring since a complete performance may require a whole lifetime ... The object of script analysis is to 'close the show and put a better one on the road.'

Berne thought scripts were the result of the repetition compulsion, a psychoanalytic concept which postulates that people have a tendency to repeat unhappy childhood events, and he felt that the task of script analysis is to free people from their compulsion to relive the situation, and start them on some other path. Berne was of the opinion that group therapy was quite useful in providing information about the script so that a few weeks in the group may have yielded more information than many months on the couch. Yet he felt that "since scripts are so complex and full of idiosyncracies, however, it is not possible to do adequate script analysis in group therapy alone."[2] and it remained to find an opportunity in individual sessions to elucidate what was learned in group.

---

[1]Berne, Eric. *Transactional Analysis in Psychotherapy*. New York: Grove Press, 1961.

[2]Bernie, Eric. *Transactional Analysis in Psychotherapy*. New York: Grove Press, 1961.

Thus Eric Berne practiced script analysis from the very beginning of his discovery of transactional analysis, but he practiced it largely in individual sessions. Over the years he gradually abandoned the practice of psychoanalysis while retaining the formal, namely weekly or biweekly, individual sessions on the couch, during which he did script analysis.

Occasionally Eric would present a segment of an ongoing script analysis; and these presentations tended to be about people who repeated certain long-term patterns over and over again on one hand, or people who seemed to have a script in which life had been programmed to last a limited number of years.

Eric Berne's Script

I met Eric Berne one Tuesday evening in 1958 at his Washington Street office and home in San Francisco. I don't recall the subject matter of that evening's discussion, but I do recall very clearly that at some time after the meeting while I was having what was to become the usual 7-Up he came to me and said, "You talk well. I hope you'll come back."

I did. And over the next years I became intimately acquainted with him. It was a slow, building relationship that took many years to warm up. There were some bad spots in it when I thought I would quit him, and many fine moments. During the last year of his life our relationship was solid, and I'm thankful that when he died it was clear to both of us that we had a deep, mutual love.

Starting sometime in 1967 Eric Berne met with a group of interested persons, mostly mental health professionals, every Tuesday evening from 8:30 to 10:00 with refreshments afterwards. If you rang the bell earlier than 8:20 he would not answer it; the evening ended when everyone (except for Eric Berne, of course) went home sometimes as late as one or two in the morning.

He was always there, except when he went on a lecture tour or vacation or (this happened very rarely) if he was sick. The seminars were led by him and many were tape-recorded. Every week's topic was prearranged and whoever presented was expected to ask a question of the group. Eric Berne would fill in when there was no one to present and sometimes he cut presentations short if they weren't going well. Sometimes he would read from forthcoming books, taking and using our feedback, sometimes he presented a meeting of one of his groups or one of the "cases" he was working with.

During meetings and in general he allowed no mystifications, no hierarchical or professional pomposity—or "jazz" as he was apt to call it. When in the presence of such mystifying behavior he would listen patiently; then, biting on his pipe and arching his eyebrows, say something like, "This is very well and good; all *I* know is that the patient is not getting cured."

He cut through professional mystifications by insisting on short words, short sentences, short papers, short meetings, short presentations. He discouraged adjectives like "passive," "hostile," "dependent," and encouraged the use of verbs in descriptions of human beings. He found words ending in "ic" (alcoholic, schizophrenic, manic) to be especially insulting.

He did everything he could to insure that during working hours of scientific meetings his and others' Adults were fully alert and maximally capable of performing their task. He discouraged physical stroking by therapists in groups, drinking coffee or alcoholic beverages during meetings, or allowing "bright ideas" (devious bids for attention) to intrude themselves into the proceedings. From scientific meetings he banned cop-outs (through excuses), glossing over (with big words), distractions (bright ideas and hypothetical examples), or slurping (of drinks).

He spent every Tuesday and Wednesday in San Francisco where he had a private practice and a couple of consulting jobs and then he flew back to Carmel where he wrote and had a second practice. He spent his weekends in Carmel and went to the beach as often as he could.

His main task seemed to be writing. I believe he put that ahead of all other things in life.

He was a man of strong principles; in his book *Transactional Analysis in Psychotherapy* the dedication reads:

In Memoriam
Patris Mei David
Medicinae Doctor Et Chirurgiae Magister
atque Pauperibus Medicus.

This description of his father signifies to me what Eric's life principles were.

His ever-present goal was: "To cure patients." Tied to this goal was his aversion of staff conferences and certain types of writing, the purpose of which, he felt, was to develop *post hoc* excuses or explanations for not doing the job.

He was proud of his father's dignified poverty as a country physician. He suspected persons whose eye was more than casually trained on making a dollar, and when he felt that making money was a primary reason in a person's pursuit of transactional analysis he did not hesitate to chide and criticize them. He often tested us in San Francisco by openly announcing requests for TA speakers which carried no honoraria, and took arch notice of who accepted such engagements and who didn't. He was self-conscious about his own earnings and became unconcerned with small expenses (such as the extra 25¢ required at Carmel's Highland Inn for Roquefort dressing or the cost of an extra fancy shirt) only after his accountant convinced him that unless he spent his money on himself it would be spent by Uncle Sam. He seemed to want to be poor and dignified. Dignity was of the utmost importance, so that while he was parsimonious with his money he was not interested in cheap, bargain basement merchandise or "getting it wholesale."

He had a strong allegiance to the brotherhood of physicians, and always wanted to maintain ties with traditional modes. This prevented him from making Parental criticism of the medical or psychiatric pro-

fessions as a whole, although his Child felt quite free
to deride and make fun of the practices of individual
members of it.

On the other hand, he was devilish, witty, naughty.
This had its most concrete but veiled expression in
the irrepressible humor found throughout his writings,
of which the article, "Who was Condom?"[1] (yes, condom as in contraceptive) was a prime example.

He was shy and he had a great interest in the fun-
loving childlike part (the Child) of other persons. His
theory came largely from his intuitive, Child ego state
(see Chapter 1). He loved and admired children and
the Child in others, but his shyness did not allow him
to express or expose his own unless things were very
safe. He loved to set up occasions for himself to get
strokes and this is why we always had a "party" after
seminars. He loved "jumping up-and-down" parties
and was very nasty to people who got in the way of
the fun by being stuffy or "grownup."

But, in my estimation, occasions where he got
strokes and had fun happened very seldom for him
and his life was work-oriented and driven by his main
purpose: writing books about curing people.

One of the brilliant ideas that Berne introduced is
that people's lives are preordained from early in life
by a script which they then follow faithfully. I believe that Eric was himself under the influence of a life
script that called for an early death of a broken heart.
This tragic ending was the result of very strong injunctions against loving others and accepting others'
love on the one hand, and equally strong attributions
to be an independent and detached individual on the
other.

I know that even he would argue with me and remind me that coronary heart disease is hereditary and
that he did everything he could to take care of his
heart; he watched his diet, exercised, and had frequent checkups. Medically, he covered all bases. But,
still, I feel otherwise. When I think of his death it has

[1]Bernstein, E. Lennard. "Who Was Condom?" *Human Fertility*
5,6 (1940): 172–76.

an eerie quality of having been a shocking surprise
and yet no surprise at all. Some part of him and me
knew it was going to happen and when. Another part
of him pretended that it wouldn't, and I went right
along with the pretense.

Berne was very interested in the phenomenon of
life spans of predetermined length. On several occasions he presented cases in which a person expected
to live only to his fortieth or sixtieth year, and, as can
be readily checked in his last book, *What Do You Say
After You Say Hello?*,[1] he was especially fascinated
by people who had a history of heart disease. In fact,
he mentions almost no cause of death other than coronary disease. The meaning of this became completely
clear to me only after he died; I knew that Berne's
father had died when he was eleven years old, and
that his mother died when she was sixty years old of a
coronary. Berne's life span turned out to be a few
days longer than his mother's, and he died for the
same reason. I believe that he had a limited life-
expectancy script which he lived out just as planned.
He never clearly stated his very conscious understanding of the possibility that he would die at age sixty,
but in retrospect everything he said about coronary
disease and limited life scripts points to the fact that
he himself was under the sway of a limited life-span
script and that he knew it. On his sixtieth birthday, at
his birthday party, he told a group of us how he had
finished the last two books that he wanted to write,
and he was now ready to enjoy life. Yet, a couple of
weeks later he announced that he was starting a new
book; a psychiatry textbook for medical students. In
my opinion, he gave himself no quarter right up to the
last day of his life, and then, just as planned, his heart
gave way.

It is true that Berne took care of his heart in some
ways, but in others he was unable to take care of it at
all. I am filled with sadness when I think of how much
he was loved and yet how little of this love benefited
him; how little reached his heart to soothe it. Berne's

---

[1] New York: Grove Press, 1972; Bantam Books, 1973.

loving relationships were short-lived and did not give
him the comfort which he needed and desired. He
defended his detached and lonely stance and pursued
his work alone. Thinking about it I can get quite
angry just as one might get angry at someone who
clearly neglects their physical health by eating too
much or smoking. The fact is that Berne may have
taken care of his heart medically (though he never
stopped smoking his pipe, from which he inhaled the
first puff whenever he lit it), but he failed to do so
emotionally.

He was not receptive to caring concern; he listened
politely when someone criticized his stroking situation or his individualism and competitiveness, but he
followed his own counsel to the end. When he required psychotherapy he did not work in a group or
consult a transactional analyst, but worked with a psychoanalyst in individual psychotherapy.

He was by no means completely passive with respect to his needs for love and human contact. He
developed important concepts related to love. His
theory was concerned with transactions between people, loving among them. He was interested in relationships. He developed the concept of strokes which
publicly was the word for the "unit of human recognition," but which we understand as the unit of human
love. During the last years of his life he wrote the
books *Sex in Human Loving*[1] and *What Do You Say
After You Say Hello?* Both of these were, in my opinion, partial attempts to break through his own personal script limitations. Unfortunately, his and my insights about strokes and scripts came too late to be of
any advantage to him personally.

In fact, in the early period of transactional analysis
(1955–1965), Berne subtly and unwittingly discouraged us from studying strokes, intimacy and scripts.
Intimacy, which is one of the ways in which human
beings can structure time according to Berne, was defined by him as a situation that develops when there

---

[1]New York: Simon and Schuster, 1971.

is no withdrawal, no rituals, no games, no pastimes, and no work. Intimacy was defined by Berne by exclusion. That is to say, it was not defined. Further, Berne believed that intimacy was a generally unattainable state, and that a person could consider themselves lucky if they experienced 15 minutes of intimacy in their lifetime. At a certain point at which the Carmel Transactional Analysis Seminar was investigating strokes and began to use techniques involving physical stroking, Eric Berne got quite alarmed and made the public pronouncement at one of the yearly conferences that "anyone who touches their patients is not doing transactional analysis."

Berne's injunction against touching in groups had a measure of reason. He worried that Transactional Analysis would become, as Gestalt seemed to be rapidly becoming, a therapy in which therapists felt free to involve themselves sexually with the people in their groups. He was a highly conscientious therapist and felt that this kind of activity would interfere with the success of therapy and give transactional analysis a bad name. It was because of this that he did not allow his followers to touch the people they worked for and with. The injunction was not really meant to prevent stroking among people, but it did tend to have that effect. He himself was not effective in obtaining for himself the strokes that he needed. It is also interesting to note that in all of his transactional analysis writings (about 2000 pages' worth) he devoted less than twenty-five pages to the topic of strokes.

With respect to scripts, he had a similar veiled attitude. Those of us who heard his presentations about his script analysis work were quite mystified by it. It seemed a complicated, in-depth, almost magical process which only Eric Berne really knew; and one that we, the younger, more practical, less individual therapy inclined colleagues either did not find really interesting or thought to be too advanced and complicated. His discussions about scripts remained couched in psychoanalytic jargon and technique unlike all the other work. Scripts were unconscious, repetition compulsion phenomena, their therapy to be pursued in one-to-one therapy.

It is my opinion that, as is the case with every great innovator, Eric Berne's personal life script set a limitation to his life and to the full exploration of the phenomena that he was interested in. In his case, the fact that he had a life-limited script, based on injunctions that stood in the way of obtaining strokes, prevented him from fully exploring scripts and strokes theoretically and caused him to throw up subtle barriers for his followers. These barriers had eventual consequences for him; his own script was unclear to him and hence unavailable for change. The injunctions concerning strokes which kept his script operative and his heart aching went unchallenged. The distance he kept from those who loved him, and whom he loved, including myself, prevented us from comforting him; he slipped out of our lives. I still feel the gap he left—he could have lived to be ninety-nine years old on the sunny beaches of Carmel.

Berne's death came suddenly. On Tuesday, June 23, 1970, we had a lively debate at the weekly San Francisco Transactional Analysis Seminar. I had arranged to present a new paper called "The Stroke Economy" at the next meeting. Eric Berne looked healthy and happy.

On Tuesday, June 30, when I arrived at the seminar I learned that he had been struck down by a heart attack. I visited him once at the hospital; he seemed improved. A second heart attack killed him on Wednesday, July 15.

I cannot say that I am objective about Eric Berne's death; when I think of him today, three years after he died, tears still well up in my eyes. Yet, I wished to record my thoughts on the subject.

Script Analysis

Berne's brilliant insights into the fact that most people live out preordained lives, and the importance that strokes have in human behavior, are insights without which script analysis and stroke theory would have never had a beginning. I feel that my contribution to script analysis and work on the Stroke Economy would not have occurred without Eric Berne's initial thoughts on scripts and strokes and, most importantly, without his constant, positive encouragement of me.

I see my work with scripts and strokes as being a continuation of Berne's work where he, due to his own scripted limitations, could not use his Adult freely. My own limitations would have prevented me from going much further than tragic script theory, due especially to my own script limitations relating to the male sex roles that I was bound to. I believe that without the input of Hogie Wyckoff in relation to the Pig Parent, the Nurturing Parent, and sex role scripting, my own work would have stopped with the Stroke Economy.

I am fortunate in that I have come to see how I, too, had plans to die in my early sixties. I have changed this plan and plan instead to live to be ninety-nine years old. I personally profit from my teachings by asking those I teach for feedback, criticism, and, when needed, therapy.

My own work with scripts started in 1965 while I was working at the Center for Special Problems in San Francisco with alcoholics. I began to see that at least the scripts of alcoholics were neither unconscious nor difficult to detect. The result of my work with alcoholics was the development of the script matrix and, following the script matrix, the development of a coherent system for the analysis of scripts. Eric Berne was enthusiastic about my work and encouraged me throughout. I later felt that the study of strokes was extraordinarily important, and while I was quite willing to follow Berne's injunction not to "touch patients" in therapy groups, I decided that strokes, especially physical strokes, needed to be studied anyway. I carried on my work on strokes outside of therapy groups and the result was the theory of the Stroke Economy.

From 1965 to 1970 Berne enthusiastically pursued

the development of script analysis based on the ideas
of the script matrix and injunctions, and in that period
of time he wrote *What Do You Say After You Say
Hello?* (1972) in which he presents his own views.
Unfortunately, I was not able, due to his death, to
share with him the thoughts on strokes, banal scripts,
and cooperation which are the main points of this
book.

The Significance of Script Analysis in Psychiatry

When people find that their lives have become un-
manageable, filled with unhappiness and emotional
pain, they have been known to turn to psychiatry
for an answer. Psychiatry, however, is not the principal form of counsel that is sought by most people—
who generally tend to go to ministers, physicians,
and friends before they resort to the use of psychiatric
help. Most Americans distrust psychiatry and resort
to psychiatric counsel only when too desperate to be
able to avoid it any longer or when they encounter a
psychiatric approach which they can relate to and
appreciate.

Mental health associations around the country are
busy convincing people that they should make use of
psychiatric services. Yet, most people avoid them, and
when in emotional difficulty make do without any
help, letting nature takes its curative course. The
fact that people in emotional difficulties do not consult psychiatrists is seen by psychiatrists to be due to
lack of judgment and is even interpreted by some
to be the result of their will to "fall (and remain) ill."
In my mind, people have, so far, shown good judgment in their rejection of the psychiatric help that is
available to most.

Of the few who do consult psychiatrists, most (in
my opinion) are not harmed. On the other hand, U.S.
Senator Tom Eagleton's short-lived bid for the Vice-
Presidential office of the United States in the 1972
elections illustrates how harmful psychiatry can be.
As Ronald Laing has pointed out, Eagleton commit-

ted the error of consulting a psychiatrist who with his diagnosis and treatment (electro-shock therapy) marked him and defeated him for any major future political aspirations. He could have chosen a psychiatrist like Eric Berne, who didn't use shock therapy and who would have helped him over his depression with other means.

Most persons who consult psychiatrists are basically "cooled out," pacified, brought back into temporary functioning; and a few are genuinely helped. I believe that psychiatrists who succeed in helping their clients do so because they reject the bulk of their psychiatric training and adopt a stance which comes out of their own experiences, personal wisdom, and humanistic convictions which overpower the oppressive and harmful teachings of psychiatric training.

Psychiatry is taught in what appears to be several different "schools of thought" with different points of view. But in my mind the minor disagreements between the different schools of psychiatric thought are negligible; actually these minor differences only serve to obscure the fact that, fundamentally, psychiatric theories agree on three main points:

1. Some people are normal, and some people are abnormal. The line of demarcation is sharp, and psychiatrists act as if they can distinguish between those who are not disturbed and those who are disturbed or "mentally ill."

2. The reason for "mental illness" and emotional disturbance is to be found within people, and psychiatric practice consists of diagnosing the illness and working with the individual to cure it. Some of the disturbances are incurable, such as alcoholism, schizophrenia or manic-depressive psychosis. Psychiatry's job is to make the "victims" of such "illness" comfortable in their misery, teaching them to adapt and cope, often with the use of drugs.

3. Persons who are mentally ill have no understanding of their illness, and very little if any control over it, just as is supposedly the case with physical diseases.

These three assumptions permeate psychiatric training and are deeply imbedded in the minds of the majority (more than 50%) of those who practice psychotherapy whether they be (in descending order of prestige) physicians, psychologists, social workers, nurses, probation officers[1] or any other trained psychotherapist.

It is little wonder that most people who get into emotional difficulties are loath to consult a psychotherapist. We do not want to hear that the trouble is to be found entirely within us and that, at the same time, we have no control or understanding of our difficulties. We do not want to hear these things about ourselves not because we are "resistant to change" or "unmotivated" for psychotherapy, but because they are not true, because they insult our intelligence, and because they rob us of our power to control our lives and destinies.

Script theory offers an alternative to this thinking. First of all, we believe that people are born O.K., that when they get into emotional difficulties they still remain O.K., and that their difficulties can be understood and solved by examining their interactions with other human beings, and by understanding the oppressive injunctions and attributions laid on them in childhood and maintained throughout life. Transactional script analysis offers an approach, not in the form of mystified theories understandable only to psychotherapists, but in the form of explanations which are commonsensical and understandable to the person who needs them, namely, the person in emotional difficulties.

Script analysis can be called a decision theory rather than a disease theory of emotional disturbance. Script theory is based on the belief that people make conscious life plans in childhood or early adolescence which influence and make predictable the rest of their lives. Persons whose lives are based on such decisions are said to have scripts. Like diseases, scripts

---

[1] The problem is more acute higher on the hierarchical ladder of psychotherapists.

have an onset, a course, and an outcome. Because of this similarity, life scripts are easily mistaken for diseases. However, because scripts are based on consciously willed decisions rather than on morbid tissue changes, they can be revoked or undecided by similarly willed decisions. Tragic life scripts such as suicide, drug addiction, or "incurable mental illnesses" such as "schizophrenia" or "manic-depressive psychosis," are the result of scripting rather than disease. Because these disturbances are scripts rather than incurable diseases it is possible to develop an understanding and approach which enables competent therapists to help their clients to, as Berne said, "close down the show and put a new one on the road." Questioning the negative assumptions of psychiatry also generates positive expectance and hope whose importance Frank[1] and Goldstein[2] have amply documented. From their studies it is clear that the assumptions of mental health workers about their clients have an extremely strong influence on the outcome of their work. Their research shows that when there exists an assumption of illness and chronicity on the part of the workers the effect is that of producing chronicity and illness in the clients, while an assumption of curability on the part of the worker will be associated with an improvement on the part of the client. Thus, considering emotional disturbance as some form of illness, as many who work with people do, is potentially harmful and may in fact be promoting illness in people who seek help from psychiatrists. On the other hand, the assumption that psychiatric disturbances are curable since they are based on reversible decisions frees in people their potent, innate tendencies to recover and overthrow their unhappiness. Workers who offer positive expectancy, coupled with problem-solving expertise, make it possible for people in emotional difficulties to take power

[1]Frank, Jerome D. "The Role of Hope in Psychotherapy." *International Journal of Psychiatry* 5 (1968): 383–95.

[2]Goldstein, Arnold P. *Therapist-Patient Expectations in Psychotherapy*. New York: Pergamon Press, 1962.

over their lives and produce their own new, satisfying life plans.

The following pages describe life scripts, and how to work with them, using transactional analysis.

SECTION 1
Transactional Analysis Theory

When organizing this book I had a difficult time deciding what to do with the next section. Logically, because it is an overview of existing transactional analysis (TA) theory, it belongs here, ahead of all the other sections.

However, it is dry, tedious, and, some even say, boring. It may give readers the impression that it is an omen of things to come and prevent them from reading on. I even thought at one time it should become an appendix at the end of the book rather than an impenetrable barrier standing in the way of the land of tragic and banal scripts and the riches of the Good Life beyond.

Obviously, though, logic won out. However, with a simple flick of the thumb, you can bypass this section —and refer to it only whenever you need to find definitions for terms mentioned later on in the book. Every new concept is italicized and referenced in the index, so you should have an easy time finding it. So read on or skip; I hope you enjoy the book.[1]

---

[1]For a much condensed version of this section you may want to read a pamphlet I have written called *TA Made Simple*, published in 1973 and obtainable for $1.25 from: TA/Simple, Box 5155, Berkeley, Ca. 94705.

1

Structural and
Transactional Analysis

The building blocks of the theory of transactional analysis (TA) are three observable forms of ego function: the Parent, the Adult, and the Child. They may seem to resemble three basic psychoanalytic concepts —the superego, the ego, and the id—but they are, in fact, quite different.

The Parent, Adult, and Child differ from the superego, ego, and id in that they are all manifestations of the ego. Thus, they represent visible behavior rather than hypothetical constructs. When a person is in one of the three ego states, for instance the Child, the observer is able to see and hear the Child sing, skip, and laugh. TA therapists focus on the ego and consciousness because they have found these concepts explain and predict social behavior better than other concepts.

Structural Analysis

A person operates in one of three distinct ego states at any one time. Diagnosis of ego states is made by observing the visible and audible characteristics of a person's appearance or ego. The ego states are distinguishable on the basis of skeletal-muscular variables and by the content of verbal utterances (words and sounds). Certain gestures, postures, mannerisms, facial expressions, and intonations, as well as certain words, are typically associated with each one of the three ego states. In addition to what she sees in the person being observed, the observer can use her own emotional reactions and thoughts as information in the diagnosis; a parental reaction in the observer may indicate that a Child ego state is being observed, while feelings of inferiority or rebelliousness may mean that the ego state being watched is Parent, and so on.

The most complete diagnosis of an ego state includes three sources of information: 1) The behavior of the person being observed; 2) the emotional reaction of the observer; and 3) the opinion of the person being observed. When diagnosing an ego state a transactional analyst doesn't say, "That's your Child!" but, "You act and sound as if you were in your Child ego state, and it feels like it is your Child because it brings out nurturing feelings in me. What do *you* think?" Naturally, if there are other observers their opinions must be taken into account as well. (See Chapter 6 for a further discussion of transactional analysis diagnosis.)

THE CHILD

The Child ego state is essentially preserved in its entirety from childhood. When a man is functioning in this ego mode, he behaves as he did when he was a little boy. It appears that the Child is never more than about seven years old and may be as young as one week or one day. When a person is in the Child state, she sits, stands, walks, and speaks as she did when she was, say, three years old. This childlike behavior is accompanied by the corresponding perceptions, thoughts, and feelings of a three-year-old.

The Child ego state tends to be fleeting in grown-ups because of a general societal injunction against "childish behavior." However, Child ego states can be observed in situations which are structured to permit childlike behavior, such as sports events, parties, and revivals. A good place to view the Child ego state in grownups is at a football game. Here, childlike expressions of joy, anger, rage, and delight can be observed, and it is easy to see how, aside from bone size and secondary sexual characteristics, a man jumping for joy when his team scores is indistinguishable from a five-year-old boy. The similarity goes further than the observable behavior since the man is not only acting as a boy, but feeling, seeing, and thinking as a boy does.

In the Child ego state, a person tends to use short words and expletives like "golly," "wow," "gee," and "nice," delivered in a high-pitched voice. He adopts stances characteristic of children: a downward tilt of the head, upturned eyes, feet apart or pigeon-toed. When sitting, the person may balance on the edge of the chair, fidgeting, rocking, or slouching. Jumping, clapping, laughing expansively, or crying are all part of the repertoire of the Child ego state.

Aside from situations which permit childlike behavior, the Child can be observed in a *fixated* form in so-called "schizophrenics" and in such persons as comedians, actors, and actresses whose profession requires them to appear habitually in a Child ego state. Of course, the Child ego state is readily observable in children.

A Child ego state much younger than a year is rarely observed, since persons who habitually express this ego state are usually severely disturbed. However, this type of a very young Child appears in "normal" persons under circumstances of severe stress, or when great pain or joy is felt.

The value of the Child should not be underestimated. It is said to be the best part of a person and the only part that can really enjoy itself. It is the source of spontaneity, sexuality, creative change, and is the mainspring of joy.

THE ADULT

The Adult ego state is essentially a computer, an impassionate organ of the personality, which gathers and processes data and makes predictions. The Adult gathers data about the world through the senses, processes them according to a logical program, and makes predictions when necessary. Its perception is diagrammatic. While the Child perceives in color, in space, and from one point of view at a time, the Adult may perceive in black and white, often in two dimensions, and from several points of view at the same time. In the Adult ego state, a person is temporarily detached from her own affective and other internal processes, a condition indispensable for the proper observation and prediction of external reality. Thus, in the Adult ego state the person "has no feelings," even though she may be able to appraise her Child or Parent feelings. Often the Parent ego state is confused with the Adult ego state especially when it is calm and appears to be acting rationally. However, the Adult is not only rational but it is also without emotion.

According to Piaget's detailed discussion of "formal operations,"[1] it appears that the Adult grows gradually during childhood as a consequence of the interaction between the person and the external world.

THE PARENT

The Parent is essentially made up of behavior copied from parents or authority figures. It is taken whole, without modification. A person in the Parent ego state is a play-back of a video tape recording of his parent or whoever was or is in place of his parents.

Thus, the Parent ego state is essentially nonperceptive and noncognitive. It is simply a constant and sometimes arbitrary basis for decisions, the repository of traditions and values, and as such it is important to the survival of children and civilizations. It operates validly when adequate information for an Adult decision is not available; but, in certain people, it operates in spite of adequate Adult information.

The Parent, while taken whole from others, is not a completely fixated ego state since it can change over

[1]Piaget, Jean. *Logic and Psychology*. New York: Basic Books, 1957.

time. Thus, a person's experiences can add to or sub-
tract from his Parent's repertoire of behavior. For instance, rearing of a first-born child will greatly increase the range of Parent responses of a person.
The Parent ego state changes throughout life, from
adolescence to old age, as the person encounters new
situations that demand parental behavior, and as the
person finds authority figures or admired persons from
whom examples for such behavior are adopted.

For instance, it is possible for people to learn nurturing Parent behavior and discard the oppressive aspects of the Parent. Some Parent behavior is geneti-
cally built into people, such as the tendency to nurse
and defend one's young, but most human Parent
behavior is learned, built as it were, on those two innate tendencies: nurture and protection.

VOICES IN THE HEAD

Structural analysis is organized around the fundamental concepts of these ego states. Some further concepts in structural analysis will be advanced.

Ego states operate one at a time; that is, a person
is always in one and only one of the three ego states.
This ego state is called the *executive*, or is said to have
executive power. While one ego state has the executive power, the person may be aware of literally
standing beside himself, observing his own behavior.
The feeling that the "self" is not the ego state in the
executive usually occurs when the Child or Parent has
executive power, while the "real self," perhaps the
Adult, observes without being able to behave. Thus,
while only one ego state is *cathected*—that is, imbued
with the energy necessary to activate muscular com-
plexes involved in behavior—it is possible for another
ego state to become conscious to the person, even
though it is unable to activate the musculature.

Since a person can be acting in one ego state while
another state observes, internal dialogues between
these ego states become possible. For example, after a
few drinks at a party, a man may be swept by the

music into an expansive, childlike dance. His Child is
now in the executive while the Parent observes his gy-
rations and mutters something like, "You're making a
fool of yourself, Charlie," or "This is all very well, but
what about your slipped disk?" Often this comment
by the nonexecutive ego state *decathects* the Child
and transfers the executive to the Parent, in which
case Charlie will stop dancing, perhaps blush, and re-
tire to his seat where the situation will be reversed
and Charlie, now in the Parent ego state, will look
disapprovingly at other dancers. Becoming aware of
the conversations that occur between the executive
and the observing state is a very important step in
therapy.

These internal dialogues can happen between any
two ego states. One specific dialogue, between the
Critical Parent and the Natural Child (see p. 53), is
most relevant to psychotherapy.

Some people find that they are constantly plagued
by statements which they perceive as voices in their
heads. These statements sometimes are even audible
and felt to come from outside the person, but they
are more commonly understood to come from within
one's own head. They are usually put-down statements like, "You're bad, stupid, ugly, crazy, and sick,"
in short, "You're not O.K.," or statements predicting
failure, or preventing action, such as, "You can't do
it," or, "That is a stupid idea, don't try it."

These internal messages have been observed by
other theorists such as Ellis[1] and Freud.[2] Ellis speaks
of "catastrophic expectations" and Freud speaks of the
"primitive, harsh superego." Wyckoff has named this
Parent ego state which is the enemy of the natural
Child, the *Pig Parent*.[3]

---

[1]Ellis, Albert. *Reason and Emotion in Psychotherapy.* New York:
Lyle Stuart, 1962.

[2]Freud, Sigmund. *New Introductory Lectures on Psychoanalysis.*
New York: Norton, 1933.

[3]Wyckoff, Hogie. "Permission." *The Radical Therapist* 2,3 (1971):
8–10. Reprinted in *Readings in Radical Psychiatry*, Claude Steiner,
ed. New York: Grove Press, 1974.

EXCLUSIONS AND CONTAMINATIONS

At times it is difficult to diagnose ego states because people tend to masquerade their Child and Parent as Adult ego states. Opinionated and judgmental attitudes are often couched in rational language. The Parent, with a straight face pretending to be Adult, may express very logical points of view. From his Adult ego state, a husband might ask his wife, "Why isn't dinner ready?" From his Parent masquerading as an Adult, he may ask the identical question. The difference, however, is that in the former case the husband is simply asking a question, while in the latter he is attempting to pressure and blame his wife for being lazy and disorganized.[1]

Sometimes two sets of muscles may seem to be powered by two separate ego states at the same time. For instance, a lecturer's voice and facial muscles may indicate an Adult ego state, while an impatient toss of the hand reveals a Parent ego state. In such cases, it is likely that the behavior is Parent in Adult disguise and therefore Parent, or that Parent and Adult are alternating rapidly.

Alternation between ego states depends on the *permeability* of the ego state boundaries. Permeability is an important variable in psychotherapy. Low permeability leads to *exclusion* of appropriate ego states. Exclusions of the Parent, Adult, and Child ego states are all problematic since they preclude the use of ego states that, in a given situation, may be more useful and advantageous than the excluding ego state.

For example, at a party the excluding Adult is less useful than the Child. The purpose of the party is to have fun, which the Child can do, but the Adult, analyzing and computing data dispassionately, would deter the party's purpose. A father with an excluding Adult prevents the more useful Parent from properly

[1]Wyckoff, Hogie. "Problem-Solving Groups for Women." *Issues in Radical Therapy* I,1 (1973).

raising his children. For example, when Johnny asks his father, "Daddy, why do I have to go to bed?" the Adult response would be a lecture about the physiology, psychology, and sociology of sleep. A more useful response might come from the Parent who might simply say, "Because you're tired, and if you don't you'll be cranky tomorrow," an answer much more appropriate to the situation.

On the other hand, extreme permeability causes another kind of problem; most often, a person's inability to remain in the Adult ego state for a sufficient period of time.

Every ego state, being a substructure of the ego, is, in its own way, an adaptive "organ" having as its function adaptation to the demands of reality. How the ego as a whole functions adaptively has been elucidated by Hartmann;[1] all three ego states share in this function, each one specially suited for specific situations. It might be said that the Parent is ideally suited where control is necessary—control of children, of unknown situations, of fears, of unwanted behavior, and of the Child. The Adult is suited to situations in which accurate prediction is necessary. The Child is ideally suited where creation is desired—creation of new ideas, procreation, creation of new experiences, recreation, and so on.

Adaptiveness here refers to the valuable function of being responsive to reality. Adaptation to the demands of oppressive persons is a special form of response which is, in most cases, except when one is under their total physical control, unhealthy and unnecessary. Thus, adaptation is generally a function which works to the person's advantage except when it occurs in response to others who may not have the person's welfare in mind. The Child ego state in an unhappy person is often completely adapted to the Pig Parent. This is the result of oppressive child-rearing situations in which parents coerce their chil-

---

[1] Hartmann, Heinz. "Ego Psychology and the Problem of Adaptation." In *Organization and Pathology of Thought*, edited by D. Rapaport. New York: Columbia University Press, 1951.

dren into submission, giving them no choices of their own.

One more concept of great importance is *contamination*. This phenomenon is characterized by an Adult ego state holding as fact certain ideas stemming from the Parent or the Child. For instance, a Parental idea such as "masturbation leads to insanity" or "women are passive creatures" could be part of a person's Adult ego state. Or, the Adult might be contaminated by an idea such as "grownups can't be trusted." Decontamination of the Adult is an early therapeutic requirement in treatment and can be accomplished through an accurately timed confrontation by the therapist's Adult with the inaccuracy of the ideas which are causing the contamination.

A very successful technique to decontaminate ego states is having the person alternately speak first for one, then another, of his ego states. This technique, originated in psychodrama and later adapted by Gestalt therapy, is a very convincing demonstration of the reality of ego states. A person who feels guilty because of masturbation could be asked to speak from his Parent about the evils of masturbation, from his Child about the guilt and fears of insanity due to his masturbation, and from his Adult about the well-known fact that masturbation is harmless and normal. Verbalizing these different points of view tends to separate the two ego states, a process which facilitates decontamination of the Adult.

Transactional Analysis

Just as the ego state is the unit of structural analysis, so the *transaction* is the unit of transactional analysis. The theory holds that a person's behavior is best understood if examined in terms of ego states, and that the behavior between two or more persons is best understood if examined in terms of transactions. A transaction consists of a *stimulus* and a *response* between two specific ego states. In a *simple transaction* only two ego states operate. One example is a transaction between two Adult ego states: "How much is five times seven?" "Thirty-five." All other combinations of ego states may occur in a transaction. However, of the nine possible combinations, four are most common and the others are seldom observed. The four common transactions are between P and C, between P and P, between A and A, and between C and C.

Transactions follow one another smoothly as long as the stimulus and response are parallel or complementary (Figure 1A).

In any series of transactions, communication proceeds if the response to a previous stimulus is addressed to the ego state that was the source of the stimulus and is emitted from the ego state to which that source addressed itself. Any other response creates a *crossed transaction* and interrupts communication. In Figure 1, transaction A is complementary and will lead to further communication, while transaction B is crossed and will break off communication. Crossed transactions not only account for the interruption of communication but also are an essential part of games. *Discounts* (see Chapter 9) are one very important kind of crossed transaction.

In addition to simple and crossed transactions, another very important form is the *duplex* or *ulterior transaction*. It operates on two levels: *social* and *psychological*. In Figure 1, the stimulus of transaction C is between A and A: "Let's work late on these accounts, Miss Smith, we'll catch dinner on the way to the office"; and between C and C: "Let's have dinner and drinks together, Sally, and maybe we'll get some work done later." In an ulterior transaction, the social level usually covers up the real (psychological) meaning of the transaction; thus interpersonal behavior is not understandable until the ulterior level and ego states involved are understood. Anyone operating on the basis of the overt communication between Sally and her co-worker would expect them to get a lot of work done that evening. A more sophisticated observer would know that another outcome is much more likely.

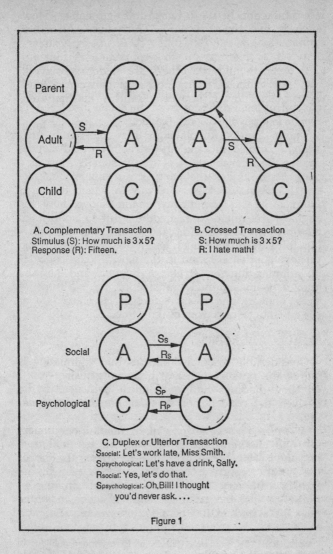

A. Complementary Transaction
Stimulus (S): How much is 3 x 5?
Response (R): Fifteen.

B. Crossed Transaction
S: How much is 3 x 5?
R: I hate math!

C. Duplex or Ulterior Transaction
Ssocial: Let's work late, Miss Smith.
Spsychological: Let's have a drink, Sally.
Rsocial: Yes, let's do that.
Spsychological: Oh, Bill! I thought
    you'd never ask. . . .

Figure 1

Games and Payoffs

A *game* is a behavioral sequence which 1) is an orderly series of transactions with a beginning and an end; 2) contains an ulterior motive, that is, a psychological level different from the social level; and 3) results in a payoff for both players.

The motivation for playing games comes from their *payoff*. To use an analogy, structural analysis describes the relevant parts of the personality, just as a parts list describes the parts of an engine. Transactional analysis describes the way in which the parts interact, just as a cutaway engine shows how the engine parts relate to each other. But to understand *why* people transact with each other at all, some driving force (like gasoline) has to be postulated; and this explanation is found in the motivational concepts of stimulus hunger, structure hunger, and position hunger. Games provide satisfaction for all three of these hungers and this satisfaction is referred to as the advantage, or payoff, of the game.

STIMULUS HUNGER

Considerable research indicates that stimulation is one of the primary needs of higher organisms. Based on these findings and on clinical evidence, Berne evolved the concepts of *stimulus hunger* and *stroking*.

A *stroke* is a special form of stimulation one person gives to another. Because strokes are essential to a person's survival, the exchange of strokes is one of the most important activities people engage in. Strokes can vary from actual physical stroking to praise, or just recognition. To be effective, a stroke must be suited to its recipient. For example, Spitz[1]

---

[1]Spitz, René. "Hospitalism, Genesis of Psychiatric Conditions in Early Childhood." *Psychoanalytic Study of the Child* 1 (1945): 53–74.

has shown that a very young child needs actual physical stroking to survive. On the other hand, adults may require only occasional, symbolic strokes such as praise, or an expression of appreciation, to remain alive. However, while it is possible to survive on minimal strokes, stroke scarcity is unhealthy both physically and emotionally; thus stroke hunger is a major driving force in people.

Stimulus hunger is satisfied by stroking or *recognition*. Stroking is a more basic need than recognition and it is said that a person needs stroking "lest his spinal cord shrivel up." Usually, the need for actual physical stroking can be complemented with symbolic stroking or recognition. Thus the average adult can satisfy her hunger for stroking through, among other things, a ritual which is essentially an exchange of recognition strokes. For example, the following is a six-stroke ritual:

A: *Hi*
B: *Hi.*
A: *How are you?*
B: *Fine, and you?*
A: *Fine. Well, see you.*
B: *Yeah, see you around.*

A game is transactionally more complex than the above ritual but it is still an exchange of strokes. It should be noted that "Go to hell!" is as much a stroke as "Hi" and people will settle for the former, negative strokes when they cannot obtain the latter positive ones.

Certain persons are prevented by their Parent from accepting overt or direct recognition, requiring more disguised forms instead. Such an example is the woman who rejects all admiration of her looks, interpreting them as sexual advances, but accepts compliments about her sewing ability while secretly resenting them. People who cannot obtain or accept direct recognition for one reason or another will tend to obtain it by playing games which are a rich source of strokes.

STRUCTURE HUNGER

The satisfaction of *structure hunger* is the social advantage of the game. To satisfy structure hunger, the individual seeks social situations within which time is structured, or organized, for the purpose of obtaining strokes. Structure hunger is the need to establish a social situation within which the person can transact with others. This need for *time structure* is an elaboration of stimulus hunger, and therefore just a more complex form of that basic need. A game structures time in many ways. For instance, a game of "If It Weren't For You" provides for considerable time structure with its endless face-to-face recriminations. It provides for additional time structure in that it makes possible the *pastime*[1] of "If It Weren't For Him (Her)," played with neighbors and relatives, and "If It Weren't For Them," played at bars and bridge clubs.

POSITION HUNGER

The satisfaction of *position hunger* is the existential advantage of the game. Position hunger is the need to vindicate certain basic, lifelong, *existential positions*. These existential positions can be illustrated with a sentence, such as, "I am no good," "They are no good," or "Nobody is any good." They are satisfied by internal transactions which take place in the mind of the player between himself and another person, usually a parent. Position hunger is satisfied by stroking or recognition received internally, from the Parent.

Thus, after a game of "Rapo"[2] the players go home and White may say to herself, "That proves men are beasts just like Dad said!" and her Parent will answer, "That's my good little girl!" This internal transaction has stroking value, and at the same time reinforces the existential position of the player. As will be elaborated

---

[1] A pastime is a series of simple, complementary transactions relating to a single subject matter.

[2] See "Rapo," p. 49.

later, every game has the added effect of advancing the *script*, or life plan of the person.

A game provides strokes for the player, without the threat of *intimacy*. The theory postulates that two or more persons can only structure time together with *work, rituals, pastimes, games, withdrawal,* or *intimacy*. Intimacy, which is a social situation free of these other time-structuring elements, is one in which strokes are given directly, and therefore most powerfully. Intimacy can be frightening to the person because it goes counter to Parental prohibitions about the exchange of strokes. Thus, a game is a carefully balanced procedure to procure strokes that are safe from Parental criticism.

It should be noted that strokes can be obtained without resorting to games, which are basically subterfuges, and that games are learned in childhood from parents as a preferred method of obtaining stimulation. Thus, a person giving up a game has to develop an alternate way of obtaining strokes and structuring time, and until he does he will be subject to despair resembling the marasmus[1] observed by Spitz in children who do not receive enough stroking.

Two games will be described in detail. The first is a "soft" (first-degree) version of the game called "Why Don't You—Yes, But," and the second is a "medium hard" version (second-degree) of "Rapo." The *softness* or *hardness* of a game refers to the intensity with which it is played and its harmfulness. First degree is the "soft" version, and third degree the "hard" version of a game.

"Why Don't You—Yes, But" (YDYB) is a common game played wherever people gather in groups, and generally proceeds as follows:

Black and White are mothers of grade-school children.
WHITE: *I sure would like to come to the PTA meeting but I can't get a baby sitter. What should I do?*

---

[1] marasmus: microscopically seen as dehydration and shrinking of central nervous system tissue. The symptoms of marasmus are apathy, weight loss, and, eventually, death.

BLACK: *Why don't you call Mary? She'd be glad to sit for you.*

WHITE: *She is a darling girl, but she is too young.*

BLACK: *Why don't you call the baby-sitting services? They have experienced ladies.*

WHITE: *Yes, but some of those old ladies look like they might be too strict.*

BLACK: *Why don't you bring the kids along to the meeting?*

WHITE: *Yes, but I would be embarrassed to be the only one to come with children.*

Finally, after several such transactions there is silence, perhaps followed by a statement by another person, such as:

GREEN: *It sure is hard to get around when you have kids.*

YDYB, the first game analyzed by Berne, fulfills the three parts of the definition of a game. It is a series of transactions with a beginning (a question) and an end (an irritated silence). It contains an ulterior motive because, at the social level, it is a series of Adult questions and Adult answers, whereas at the psychological level it is a series of questions by a demanding, reluctant Child unable to solve a problem and a series of answers by an increasingly irritated Parent, anxious to help and in a quandary.

Finally, the payoff of the game is as follows: It is a rich source of strokes as it provides a readily usable form of time structure wherever people congregate and it reinforces the existential positions of people in the group. The position, in this case, is exemplified by Green's statement, "It sure is hard to get around when you have kids." For White, the game proves that parent types (advice givers) are no good and always want to dominate you, and at the same time proves that children are no good and prevent you from doing things. For Black, the game proves that children, or grownups who behave like children, are ungrateful and unwilling to cooperate. For both Black and White, the existential advantage fits into their script. Both White and Black come away from the game feeling angry or depressed according to what their favorite feeling racket (see below) is. After a long enough succession of YDYB and similar games, White or Black may feel justified in doing something drastic such as getting drunk, going to a mental hospital, attempting suicide, or simply giving up.

While YDYB can be played by almost anyone, the psychological content of "Rapo" attracts fewer persons. It is a sexual game, so it requires a man and a woman, although it may be played between members of the same sex.[1] It proceeds, typically, as follows:

At a party, after considerable flirtation, White and Black find themselves in the bedroom with Black reading from the Joy of Sex.[2] Aroused by the inviting situation, Black makes an advance and attempts to kiss White. White rebuffs Black and leaves abruptly.

Again we have a series of transactions, this time beginning with a sexual invitation and ending with a sexual rebuff. On the social level, the game looks like a straightforward flirtation ended by Black's breach of etiquette, self-righteously rebuffed by White. On the psychological level, between Child and Child, White has first enticed and then humiliated Black.

The payoff, again, consists of strokes, a way to structure time, and existentially, a validation of the position "Women (men) are no good," followed by feelings of anger or depression, according to the feeling racket (see below) called for by the script. Again, the script is advanced since enough episodes of this game may justify a murder, rape, suicide, or depression for the players.

Related to the payoff in games is the concept colloquially called "*trading stamps.*" Trading stamps, or enduring, non-genuine feelings such as sadness or

[1]Zechnick, Robert. "Social Rapo—Description and Cure." *Transactional Analysis Journal* III,4 (1973): 18–21.
[2]Comfort, Alex, ed. *The Joy of Sex.* New York: Crown Publishers, 1972.

guilt[1] are "collected" and saved up by persons who
play games so that when enough are accumulated
they can be traded in for a "free" blow-up, drunken
binge, suicide attempt, or some other script milestone.

A *racket* is the person's basis or reason for collecting
trading stamps. The person, for instance, whose
existential position is "I'm no good" can continually
promote her low self-esteem racket by collecting gray
stamps, while the person whose position is "You're no
good" can do the same through the collection of anger
stamps (red stamps) in an anger racket.

ROLES AND DEGREES

As mentioned above games can be played soft or
hard. The example of YDYB given is the softest (first-
degree) version of the game because it is relatively
harmless. The hard (third-degree) version of this
game might be played by an alcoholic who "Yes,
buts" every suggestion to his dying moment.

Third-degree games involve tissue damage. The
game of "Rapo," described above, is a second-degree
game. The first-degree of "Rapo" is often played at
cocktail parties in the form of a series of flirtations
and put-downs, while the much more rare, third-
degree level of the game might end up in a courtroom
or even at the morgue.

Each person playing a game is playing a *role* in it.
For instance, the Alcoholic game has five roles: the
Alcoholic, the Rescuer, the Persecutor, the Patsy, the
Connection. There are three basic game roles, how-
ever, as noted by Karpman,[2] and they are the *Per-
secutor*, the *Rescuer* and the *Victim*.

---

[1]Genuine feelings are related to events and tend not to endure unless their causes endure. Despair may endure for some time after a
great loss. Joy and anger tend to have peaks and subside. Anger is
a genuine and important emotion but it may be a racket if it endures
beyond the events that cause it.

[2]Karpman, Stephen B. "Script Drama Analysis." *Transactional
Analysis Bulletin* 7,26 (1968): 39–43.

2

Second-Order
Structural Analysis

Script Analysis requires an understanding of *second-order structural analysis,* or the analysis of the structure of the Child.[1]

Let us consider a five-year-old child, Mary (Figure 2A), who is capable of operating in three ego states. In her Parent ego state (P_1) she scolds and cuddles her little brother as she sees her mother do; in her Adult ego state (A_1), the *Little Professor,* she asks difficult questions ("What is sex, Daddy?" "What is blood for?"); in her Child ego state (C_1) she behaves as she did when she was two years old—she talks baby talk, throws a tantrum, or rolls around on the floor.

Thirty years later, Mary (Figure 2B) is still capable of behaving in three separate ego states. The Parent (P_2) cares for her husband or nurses her newborn baby; her Adult (A_2) knows how to cook, perform an appendectomy, and make accurate predictions about events and people; her Child (C_2) is identical with the five-year-old Mary described above. Of the three modes of the Child in the thirty-five-year-old Mary, one of them is likely to be apparent more often than the other two; Mary's personality, as it is known to others, will depend on which of the three possible Child ego states is usually cathected.

---

[1] On the subject of second-order structural analysis most transactional analysts part company with each other. The following represents my views.

51

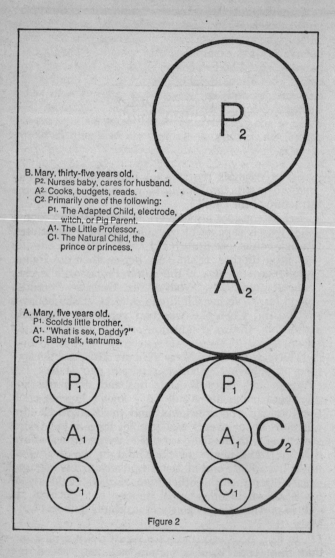

B. Mary, thirty-five years old.
  P_2. Nurses baby, cares for husband.
  A_2. Cooks, budgets, reads.
  C_2. Primarily one of the following:
    P_1. The Adapted Child, electrode,
      witch, or Pig Parent.
    A_1. The Little Professor.
    C_1. The Natural Child, the
      prince or princess.

A. Mary, five years old.
  P_1. Scolds little brother.
  A_1. "What is sex, Daddy?"
  C_1. Baby talk, tantrums.

Figure 2

If her Child (C_2) is primarily P_1, she is likely to have a script which is the result of her parents' behavior when Mary was, say, five years old. She will behave in ways exemplified and forced on her by her parents. This Child ego state, P_1 in C_2, has also been called the Adapted Child because it is molded to parental demands. In the case of persons with self-destructive scripts it is also called the *"electrode"* because of the electrifying manner in which it seems to control the person's mental life and behavior. In these cases P_1 in C_2 is also called the *"witch"* or *"ogre"* because it seems to have supernatural qualities similar to the witches and ogres in fairy tales. The P_1 in C_2 is also called the *Pig Parent* because it makes people feel not O.K. and because its function is to force them to do things they don't want to do. Its only usefulness is in situations in which people need to oppress or take things away from each other.

If Mary's Child (C_2) behaves mostly as A_1, the Little Professor, she will be inquisitive and lively ("bright-eyed and bushy-tailed") as contrasted to the more emotive, powerful, perhaps overwhelming behavior of C_1 which is called the *Natural Child,* or the *"prince"* or *"princess."* The Little Professor is the ego state which Berne first explored in his studies on intuition when he guessed the occupations of people by using his own intuition (see p. 13–14).

When in the Natural Child ego state (C_1) the individual is "turned on" or in a "peak experience." Some people's Child is exclusively the Natural Child; but as societal strictures against this form of behavior are strong, the Child of very few people operates at that level. The acute "psychotic" state in which a confused Natural Child takes over completely is, in essence, the breakthrough of the Natural Child after a period of domination by the Parent.

It is important to distinguish, in thirty-five-year-old Mary, the Parent (P_2) from the Parent in the Child (P_1 in C_2). Both ego states are superficially similar in that they both involve certain behavior which is parental, such as finger wagging and certain words such as "ought, "should," etc. Upon close examination, however, important differences become clear. P_1 in C_2 is a little girl acting like a mother while P_2 *is* a mother.

P_1 in C_2 wants to be like mother and imitates her ("Johnny, you better be good"), all the while checking for reassurance from the parents ("How am I doing, Mommy?").

The difference between the Parent (P_2) and the Pig Parent, bad witch, mother ogre, electrode, or Adapted Child (P_1 in C_2) needs to be closely examined.

Superficially, they are similar; they both are Parent ego states and share the fact that they are taken whole from others. They both have nurturing and protective qualities. The fundamental difference between them is their potency, their value in human relationships, or, for lack of a "scientific" word, their goodness.

The Parent (P_2) is also called the Nurturing Parent. Its function (see Figure 3) is nurturance and protection and it is both convincing and potent in these functions, while the Pig Parent is neither truly nurturing nor protective.

For example, the Nurturing Parent will say, "Take care of yourself, don't love a man who doesn't respect you," while the Pig Parent will say, "Take care of yourself, men are pigs." Inside of the head the Nurturing Parent defends the Natural Child from the Pig Parent; for instance, if the Pig Parent says, "You're stupid," the Nurturing Parent says, "Don't listen to that, you're very smart and I love you."

The difference between P_2 and P_1 in C_2 can be seen clearly in policemen who because of their work have to operate in their Parent ego state a great deal of the time. Some habitually operate from their Nurturing Parent and then they are Peace Officers, who are protective and nurturing to the people they work for who in turn will respect and appreciate them. Others operate from their Pig Parent and then they "protect" people from what does not harm them or even from what is good for them. Their "protection" is oppressive, often based on bribes, and they are angry and scared

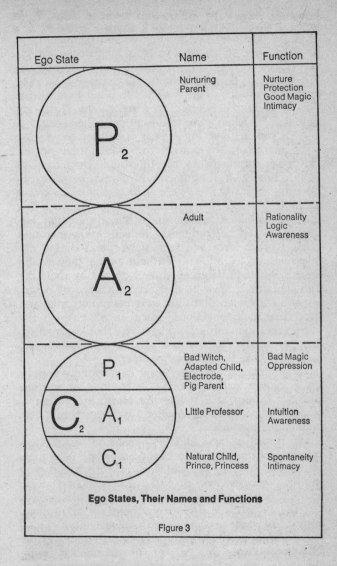

Ego State	Name	Function
P₂	Nurturing Parent	Nurture Protection Good Magic Intimacy
A₂	Adult	Rationality Logic Awareness
P₁	Bad Witch, Adapted Child, Electrode, Pig Parent	Bad Magic Oppression
C₂ A₁	Little Professor	Intuition Awareness
C₁	Natural Child, Prince, Princess	Spontaneity Intimacy

Ego States, Their Names and Functions

Figure 3

and therefore feared and hated by people, which tends to keep them scared and angry.

To be sure, any policeman who has to uphold oppressive laws, or whose back is up against the wall, is very likely to get angry or scared and lapse into the Pig Parent so that his behavior depends a great deal on the conditions of his work. The point here is that the difference between Pig Parent and Nurturing Parent is especially clear in the case of policemen.

A person in their Pig Parent is neither convincing nor potent except to someone over which it has power. No one is impressed by the "hell and damnation" of Holy Hubert, a fundamentalist street preacher in Berkeley. He is O.K. as long as he is powerless; but if he had power in the community, as many such Pig Parent dominated persons have had throughout history, he would be frightening indeed. Many men and a few women have had such power, and caused untold miseries to millions. Without power they would have been small, frightened, and crazed by their Pig Parents; and, it must be remarked, always well-meaning and convinced that they were being nurturing and protective in their actions. Power is what makes the Pig Parent dangerous, oppressive, and destructive. Stripped of their power evil persons can, once again, be seen as O.K. though angry or scared.

To summarize, the Pig Parent is a scared or angry Child ego state that attempts to protect or nurture and is a failure at it, while the Nurturing Parent is confident, loving, and competent in the nurturing and protective functions.

The Parent in the Child (P_1) seems to be a fixated ego state not amenable to change or worth changing. Unlike the Parent (P_2) which, as was explained previously, changes over time, P_1 in C_2 is best dealt with by decommissioning it. In therapy this implies that the P_1 in C_2 is decathected and not allowed to exert its influence on the rest of the personality.

The Adult in the Child (A_1) is called the Little Professor because this part of the personality, intuition, is thought to have an extremely accurate grasp and understanding of the major variables that enter

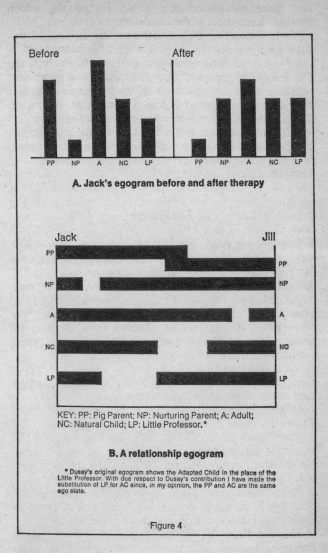

A. Jack's egogram before and after therapy

KEY: PP: Pig Parent; NP: Nurturing Parent; A: Adult;
NC: Natural Child; LP: Little Professor.*

B. A relationship egogram

* Dusay's original egogram shows the Adapted Child in the place of the Little Professor. With due respect to Dusay's contribution I have made the substitution of LP for AC since, in my opinion, the PP and AC are the same ego state.

Figure 4

into interpersonal relationships (Figure 3). This grasp is manifested in the capacity to detect the "real" (covert) meaning of transactions. The Little Professor is able to understand that which the second-order Adult (A_2) misses. However, in matters other than psychological transactions, the Professor operates with limited information. A good analogy to clarify this point can be found in a very shrewd peasant who is able to hold his own in any personal situation in his hometown, but who when he goes to the big city is simply not able to cope with the much more complex situation requiring a great deal of information not available to him.

Egograms

One more concept is of great usefulness in transactional analysis: the egogram.[1] The egogram is a simple diagram showing the relative strength of the Pig Parent, Nurturing Parent, Adult, Natural Child, and Adapted Child (Figure 4). This diagram is useful in showing, at a glance, which ego states dominate the personality. It can also be used to show changes in personality as well as the way in which two persons in a relationship compare.[2]

---

[1]Dusay, John M. "Ego Games and the Constancy Hypothesis." *Transactional Analysis Journal* II,3 (1972): 37–41.
[2]Karpman, Stephen B. "Fingograms." *Transactional Analysis Journal* III,4 (1973): 30–33.

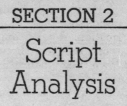

SECTION 2
Script
Analysis

3

Oedipus Revisited

A script is essentially the blueprint for a life course. Like theatrical tragedy, the life scripts follow Aristotle's principles of drama. According to Aristotle, the plot of good tragedy contains three parts: prologue, climax, and catastrophe. To use the example of depression ending in suicide, the prologue in the person's life is his childhood, and its protagonists are he and his two parents. The climax is the period in adulthood during which the person struggles against the script and appears to be escaping his destiny or catastrophe (suicide) by achieving a measure of happiness. The climax is a highly unstable situation, however. It represents the battle between two forces: the script or self-destructive tendency, and the wish to avoid the catastrophe. The climax in the form of a happy relationship or a period of prosperity suddenly yields to the catastrophe when the person relaxes his battle against the script and destiny takes its course, depression wins, despair takes over, and the person kills himself.

In addition to this three-part requirement for the plot of good tragic drama, Aristotle postulates that the tragic hero is a good man who commits a tragic error *(hamartia)*.[1] The tragic error in tragic drama is walking in blindness[2] so that the tragic hero who in-

---

[1] Aristotle. *Poetics.* New York: The Modern Library, 1954.

[2] Frumker, Sanford C. "Hamartia: Aristotle's Meaning of the Word & Its Relation to Tragic Scripts." *Transactional Analysis Journal* III,1 (1973): 29–30.

tends to accomplish a certain result with his actions accomplished the exact opposite *(peripeteia)*. After the hero works in blindness to his own defeat he suddenly comes to "the realization of the truth, the opening of the eyes, the sudden lightning flash in the darkness" *(anagnorisis)*[1] as he recognizes what he has done to himself.

Certain persons' lives follow the same path that Aristotle prescribes for "good" tragedy, and that is why their scripts are called *hamartic*. Their lives are walked in blindness, following someone else's dictates which lead them to destruction. Some have an awakening, when it is too late or as they are dying, in which they see what has happened to them. Some die never knowing what life could have held for them.[2] Their audience watches in horror, unable to avert the tragic ending; and to those who can see what is happening the protagonist seems to be destroying himself willingly. Alcoholism and other drug abuse, lifelong depression ending in suicide, madness, all have the qualities of hamartic scripts.

Once the similarity between modern life courses and ancient Greek tragedies is seen, it is possible to better understand human afflictions by looking into the thoughts which Aristotle and, subsequently, Freud had on the subject of tragedy.

In all tragic scripts, and in the *Oedipus Rex* cycle in particular, a hero, well-known to all, does something that is known to all beforehand, and does it in a relentless, predictable, fatal way, as if walking blindfolded off a precipice's edge. From the outset, the audience knows of the hero's eventual demise or change of fortune, yet is fascinated not only by the similarity between events occurring in the tragedy and the events in their own lives, but also by the manner in which the script unfolds in a predictable and relentless manner.

---

[1]Lucas, F. L. *Tragedy, Serious Drama in Relation to Aristotle's Poetics*. London: Hogarth Press, 1971, pp. 109–123.

[2]Thanks are due to Sanford Frumker for his clarification of the concept of *hamartia*.

The tragic deeds and outcome of Sophocles' *Oedipus* are not only known by most audiences before viewing, but within the tragedy itself, three different oracles concur that Oedipus will commit patricide and incest. In addition, Tiresias predicts the events of the play when he says:

But it will be shown that [Laius' murderer] is a Theban
A revelation that will fail to please a blind man
Who has his eyes now; a penniless man who is rich
now.[1]

All predictions of the tragedy come true, and this inevitably adds to the fascination of the Oedipus cycle.

In scripts, too, a prediction is made of what is to come. For instance, a forty-five-year-old alcoholic man reported to me that he believed that his alcoholism was the result of a prediction made by a Siamese sage fifteen years before we met. He explained that as a young man on leave from his aircraft carrier, he had visited Siam and been to a soothsayer. The old man predicted, after a few words with him, that he would die an alcoholic. Fifteen years later he found himself irresistibly driven to drink and fearing that he would indeed die an alcoholic. He realized (his Adult knew) that it does not make sense to believe his alcoholism was caused by the old man's prediction, but he nevertheless felt (his Child believed) that it was, and that he was powerless in the face of the apparently inevitable outcome. This man was like the spectator of a tragedy on the stage. For him, the events of his life unfolded according to the prophesies of an oracle, just as Oedipus unbelievingly saw Tiresias' prediction come to pass.

A script is a life plan, containing within its lines what of significance will happen to the person; a plan not decided upon by the gods, but finding its origin early in life, in a premature decision by the youngster.

---

[1]Sophocles. *The Oedipus Cycle.* New York: Harcourt, Brace and World, 1949.

It could be speculated that, with the above alcoholic, the wise old man was able to see the patient's self-destructive bent, which was later to unfold; it is common for persons like clinic intake workers, who interview large numbers of people, to see self-destructive life paths long before the protagonist himself recognizes them. The script guides the person's behavior from late childhood throughout life, determining its general but most basic outlines, and the trained observer is often able to detect and predict the course of a person's life quite accurately.

The concept of childhood life decisions is hardly surprising to anyone who has heard the life plans made by young children who later become engineers, lawyers, or doctors. In the area of successful achievement, it is understood that the young child often makes a decision about his life career, but the statement is much more startling when used without prejudice on all life careers, the alcoholic and the suicidal as well as the engineer and lawyer.

Until Freud wrote about *Oedipus Rex*, judging from his comments in *The Interpretation of Dreams*,[1] the myth was seen as a tragedy of destiny, one ". . . whose tragic effect is said to lie in the contrast between the supreme will of the gods and the vain attempts of mankind to escape the evils that threaten them." This destiny view has its origin in Aristotle's *Poetics*;[2] Freud rejected it in favor of his hypothesis that it is the incestuous content of the tragedy which moves audiences rather than the tragedy-of-destiny content.

Freud postulated that the frequent wish of his male patients to kill their fathers and bed down with their mothers had its counterparts in the Oedipus tale.[3] According to Freud, the Oedipus cycle is a source of vicarious fear and pity because it reflects a basic household drama experienced by all children who grow up with their parents.

[1]Freud, Sigmund. *The Interpretation of Dreams*. In *The Basic Writings*. New York: Modern Library, 1938.
[2]Aristotle. *Poetics*. New York: The Modern Library, 1954.
[3]Freud, Sigmund. *The Interpretation of Dreams*. In *The Basic Writings*. New York: The Modern Library, 1938.

However, a script analysis of the Oedipus complex would focus rather on the fated, predicted, ongoing destiny-aspect of *Oedipus Rex*. It would bid the reader to observe and reconsider the theory rejected by Freud that the message which spectators glean from the tragedy and the experience which deeply moves them is the realization of, and submission to, divine will and the realization of their own impotence in the face of fate.

The Child in the spectator is moved both by the similarity of the Oedipus tragedy and the events in his own household, and by the manner in which certain specified destinies unfold in what seems an irrevocable manner. The psychologist as a spectator, both of the Greek tragedies and of present-day human tragedy, learns, or should learn, that human beings are deeply affected by and submissive to the will of the specific divinities of their household—their parents—whose injunctions they are impotent against as they blindly follow them through life, sometimes to their self-destruction.

4

The Existential
Predicament of Children

Each succeeding generation of human beings produces the raw material—an O.K. child. Children are, therefore, born automatically into a great predicament because there is always a discrepancy between the possibilities of what they could become and what they are permitted to achieve. The discrepancy can be enormous—some children are born and their potential is immediately snuffed. Other children may be allowed quite a wide range of development.

The script is based on a decision made by the Adult in the young person who, with all of the information at her disposal at the time, decides that a certain position, expectations, and life course are a reasonable solution to the existential predicament in which she finds herself. Her predicament comes from the conflict between her own autonomous tendencies and the injunction received from her primary family group.

The most important influence or pressure impinging upon the youngster originates from the parental Child (Figure 5A). That is, *the Child ego states of the parents of the person are the main determining factors in the formation of scripts.*

Witches, Ogres, and Curses

The world of fairy tales provides us with useful clues to personality. Fairy tales tend to include a bad witch or an ogre as well as a good witch or fairy

mother or male protector,[1] a fact which—as in the
case of the Oedipus tragedy—is an intuitive bull's-eye.
The household parallel corresponding to witches is, of
course, mothers and fathers. That is, some children
are affected by their mothers or fathers as if by witches, good and bad, and this view of them can become
an important factor in the make-up of their personality.

Every person has three ego states, and in trying to
understand a person, the three ego states of both his
mother and father have to be understood as well
(Figure 5A). For persons with self-destructive scripts,
the Child ego state in father or mother (C_F or C_M)
has essentially all the features of a bad witch. This
witch, also known as the parent's "crazy Child," has a
most profound influence on the offspring. In these
cases, the young three- or four-year-old is under the
unquestioned and unquestionable rule of a confused,
scared, often wanton, and always irrational Child ego
state.

Crossman[2] points out that the child in a good
household is nurtured, protected, and raised by the
Parent ego state of his parents, with their Adult and
Child playing lesser roles. These lesser roles, however,
are not unimportant since the Adult in the parent encourages the offspring to learn the rules of logic and
the Child ego state of the parent plays an extremely
important part in exciting and encouraging the Natural Child. Nevertheless, the Nurturing Parent ego
state of the parents is the one that carries the burden
of child-rearing and neither the Child nor the Adult
is allowed to take full command in the situation.

The Nurturing Parent has as its main interest to

---

[1]Witches are in actuality powerful men or women and can use
their powers for good or bad purposes. Thus, I will use the terms
"bad witch" and "good witch" in this book and no longer distinguish
them along gender lines. This usage is not only more accurate, but
it also avoids a common misinterpretation of the oft-used term
"witch mother" by mothers who take the term to refer to themselves
when, in fact, it refers to an ego state in all people.

[2]Crossman, Patricia. "Permission and Protection." *Transactional
Analysis Bulletin* 5,19 (1966): 152–53.

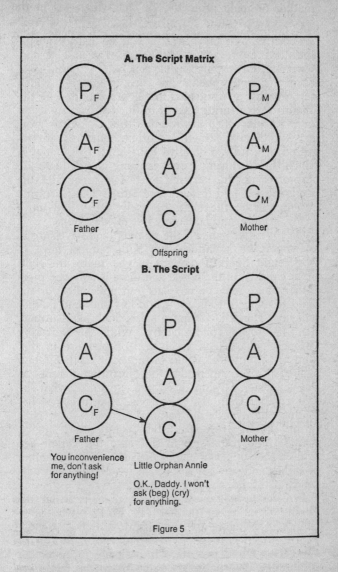

A. The Script Matrix

P_F

A_F

C_F

Father

P

A

C

Offspring

P_M

A_M

C_M

Mother

B. The Script

P

A

C_F

Father

You inconvenience
me, don't ask
for anything!

P

A

C

Little Orphan Annie

O.K., Daddy. I won't
ask (beg) (cry)
for anything.

P

A

C

Mother

Figure 5

support, to keep going, to take care of, to protect the
Child. The reaction of the Nurturing Parent to the
newborn is, "I'll take care of you no matter what."
This nurturing response is both instinctive and learned.
A woman, for instance, when her baby is born, has a
set of instinctive behaviors such as nursing which
start out by guaranteeing basic protection. But the
amount of Nurturing that is instinctive isn't sufficient
for the years which are required for a child to grow
up. Additional, learned nurturing behaviors are required in a fully protective household. In a home in
which the Nurturing Parent is doing an adequate job
of protecting, the parental nurturing supersedes the
needs of the Child in mother or father. The Nurturing
Parent will let the child be itself; speak and move
freely, explore, and be largely free of constraints.

On the other hand, if the parents themselves are in
an oppressive situation—say, both parents have to
work eight hours a day, or maybe there are eight
other children in the house and there is only one room
—then there may be no place, no possibility for the
child to express itself; the Child in father and mother
will say, "Don't! Don't make noise, don't bang around,
don't laugh, sing, or be happy." While the Nurturing
Parent would take a great deal of pleasure in that
kind of activity, the Child in father or mother rebels
against it, and supersedes the Nurturing Parent. As
the youngster develops her three ego states, what she
sees coming from the parents is what becomes her
Parent. She records the parental responses—not Nurturing Parent responses but competitive, angry,
scared Child responses. In this case the Parent ego
state in the youngster comes from the Child in mother
or father and we call it the bad witch, the electrode,
the Crazy Child, or the Pig Parent.

In a *hamartia-genic* household, then, it is not the
Parent of father or mother (P_F or P_M) who is in
charge of bringing up the offspring, but a pseudo-
Parent which is in reality a Child ego state (C_F or
C_M). This Child ego state is basically incapable of
performing the necessary function of a father or
mother, and where the Child becomes a pseudo-Par-

ent, the offspring generally develops a significant
script.

The child's predicament in a hamartia-genic household is illustrated in Figure 5B. In this example, the
father of a four-year-old, who later became Little Orphan Annie, allowed his own Child (C_F) to become a
pseudo-Parent. This man's Child was annoyed by his
daughter's needs. He also believed that the best way
to build character in a little girl and to avoid spoiling
her was to deny her everything she wanted, and to
give her something else in its place. If the little girl
wanted a teddy bear for Christmas and he knew it, he
would get her an equally lovely toy that she didn't
want, believing that this would be "good for her." The
little girl soon saw that her wishes never came true.

Her predicament, then, was that circumstances completely beyond her control made everything she allowed herself to desire automatically unobtainable.
She learned that if she did not express her wishes, the
chance they might come true was enhanced. She also
observed that even if she kept her wishes secret, she
might unwittingly reveal what she wanted by crying
when she was disappointed. As a consequence, in order to keep her father from noticing or deducing what
her wishes were, she decided that crying was undesirable. Her father basically and consistently enjoined
her not to want anything, not to ask for anything, and
not to cry when disappointed. This *injunction* coming
from father's Child (C_F) became the little girl's Parent
(P_1). This little girl became a grown woman, but until she gave up her script she carried inside her Child
her father's injunction, "Don't ask for anything." It
became a relentless influence which guided every one
of her significant actions for years.

Restrictive injunctions and attributions are passed
on to children in order to satisfy or comfort the parents. In another example, the mother of a boy was
very scared of aggressive males because her husband,
an aggressive male, had beaten her and left her. When
her son was born she did not want him to be an aggressive, masculine man. So she used injunctions "don't
be aggressive," "don't be assertive," and attributions

"you are gentle," "you are quiet," to affect his behavior, and he grew up to be non-masculine with many female role characteristics. He developed being different from other little boys, and the other little boys made fun of him, so that sooner or later someone called him "queer," and he connected the word queer with being a homosexual. He looked up "homosexual" in the dictionary and found that a homosexual is a man who has sexual relations with another man. One day he was walking through the park and was approached by a man and had a homosexual experience which he enjoyed, and at that point decided that he *was* a homosexual and proceeded to pursue a homosexual life course. Thus, he went from getting a set of injunctions and attributions to deciding that he was something that he didn't have to be, with very little choice in the matter. He did not freely choose to be a homosexual; the pressures of his household plus other circumstances forced that choice on him. He was, for instance, not free to have sexual relations with women: script analysis eventually freed him to be able to choose to have sexual and loving relationships with women as well as men.

This is how household pressures, over a period of years, combine with a set of circumstances so that people make life decisions. Other children are pressured to be unhappy, stupid, or clumsy for similar reasons.

It might be interesting to speculate why a parent would want his child to be clumsy or stupid. Imagine a child is born that is not wanted. Mother, who had had three children and didn't want to have any more, got pregnant one night when her husband came home drunk and raped her, forcing her to have intercourse against her will. Her husband didn't believe in abortions so the baby was born, and it was a difficult birth. The child was an annoyance from the start. It took fifteen stitches to sew mother up—clumsy from the very beginning. This kid was seen as a clumsy kid; he started all wrong and he reminded mother of her brother who is clumsy, too. So she often thought and said: "This kid is just like Uncle Charlie, who is a clumsy man." Soon mother and father started calling him "Clums" in jest whenever he made mistakes. It suited these parents' needs to think of this particular son as a clumsy boy, because it gave them a place to vent their anger and an excuse for not taking good care of him.

Injunctions

The injunction, or in fairy-tale language, the "curse," is a prohibition, or an inhibition of the free behavior of the child. It is always the negation of an activity. The injunction reflects the fears, wishes, anger, and desires of the Child in the parent (C_F or C_M). Injunctions vary in range, intensity, area of restriction, and malignancy. Some injunctions affect a very small range of behavior, such as "don't sing," or "don't laugh loudly," or "don't eat too many sweets." Others are extremely comprehensive in range, such as "don't be happy," "don't think," or "don't do anything."

The intensity of injunctions varies in proportion to the consequences of disobedience. Thus, the injunction "don't be happy" can be given with great intensity, in which case the least expression of happiness can bring severe repercussions; or it can be given with minimal intensity, in which case only minor disapproval is expressed when the injunction is broken. The area of behavior that the injunction restricts depends upon the witch mother's or ogre's specific and delineated focus: the injunction might be "don't think," "don't be happy," "don't enjoy sex," "don't show anger," "don't be healthy," or "don't accept strokes," "don't reject strokes," "don't give strokes."

As to malignancy, some injunctions have destructive long-range effects, while others do not. They can be classified like games in terms of degrees. For instance, the third-degree injunction of Mr. Bruto, an alcoholic man, was "never be idle." This was not only a long-range injunction, but one so malignant that he eventually found himself unable to avoid a job he intensely disliked except by knocking himself out through drinking.

On the other hand, many parental injunctions are neither destructive nor long-range in their effects. For instance, mother may say to child, "never touch the electrical outlet on the wall!" This first-degree injunction may be quite effective in controlling the child's behavior but it hardly seems malignant. Unless it is part of a larger injunction such as "don't touch anything," or "don't play with anything electrical or mechanical (it's men's work)," it will probably only last as long as it takes the child to learn how to use electrical wall outlets safely.

Attributions

Tragic scripts tend to be based on negative injunctions, accompanied by severe punishments. But children are also powerfully affected by attributions. The concept of attributions, developed by Ronald Laing, serves to explain how parents affect children *to do* rather than not do things. In Laing's words:

One way to get someone to do what one wants, is to give an order. To get someone to be what one wants him to be, or supposes he is or is afraid he is (whether or not this is what one wants), that is, to get him to embody one's projection, is another matter. In a hypnotic (or similar) context, one does not tell him what to be, but tells him what he is. Such attributions, in context, are many times more powerful than orders (or other forms of coercion or persuasion). An instruction need not be defined as an instruction. It is my impression that we receive most of our earliest and most lasting instructions in the form of attributions. We are told such and such is the case. One is, say, told one is a good or a bad boy or girl, not only instructed to be a good or bad boy or girl. One may be subject to both, but if one is (this or that), it is not necessary to be told to be what one

*has already been "given to understand" one is. The
key medium for communication of this kind is
probably not verbal language. When attributions have
the function of instructions or injunctions, this function
may be denied, giving rise to one type of mystification,
akin to, or identical with, hypnotic suggestion . . .*

*One may tell someone to feel something and not to
remember he has been told. Simply tell him he
feels it. Better still, tell a third party, in front of him,
that he feels it.*

*Under hypnosis, he feels it; and does not know
that he has been hypnotized to feel it. How much
of what we ordinarily feel, is what we have all been
hypnotized to feel? How much of who we are, is what
we have been hypnotized to be?*

*Your word is my command. A relationship of one
to another may be of such power that you become
what I take you to be, at my glance, at my touch, at
my cough. I do not need to say anything. An
attribution, as I am using the term, may be kinetic,
tactile, olfactory, visual. Such an attribution is
equivalent to an instruction to be obeyed "implicitly."*

*So, if I hypnotize you, I do not say, "I order you
to feel cold." I indicate it is cold. You immediately
feel cold. I think many children begin in a state
like this.*

*We indicate to them how it is: they take up their
positions in the space we define. They may then
choose to become a fragment of that fragment of
their possibilities we indicate they are.*

*What we explicitly tell them is, I suspect, of less
account.*

*What we indicate they are, is, in effect, an
instruction for a drama: a scenario . . .*

*The clinical hypnotist knows what he is doing;
the family hypnotist almost never. A few parents have
described this technique to me as a deliberate
stratagem.*

*More often parents are themselves confused by a
child who does x, when they tell him to do y and
indicate he is x.*

*"I'm always trying to get him to make more friends,
but he is so self-conscious. Isn't that right, dear?*
*"I keep telling him to be more careful, but he's so
careless, aren't you?"*

I quote Laing at length to show the eloquence of his
writing and the brilliance of his thinking. I consider
his book *The Politics of the Family*[1]—from which the
above is taken—essential to the understanding of
scripts.

Attributions, then, tell the child what she must do
and injunctions tell what she must not do in order to
remain in the parent's favor. They are the age-old
behavior modification program of the nuclear family.
Attributions when followed are reinforced, injunctions
when disobeyed are punished. Familial reinforcement
schedules control children's behavior in the same manner in which psychologists control the behavior of rats
by selective rewards and punishments.

Parental attributions, like curses, are often introduced into a person's life at the day of birth. For
example, parents often predict that a certain child is
going to be healthy, unhealthy, smart, stupid, lucky,
or unlucky. One alcoholic's mother read his future alcoholism in the stars, a finding which she often repeated
to him in his childhood. Myths containing the elements of what the parents would like the child to do
in life are often passed down to children. One man,
who prides himself on being extremely perceptive of
other's feelings, was told that as soon as he emerged
from the womb he opened his eyes and looked around.
Whenever something bad happened to another, he
was reminded that he was born on Friday the thir-
teenth, and could expect bad luck all his life. Characteristically, the grown person believes that his state is
fated rather than produced by the parental prediction.
The effect of a prediction of this sort has been amply
explored in the concept of the self-fulfilling prophecy.[2]

[1]Laing, Ronald D. *The Politics of the Family and Other Essays.*
New York: Pantheon Books, a division of Random House, 1971.
[2]Merton, Robert K. *Social Theory and Social Structure.* Glencoe,
Illinois: Free Press, 1957.

In general, expected behavior is likely to occur simply because it is expected.

Names often subtly suggest to the child what parents expect of him: John, Jr. is expected to follow in his father's footsteps; Jesse is expected to raise hell; Gigi is expected to be sexy; and Alfred is expected to be well-ordered and neat. Berne provides an excellent discussion of the ways in which a forename can be the source of script programming in *What Do You Say After You Say Hello?* He also speaks of the relevance of two main *birth scripts*—The Foundling Script and The Torn Mother Script—which he has observed, and which play an important part in people's lives. The former is a belief of being a foundling, therefore not really a blood relation of the parents; the latter is a belief that the person severely hurt, invalided, or crippled his mother at birth. These birth scripts, real or imagined, can have a lasting effect. I have found that the Foundling Script can have two forms: "daughter (or son) of a King (or Queen)" or "son (or daughter) of A Whore (or Bum)." I have found the latter when it is present, especially "daughter of a Whore," to be an extremely compelling force; and Berne points out that " 'Mother died at childbirth' (mine) is almost too much for anyone to bear without good help."

Witchcraft

Transactional analysis and script analysis are concerned with the understanding and analysis of transactions at two levels: the social level (the audible, visible, and obviously perceptible level of transactions between people) and the psychological level (the hidden, covert, non-explicit communication that may accompany the social level of transactions).

The accurate understanding and prediction of people's behavior depends on an acuity of perception of the psychological level of transactions; without it only the most superficial aspects of people's transactions will be understood. In the analysis of games the social level, which is clearly explicit, is easily understood by the observer; but the psychological level is understood only through intuitive, perceptual powers which are neither easily explained nor taught.

Script analysis, which is the study of people's decisions early in life based on the injunctions and attributions of their parents, requires an understanding of the way in which parents transmit information to their children about what it is they want them and do not want them to do. It is seldom found that a parent said to his child something as explicit as "I want you to die," or "I don't want you to think," or "You are absolutely no good." Rather, one finds that those kinds of statements are given to children in the form of veiled communication which is at times very crude but is often extremely subtle. In any case, whatever the subtlety of such attributions and injunctions, they are known as witch messages; messages which affect these children for the rest of their lives with magical, uncanny powers.

The power of parents to influence their children—the power to mold them, the power to make them do things and prevent them from doing things—according to their wishes is an aspect of a more general capacity which all human beings have, the capacity for witchcraft. The analysis of witchcraft is a subheading of transactional analysis in that it deals with the analysis of covert or ulterior messages and their effect and power.

People can be influenced for better or for worse and the power to do either may be called good magic or bad magic. The two faculties which are involved in good and bad magic are the Nurturing Parent and the Pig Parent.

Good Magic

The Nurturing Parent can instill people with power, cause them to feel and be intelligent, good, perceptive, beautiful, healthy.

Two, three, or more persons can be involved. The Witch or sender, It or the receiver, and a Third Person or transmitter. Witch messages can be given directly from the Witch to It or indirectly from the Witch to It through the Third Person. It is also possible that Fourth, Fifth, and Sixth Persons are involved as well; in fact, a whole group can become a transmitter of messages of this sort.

Good witch messages function as encouragement and attributions of intelligence, goodness, perceptiveness, beauty, health, etc. Thus, the Witch can say to It: "I love how smart you are," or "You are *sooo* beautiful," or "You are *very* healthy," or, through a Third Person, "Isn't she smart?" or "Jill has beautiful eyes," or "The doctor says Jack is really healthy." Third Person messages have the same or even larger effect on It as if said directly to It. For instance, Jack, above, is affected in two ways: 1) because he hears, and believes, the statement ("Jack is healthy") addressed at the Third Person; and 2) through the effect that the statement has on the Third Person who eventually comes to think and believe the same as the Witch does. This latter process can occur in the absence of It, so that if the Witch speaks to a Third Person about Jill's intelligence, beauty, or health, the message will be transmitted from the Third Person to Jill whenever they come together.

A property of witch messages is that their power does not necessarily depend on the words used. The words themselves are only a vehicle. "I love how *smart* you are" could actually be a bad message about being *too* smart; while "I *love* how smart you are" means quite something else. Certain parts of the statement are energized and some are de-energized; and these fluctuations of energy have important meanings, more important, at times, than the words.

The origin of good magic is the Nurturing Parent, which is a faculty or ego state of human beings geared to the protection and nurturing of other people. The net effect of the nurturing magic messages is to increase the power of people and to liberate them from their own oppressive influences (the Pig Parent) as well as to give them power to liberate themselves from the oppressive influence of others. It has been known to people as the Guardian Angel, the good fairy, or fairy godmother who protects them from Evil.

Nurturing messages can be stored by a person in her or his own Nurturing Parent and can be used for self-nurturing, which is also a powerful source of O.K. feelings. Self-nurturing, however, depends on the nurturing of others and eventually loses power if it isn't reinforced by external nurturing messages.

Bad Magic

Everything that has been said about good magic is true about bad magic except that the source and purpose of bad magic are different. Good magic can be distinguished from bad magic by the effect that it has on its recipient. If it has the effect of adding power to the recipient it is good; if it decreases power it is bad.

It is important to realize that bad witchcraft in the form of attribution is often used for the recipient's "own good" as judged by the witch; any attribution, no matter how good it looks or sounds, can be bad for the recipient. For instance, the attribution of beauty may be harmful to a woman who is a "media beauty" because it stands in the way of being seen as and becoming intelligent or powerful.

Thus, while bad witchcraft is usually clearly bad, some witchcraft that appears to be good may in fact be bad because it is not wanted by the recipient, or because even though wanted it diminishes her power in some way.

The exercise of power over people for the purpose of harming them seems to have two basic sources. The first source is scarcity. When scarcity of something needed exists so that there is less of it than would be necessary to satisfy all of the people in a situation, then it is inevitable that certain people who have more power will use that power against other people to take away their fair share. The power used can be crude physical force, as when one kills people and takes their food or land; but it also can take the form of psychic force where the powerful person creates a situation in the powerless person so that the powerless person will give up his fair share without resistance, thus not needing to be coerced. This is what is called "mystified oppression,"[1] a situation where people allow others to oppress them because they accept the deceptions which justify the oppression.

The second reason why people use power over other people is what has been aptly called by Fanita English[2] the "hot potato." It is done as a defense against accusations of worthlessness from within oneself or from the outside. That is to say, in a situation in which one feels worthless or not O.K., this feeling can be passed on to another person as in a game of "hot potato" so that proving that another person is not O.K. relieves one of the feeling. Also, a person will often feel stronger, more vital, and powerful if he can control and influence others. In other words, if he can make another person feel less O.K. than he does, then, relatively speaking, he is O.K.

The two situations of bad magic which have been described above are best understood in the context of a child entering a family. Let us assume a child is born into a family living in a ghetto. The family consists of a mother, a father and a grandfather, as well as two boys and two girls ages 10, 8, 6, and 4, all living in a three-room apartment. The family lives on welfare, the grandfather is an alcoholic, and the two older children are in trouble with the law. At this point, a new child, Ultimo, is born into the family.

Clearly, the essential ingredients for physical comfort are not available in this situation. There is not enough space, not enough food, not enough strokes, not enough time, not enough energy, to take care of Ultimo. Everyone in the family is aware of the fact that this newborn child is going to diminish their

[1]Steiner, Claude M. "Radical Psychiatry." In *Going Crazy*, ed. by Hendrik M. Ruitenbeek. New York: Bantam Books, 1972.

[2]English, Fanita. "Episcript and the 'Hot Potato' Game." *Transactional Analysis Bulletin*, Vol. 8, October, 1969, pp. 77–82.

share of space, food, energy, strokes; and while every
newborn child is given a period of respite in which it
is offered a plenitude of what it needs, a day comes,
usually around the first birthday, when the scarcity of
the situation begins to affect Ultimo. The situation
quickly becomes a dog-eat-dog affair in which everyone fends for himself, and the devil take the hindmost.
Direct physical force will be applied on Ultimo to prevent him from getting his fair share of what he needs,
as well as psychic force in the form of messages such
as "You're stupid," "You move around too much," "You
make too much noise," "Get out of here," "Go play in
the freeway (haha)," "You're a bad boy," etc., all of
which are designed to diminish his range of power
and prevent him from making a claim to what is
rightfully his. This is an example of scarcity witchcraft.

At the same time that there is physical scarcity
which calls for both physical and psychic oppression,
there may also exist a situation in which the grownups
in the family have various degrees of feelings of worthlessness. For example, father has not been able to get
a decent job and feels that he is a failure. His wife
called him a "no-good bum" this morning. During an
afternoon in which father feels that he is supposed to
go looking for work but is instead watching television,
Ultimo, on vacation from school, might be hanging
around listening to records. Father, who feels not O.K.
and ashamed about his own behavior, becomes annoyed at his son and demands that he do the dishes.
When his son, following his father's example, refuses,
father calls *him* "a no-good, lazy bum." At that particular point he is passing the "hot potato" from himself
to his son, and he enjoys a short period of relief from
worthlessness. At another time, when mother sets the
food on the table while feeling that she is a bad pro-
vider because there is nothing but starches for dinner,
Ultimo says, "Mom, I learned in school that you're
supposed to eat meat at least once a day." At this
point, mother looks at him angrily, "Shut your smart
mouth, boy." Again the "hot potato," the feeling of not
O.K. in mother, is passed on to the son. For a brief

period mother feels freedom from guilt, which has been replaced by self-righteous indignation at Ultimo's insolence. Ultimo feels he has done something very bad. He feels not O.K. and comes away from the situation feeling guilty, selfish, and bad. All of these feelings become part of his Pig Parent and could plague him as long as he lives.

Bad witchcraft is known elsewhere as curses, voodoo, or the pox. The power of witchcraft is enormous, especially if a group of people all apply it to one person. Voodoo death is a case in point, in which a person is killed when all of the members of his village give him the "evil eye." Madness, or so-called schizophrenia, is our "civilized" counterpart of voodoo death —the psychic murder of people by collective bad witchcraft.

It is very important to realize the basic defenselessness of the offspring in the face of the bad witch's curse. Household situations where the Child ego state (P_F or P_M) operates as a pseudo-Parent can be compared, in more severe cases, with a concentration camp in which a pair of hundred-and-fifty-pound prison guards physically and psychologically terrorize a forty-pound three-year-old into submission. The severity of some of the injunctions found in hamartic scripts cannot be minimized. This point will be discussed further in the chapter on therapy.

The script, then, is a decision the young person makes by choosing between his own autonomous needs and expectations, and the pressures of injunctions he encounters in his primary family group. The script matrix (Figure 5) is extremely useful to visualize the different forces which influence the child to make its decision. The diagram implies that the effect of the parents (or their substitutes) is paramount in the kind of decision that will be made, the more so in early life when others have little access to or influence on the child. This view stands somewhere between the extreme sociological one that sees a person's behavior as the result of cultural influences only, and the view that regards behavior as strictly the consequence of forces and dynamics inside of the child.

5

Decisions

When a youngster's inborn expectations of protection to develop as he will aren't met, adoption of a script occurs. To the Child it is as if alien forces were applying pressure against his growth; unless he yields to these pressures life becomes extremely difficult. Thus, the Child is forced to abdicate his birthright, and he does this by readjusting his expectations and wishes to fit the situation. This process is a crucial point in the development of scripts and is called the *decision*.

The script decision is made when the youngster, applying all her adaptive resources, modifies her expectations and tries to align them with the realities of the home situation.

Time of the Decision

The age at which the decision is made varies from person to person. In a life course which develops normally, a decision of such importance as what one's identity is to be and what goals one will pursue should be made late enough in life so that a certain measure of knowledge informs the choice. In a situation where a youngster is under no unreasonable pressure, important decisions about life will occur no earlier than adolescence.

A script results from a decision which is both premature and forced, because it is made under pressure

and therefore long before a decision can be properly
made.

Emotional disturbances can be graded on a list by
degree of malignancy. Psychosis, whether "schizophrenic" or depressive, as well as tissue self-destruction, such as alcoholism, are third-degree, tragic
scripts; they are based on third-degree injunction and
the decisions they are based on come early in life. So-
called "neurotic" disturbances and just plain common
ordinary unhappiness are first- and second-degree
banal scripts[1] and they are based on first- and second-
degree injunctions and/or attributions; their decisions may come as late as adolescence.

The decision is as good and as viable as the skills
of the Little Professor at the time of the decision. The
Little Professor operates at a different level of logic,
perception, and cognition than the Adult of the grownup. In addition, the Little Professor is forced to
operate with incomplete data because of its limited
sources of information. In general, the younger the
person making the decision, the more likely that the
Little Professor operated on incomplete data and im-
perfect logic.

Making the decision eases pressure and increases
short-term satisfaction. For example, the young man
mentioned on pages 69–70 recalls that when he was a
little boy his mother showed great discomfort when he
played with the rough children in the neighborhood.
He also noticed that if he imitated those rough boys,
his mother expressed considerable disapproval. He
found no support for any boyish behavior from his
father who acquiesced in his mother's dislike of "man-
liness" and vigorous activity. He wanted to be "one of
the boys," but this wish encountered so much resistance and pressure that he recalled deciding on a
specific day of a specific week of a specific year that
he would be his "mother's good little boy," a decision
which very obviously made life easier for him. When

---

[1] Thanks are due to Kathy Dusay for suggesting the word "banal"
for everyday, "garden variety" scripts.

he presented himself for therapy at age thirty-five, he was indeed mother's good little boy—neatly dressed, clean, polite, well-groomed, considerate, and respectful. Unfortunately, the decisions which had been adaptive and comfortable at age ten were now completely outdated and responsible for much discomfort. The decision had affected his sex life, in that he practiced a sort of depersonalized sex, voyeurism, and masturbation, which was an adaptation to his mother's wishes that he be a good, quiet, little boy. His decision also affected his work because he saw all work as an acquiescence to a motherly demand. This resulted in a childlike approach to his endeavors, always tainted by acquiescence, mixed with bitterness. The bitterness came from the fact that even though he had decided to be mother's good little boy, the decision had been made with considerable anger and resentment.

It might be noted here that what psychoanalysts call traumatic neuroses—neurosis caused by a traumatic event—are situations in which the pressures on the youngster making the decision are sudden rather than extending over a long period of time. Here the crux of the script is still the decision, but one made in response to an acutely uncomfortable situation as opposed to one made as a result of long-standing and enduring pressures.

A very important set of injunctions and attributions which affect children from the earliest day on causing premature script decisions is the gender-linked programming called sex roles. According to these, boys and girls are separated into two human camps which are expected to be different along a number of extremely important dimensions. Sex role scripting can have, in my opinion, severely damaging, malignant, and far-reaching consequences as will be shown in the section on Men and Women's Banal Scripts.

"Good" scripts, or life plans which have socially redeeming qualities (such as the script of a martyr or hero, an engineer, doctor, politician, or priest), can be premature and forced decisions as well; their outcome may seem to be generally positive, but the decision is

often made without necessary information and autonomy.

Decisions which lead to healthy personality development must be both timely and autonomous. Thus, in
proper script-free ego formation, the date of decision
is such that it provides for sufficient information, lack
of pressure, and autonomy.

Form of the Decision

Erik Erikson[1] speaks of the position with which
children are born into the world as one of *basic trust*.
As he describes it, basic trust comes from a state of
affairs in which the infant feels that she is at one with
the world and that everything is at one with her. It
is clearest when mother and child are interacting most
basically, as when feeding or nursing at the breast;
even more basic is the mutuality of mother and offspring *in utero*.

Transactional analysis would describe this feeling of
basic trust as the first of four possible existential posi-
tions a person can assume. The four positions are "I'm
O.K., you're O.K.," "I'm not O.K., you're O.K.," "I'm
O.K., you're not O.K.," and "I'm not O.K., you're not
O.K."

The original position, "I'm O.K., you're O.K.," is
rooted in the biological mutuality of mother and child
which provides for the unconditional response of the
mother to the child's needs. How a mother responds
unconditionally to the demands of a child can be
clearly understood by observing a cat and her kittens
in the act of feeding. When a hungry kitten meows the
mother cat will seek out the kitten and try to start
the nursing process. This can be interpreted as an
expression of a mothering instinct, but it can also be
seen as an automatic, stimulus-bound behavior pattern: the unpleasant meowing of the kitten produces

---

[1]Erickson, Erik H. *Identity: Youth and Crisis.* New York: W. W.
Norton, 1968.

an urge in the mother cat to offer herself for nursing in order to stop the unpleasant stimulus. This example is given to emphasize that there is a biologically given responsiveness in the mother to a hungry offspring, and that this universal biological responsiveness almost guarantees a primary mutuality which, in human beings, generates a basic trust or a position of "I'm O.K., you're O.K."

This basic trust position, "I'm O.K., you're O.K.," categorizes what we call the position of the "prince" or "princess," and this position is one that the infant tends to adhere to.[1] The only reason a youngster gives up this position for either "I'm not O.K.," or "You're not O.K.," or both, is that the original, primary mutuality is interrupted, and that the protection which at first was given unconditionally (in utero at the very least) is withdrawn. The insecurity of uncertain protection with conditions brings the youngster to the conclusion that either he is not O.K., mother is not O.K., or both are not O.K. Needless to say, this decision is not reached without a struggle. It requires considerable pressure to convince the prince that he is not, after all, a prince and to cause him to believe that he is, instead, a frog.[2] It is important to note the difference between a youngster who still feels that he is O.K., though he is uncomfortable because of the circumstances in which he finds himself, and the youngster who adapts to the discomfort of his surroundings by deciding that he is not O.K., and thereby becomes comfortable. In a situation of this nature, the choice seems to be whether to remain an uncomfortable prince or to become a comfortable frog.

Becoming a frog requires not only a transition from "I'm O.K." to "I'm not O.K.," but also the adoption of a conscious fantasy about the kind of frog the youngster finds he is.

[1] In transactional analysis, children are seen as princes and princesses until their parents turn them into frogs.

[2] The reader will note that this view is in disagreement with the Harris's (I'm OK—You're OK) who believe that the first, universal position is "I'm not O.K., you're O.K."

Frogs, Princes, and Princesses

Scripts cause the person to act as if he were someone other than himself. This is much more than mere
acting or surface masking. The youngster who finds
himself unable to make sense of the pressures under
which he lives needs to synthesize his decision in
terms of a consciously understood model. This model
is usually based on a person in fiction, mythology,
comic books, movies, television, or possibly real life.
The mythical person embodies a solution to the
dilemma in which the youngster finds herself. For
example, one man, Mr. Salvador, consciously thought
he was Jesus Christ, and recalls that as a young boy
his parents had accused him of killing his younger
brother. Their exact reasons for doing this are not
clear, and whether they meant it as a joke or seriously
was never understood. However, Mr. Salvador as a
youngster found himself having to make sense of this
accusation. Reared as a Catholic he knew his catechism, and he decided that he was like Jesus Christ
and would redeem himself of his original sin by living
a pure life, such as that lived by Him. Thus, Mr.
Salvador's script was based on the life of Jesus Christ,
a good example of the way youngsters synthesize and
make comprehensible their home situation by way of
a commonly available myth or fairy tale. This identity
was consciously maintained throughout his life, and
Mr. Salvador reported that three or four times during
any one day he would have conscious thoughts about
his Christlike identity. As an example, when he was
once seeking an overnight sleeping place at a friend's
house and was turned down, he thought, "No room
at the inn." On another occasion, at a particularly
unhappy time in his life, he severely hurt his fore-
head which drew blood above his eyes, and he
formed a vision of the crown of thorns; once again
this was a conscious identification. Incidents like this,
in which the script's mythical character becomes a

consciously understood identity, are commonplace phenomena in scripts.

The character chosen for imitation can be a highly stylized, completely mythical individual at one extreme, or a live, flesh-and-blood person at the other. Thus, Mr. Junior's mythical character was his father, who had died when he was seven years old. Mr. Junior knew his father partially through his own dim recollections and partially through the bittersweet memories of his mother. By contrast, Mr. Niet chose as his mythical character Captain Marvel, as understood by him at age twelve, through his reading of comic books. Mr. Junior, when behaving as he thought his dead father behaved, had a human, flesh-and-blood appearance; Mr. Niet, on the other hand, had an extremely unreal, rigid, and almost robotlike appearance.

The mythical character chosen can also vary in complexity. For example, recall Mr. Salvador, who chose Jesus Christ as his mythical character. His view of Jesus was a fairly complex elaboration of what he knew about Him at the time he made his decision. He gained his understanding of the personality of Jesus Christ by reading the catechism and the Bible, but his extensive elaboration made his portrayal considerably different from what anyone might expect. For example, as a boy he had come to the conclusion that Jesus "was making it with Mary Magdalene" and that, in general, He was not chaste, but a sexually active rescuer who got involved with females in distress and tended to protect and care for them. Mr. Salvador's particular understanding of the mythical character was later turned into action and he was therefore quite sexually active with females who required him to protect them.

On the other hand, Mr. Bruto based his choice of a mythical character on a painting, *The Man with a Hoe*, which represented simply an overwhelmingly burdened, almost subhuman male. Mr. Bruto consequently lived a life of hard work, which he never questioned or rebelled against.

It should be noted at this point that youngsters

choosing a mythical character always elaborate the available material and adapt it to fit their own circumstances, needs, and information. Because of this, it is important in diagnosing a script to know how to retrieve the person's interpretation of the character she has adopted, and not to make the mistake of assuming the well-known, popular version.

Parents are often shocked by their children's script behavior and have trouble seeing the part they play in it. Parents want their children to behave in a certain way, but when the children follow the injunctions, modified by their own elaborations, the parents often are horrified at the results. A classic example is the case of Buddy, an eighteen-year-old boy, who decided that "I ain't taking nothing from nobody." This decision translated itself into such extreme sensitivity and violent reaction to pressure from parental figures that he would fly into uncontrollable rages when pushed beyond his limits. These rages were so extreme that he had been hospitalized or confined from age fourteen on. Buddy recalls that as a six-year-old, while chasing his older sister with a butcher knife, his mother reprimanded him by saying indignantly, and in an injured tone, "Buddy, you are *too young* to be chasing your sister with a meat cleaver!" It is clear in this situation that mother, who would consider this kind of behavior appropriate at age eighteen, yelled "Foul!" when Buddy, a precocious young man, engaged in it at age six. Similarly, a man who is sexually attracted to his daughter may urge her to dress and act sexy and then be sexually suggestive toward her. When he finds himself with a thirteen-year-old pregnant child on his hands, he has difficulty recognizing that the girl had simply followed his instructions, with only minor variations. The same situation is found over and over again in the case histories of alcoholics and other drug abusers who describe their parents' dismay when they discover their offsprings' drug abuse after years of encouraging the use of alcohol or other drugs to deal with stress, and of condoning drug abuse in themselves and others.

6

Transactional Analysis
of Scripts

Scripts are being studied by a growing number of investigators, each one of which (or each group of which) may have a different emphasis.

I intend to pursue a certain line of investigation which I call "transactional analysis of life scripts" in order to emphasize the transactional focus of my interest. This should distinguish it from, among others, the *structural* analysis of scripts—which, in my mind, is closer to psychoanalysis than it is to transactional analysis.

A great deal has been written recently about the structural analysis of scripts. This line of research focused in detail on the script matrix, investigating the sources and content of injunctions; interested readers can find many articles on that subject in the last three years' issues of the *Transactional Analysis Journal*.

My interest in script theory derives from my wish to help people gain autonomy from harmful parental and societal programming. Script analysis, to me, is meant to provide information and suggest strategies for redecision and change. The detailed study of historical and structural aspects of the script strikes me as distractions from that task. Some structural information is necessary for good problem solving work and a certain additional amount has esthetic value in that it provides elegant explanations for past and present events. But, as I see it, the most important fact in transactional script analysis is "here and now" transactions.

Thus, I am more interested in the answer to the question, "What can you do now to free yourself from a decision to never trust anyone?" than to the question, "Was your decision not to trust anyone made due to a maternal injunction or a paternal injunction?" or, "Did the injunction come from P_1, P_2, C_1 or C_2 in your mother or father?"

Structural analysis of scripts leads to a proliferation of subdivisions of ego states on the script matrix (the record so far is 28). Transactional analysis of scripts leads to a proliferation of *techniques* which can be used by therapists in problem solving groups to do contractual transactional analysis. Structural analysis of scripts can be pursued in one-to-one or individual psychotherapy; transactional analysis of scripts is best done in groups because it is based on the analysis of transaction between people.

The Three Basic Life Scripts

In order to devise a strategy for change, it is not only important to know the components of a script, but it is also important to examine a person's life script in terms of much broader aspects, as follows.

There are three basic ways in which people's autonomous lives are thwarted and distorted into scripts. Looking over the many unhappy life styles that have come to my attention, and taking their extremes, I find that people can either become depressed to the point of suicide, go mad, or become addicted to some sort of drug. Depression, madness, and drug addiction are the three basic life disturbances and I call the scripts that correspond to these disturbances Lovelessness, Mindlessness, and Joylessness; or, for short, No Love, No Mind, and No Joy scripts.

DEPRESSION, OR NO LOVE SCRIPT

Large numbers of people in this country are in a constant unsuccessful quest for a successful, loving relationship. This is a difficulty that seems to affect women more often than men, probably because women are more sensitized to their needs for love and less capable of adapting to Lovelessness. Lack of adequate stroking, which leads to chronic stroke hunger and various degrees of depression, culminating either in suicide or in the most extreme form of depression —catatonia—is one large strand of human suffering. The Lovelessness script is based on the Stroke Economy, a set of early childhood injunctions addressed to the stroking capacities of children. Those injunctions very effectively cripple the growing child's normal tendencies and skills for getting strokes. The result is various degrees of depression with feelings of being unloved and/or unlovable.

MADNESS, OR NO MIND SCRIPT

Another large portion of people live with the ever-present fear that they are going crazy and, according to statistics, about 1% are actually hospitalized. Every town across this country has within easy reach one or more mental hospitals—Ypsilanti in Ann Arbor, Belle-vue in New York, Napa and Agnew in the San Francisco Bay Area, La Casteñeda in Mexico City. Most people have, very much in the front of their minds, the awareness of the regional "nut house" or "funny farm" to which they might be relegated should they go mad; the fear of madness is present in large numbers of people.

Going crazy is the most extreme expression of the No Mind script. Mindlessness, or incapacity to cope in the world, the feeling that one has no control over one's life—seen in folk terms as having no will power, being lazy, not knowing what one wants, being stupid or crazy—is based on early childhood injunctions which attack the child's capacity to think and to figure out the world. Training against the use of the

Adult in the early years of life is the foundation for the No Mind script with the *discounting transaction* as its cornerstone.

DRUG ADDICTION, OR NO JOY SCRIPT

Large numbers of human beings in this country are in one way or another addicted to drugs. I'm not speaking here only of the visible, clearly self-destructive drug addictions such as alcoholism or heroin addiction, but also of the less visible but much more common reliance on drugs for the production of desired bodily feelings. The use of drugs for the attainment of bodily well-being includes drinking coffee, smoking cigarettes, taking aspirin, and, of course, using barbiturates, sedatives, and amphetamines, as well as over-the-counter drugs which are taken to modify bodily feelings. People are, from early in their lives, prevented from experiencing their bodies and from knowing what will feel good or bad to them.

If a person gets a headache, the usual question is not, "Why did I get a headache? What specific injury or injurious situation have I exposed my body to that is now producing a headache?" but, "Where is the aspirin?" This basic pattern is the pattern of all drug taking. People do not reflect why they need to have a drink after they come home from work, or why they need to take a pill in order to go to sleep, or why they need to take another pill in order to wake up. If they asked themselves these questions and remained in good touch with their bodies, the answers would be readily accessible. Instead, people are trained, from early in life, to disregard their bodily sensations and messages, whether pleasant or unpleasant. Unpleasant bodily sensations are medicated away whenever possible or passively tolerated whenever there is no medication which could affect them. Pleasant bodily sensations are not indulged in, and constant pressure is exerted to prevent children from being in touch with the exhilaration, the joy of a full bodily experience, and to distract them from their bodily feelings, pleasures and pains. The result is that many people are disconnected from their bodily sensations, their bodies are split off from their centers, they have lost agency over their physical selves, and are joyless.

People may be racked by some sort of pain with which they are out of touch and don't really feel. They are also out of touch with the joyful experiences which their body could afford them. The extreme of this alienation from the body is drug addiction; but, intermediately, people, especially men, although many women as well, are out of touch with their feelings—good or bad. They're incapable of feeling love, incapable of feeling ecstasy, incapable of crying, incapable of hating, and live for the most part in their heads, disconnected from the rest of their bodies. The head is seen as the Center, the switchboard, the computer which reigns over the rest of the body which is just a machine designed to work or execute certain functions. Feelings, good or bad, are considered to be hindrances to proper functioning.

These three life scripts—No Love, No Mind, No Joy—are, as I said earlier, exemplified in their extreme form by being completely and catatonically depressed, by going crazy, or by becoming addicted to a drug. Much more common in everyday life, though, is some intermediate outcome, such as going from one unsuccessful loving relationship to another, eventually living alone as an "old maid" or bachelor; or being a hardened, unfeeling, cigarette and coffee addicted, hard-drinking, unhappy person; or being constantly in the throes of crises due to incapacity for managing everyday problems. These banal manifestations of the three major scripts can also be mixed so that a person can be under the influence of a Loveless as well as Joyless script, or under the influence of a Loveless and Mindless script, or under the influence of all three.

Each of these three oppressive scripts is based on very specific injunctions and attributions which are laid down by parents on their children, and each of these three scripts can be effectively analyzed and given up in a group therapy situation.

Generally speaking, every person is affected in some degree by every one of these three scripts, even though he may manifest one of them most prominently. People can work through the early childhood injunctions, attributions, and decisions that affect their loving capacities, their capacities to experience their bodies fully, and their capacities to experience and control the world, and free themselves of these oppressive scripts.

Transactional Analysis Diagnosis

The word "diagnosis," which means knowing a difference or being able to distinguish between two different situations, is an important word to anyone who wishes to solve a problem or remedy an undesirable situation. In medicine, being able to tell the difference between two diseases so that treatment can be aimed at the specific disease process which is causing the illness is of utmost importance. However, the word "diagnosis" is not used only by physicians. Automobile mechanics use "diagnosis" to decide what part of a car to replace or adjust. Psychologists use the word in connection with psychological tests to diagnose emotional disturbance or "mental illness." I will use it in this book in connection with the identification of scripts.

Let me say, at this point, that I thoroughly object to the manner in which mental health professionals diagnose "psychopathology."

I believe it is one thing to look at a car and, after performing certain tests, declare that the difficulty with it is that it requires a new set of spark plugs rather than a carburetor overhaul. This seems as it should be, since it is not possible to ask the automobile any questions; so the only validation for the diagnosis is to change the plugs and then see whether the difficulty disappears. A diagnostician working with automobiles would probably be able to improve on her guesses if another person, as skilled as herself, took an independent look at the automobile and

came up with a diagnosis of his own. Two, three, or
four such independent diagnoses could be checked
against each other and, if a number of them agreed,
the likelihood would increase that the diagnosis was
correct. Still, no matter how often diagnosticians
agreed on spark plugs or carburetor, the final test of
the diagnosis would be whether the difficulty disap-
peared when repairs were made. A similar process is
reasonably followed by physicians when diagnosing
physical illness.

Psychologists and psychiatrists are, in my mind,
most reprehensibly guilty of misusing the process of
diagnosis as follows: first of all, if psychological tests
are used, the scientific literature regarding psychological tests is pretty well settled on the conclusion
that projective psychological tests, which are the type
mostly used, when given by different diagnosticians,
generally result in different conclusions. Their re-
liability is low, and this makes them useless as guide-
lines for therapy.[1] But even if four diagnosticians
agreed on a diagnosis, say anxiety neurosis, no agreement would exist about what therapeutic strategy
should be used.

Because the results of psychological tests tend not
to agree with each other there is a tendency for
diagnosticians not to check their conclusions against
each other, probably because this would prove to be
too embarrassing. My experience is that when two
diagnosticians talk about the same case they avoid
confrontations and tend instead to gloss over their differences. Diagnosticians act in many ways like politicians who may overtly take their differences very seriously but are always willing to shake hands in a
smoke-filled room.

My main objection to psychological and psychiatric
diagnosis, however, is that it completely ignores the
opinions and point of view of the person being diag-

---

[1]The result of any one of empirical tests (as opposed to projective), because they are automated and don't involve a human factor,
tends to come out the same no matter who gives it; but the different tests don't agree with each other either, nor do they suggest
specific remedies, if they happen, by chance, to agree.

nosed. After a diagnostician comes to the conclusion that the person suffers from an "hysterical neurosis; dissociative type," or from "schizophrenia; schizo-affective type, depressed," the absolutely last thing that he will do is ask the subject what she thinks about the diagnosis. In fact, diagnoses are elaborately hidden from their subjects; so much so that in certain circles it is considered a breach of ethics to actually communicate the diagnosis to the subject. This is justified on the basis of rationalizations to the effect that "patients" cannot properly understand diagnoses and that they would be too upset by them. I suppose that the reasons given are actually correct, since the fact is that most people would not be able to understand most diagnoses (I never really understood them myself even after years of studying and affixing them to psychiatric "patients"). Further, these diagnoses have a very obnoxious ring (how would *you* like to be called a Passive-Aggressive or Inadequate Personality?), being also often damaging to people because of the way they stick once they are made, and thus I suppose it's true that people would be upset by them —and rightfully so.

I personally consider some diagnoses insulting enough that if placed upon me or a person I'm close to it might cause me to react quite defensively, just as if we had been called a less sophisticated, insulting name such as "idiot" or "asshole." I have often said that anyone who calls a friend of mine a schizophrenic would have to deal with me just as if he had insulted her and I would expect the insult to be retracted.

Transactional analysis diagnoses can be as obnoxious as any other kind. Being told that you have a tragic loser script, with an injunction from your witch mother not to think, perpetuated by a game of "Stupid," doesn't sound any better to me than being called a "schizophrenic; chronic undifferentiated."

What makes a transactional analysis script diagnosis an instructive, human, and helpful statement is the manner in which it is arrived at and communicated.

In transactional script analysis a diagnosis of, say,

a certain kind of script, injunction, attribution, time
of decision, or somatic component, is arrived at by
culling information from a number of different
sources:

1. *The diagnostician's conclusions.* These are usually
arrived at by an intuitive blending of the Adult information. (This process is the same used by Berne
to guess the professions of Army dischargees and the
same process that he later used to diagnose ego states;
it is centered in the Little Professor in the Child as
well as the Adult of the diagnostician.)

2. *The subject's own reaction to the diagnosis.* This
element in a script analysis diagnosis is of utmost
importance. No matter how convinced the diagnostician is of her diagnosis, the final test of any diagnosis
is the extent to which the subject of it finds it to be
accurate, to feel right, to sit well, and to make sense.

3. *The reaction of other members of the therapy
group.* It is an essential distinguishing feature of a
transactional diagnosis that it is arrived at cooperatively between the therapist, the subject, and other
people in the group.

Consider the following exchanges.

JEDER: *I feel very bad because I'm letting a lot
of people down. I promised my daughter I'd take
her to the circus, and I'm supposed to paint the
living room. And I promised Mary I'd help her
balance her books. I don't seem to be able to keep
my commitments to people.*
THERAPIST: *You have an injunction from your
mother. "Never say no."*
JEDER: *Oh, no. I have a very easy time saying no.
Look at the way I discipline Johnny, and when the
Fuller Brush salesman came to the door I absolutely
refused to buy anything.*
THERAPIST: *I don't want to argue about it. That's
my opinion, and you may take it or leave it.*
JEDER: *I guess you are right. . . .*

Contrast the above conversation with the following:

JEDER: *I feel very bad because I'm letting a lot of people down. I promised my daughter I'd take her to the circus, and I'm supposed to paint the living room. And I promised Mary I'd help her balance her books. I don't seem to be able to keep my commitments to people.*

THERAPIST: *I have an idea about your script injunction. Would you like to hear it?*

JEDER: *Yes.*

THERAPIST: *I think that your mother gave you a script injunction never to say no.*

JEDER: *Oh, no. I have a very easy time saying no. Look at the way I discipline Johnny, and when the Fuller Brush salesman came to the door I absolutely refused to buy anything.*

THERAPIST: *I see what you mean. Well, maybe your mother's injunction was never to say no to women. Actually it does look as though you are quite capable of saying no to men. What do you think about that?*

JEDER: *Well, I don't know. It seems too simple.*

JACK (group member): *That's true about you, I think. I've noticed that if a man says something in this group you disagree with it, and when a woman says it you're much more likely to go along with it.*

JEDER: *(Says nothing—seems to be thinking)*

MARY (group member): *I agree. I think that's really true. I think your mother did give you an injunction against saying no to women.*

JEDER: *Well, it's embarrassing because it makes me feel like I am tied to my mother's apron strings, but I guess it is true. I can see it now that I look at it. . . .*

The above two interactions exemplify how not to and how to arrive at a transactional script analysis diagnosis. You will notice that in the first exchange the therapist's diagnosis was actually incorrect, although it was partially correct. The ensuing exchange does not seem helpful especially because Jeder, though superficially accepting the diagnosis, rejected it inwardly.

The second exchange has several distinguishing characteristics. The therapist asked Jeder whether he wanted a diagnosis made at that particular point. Having received his approval, the therapist made a tentative diagnosis. With the help of the group members the diagnosis was refined until it finally was acceptable to Jeder as being true. Acceptance of a diagnosis, let me hasten to say, is not necessarily an index of its validity; occasionally a person will accept any diagnosis that a therapist makes, no matter what it is. This is usually part of a game of "Gee, You're Wonderful, Professor," in which the subject comes on as a poor little Victim and the therapist comes on as a wonderful, all-knowing Rescuer. This kind of game is absolutely fruitless and often ends up with the person not really getting anything out of therapy and the therapist being angry and switching to frustrated Persecutor. Anytime a therapist finds himself being "right on" a great deal of the time with any one person he should check out the possibility of such a game being in progress.

I cannot emphasize enough that transactional analysis diagnosis has as its principal goal to suggest therapeutic approaches to fulfilling the therapeutic contract, that is, solving the person's problem. The basic therapeutic operation in script analysis is Permission. How a therapist gives Permission is explored in the chapter on therapy; at this point it is sufficient to say that Permission is a therapeutic transaction which enables a person to revoke his decision to follow the parental injunctions. The therapist is aided in giving Permission by an understanding of the person's parental injunctions and attributions, their source, and content. She should be able to distinguish the counterscript from a genuine change in the script. Further, she should have a clear understanding of the aspects of the person's decision affecting his everyday life, namely, his mythical hero, somatic component, and sweatshirt, as well as his central game. A list of relevant data will be supplied later in the Script Checklist (page 119). Keeping in mind my comments about the relative importance of this information, let me elaborate below:

Injunctions and Attributions

The main injunctions and attributions tend to come from one of the parents, and the parent of the *opposite* sex is often the source. The parent of the same sex then teaches the youngster how to comply with these injunctions and attributions. Thus, if mother dislikes assertive behavior in men and boys and enjoys sensitivity and warmth, she will enjoin her sons not to be assertive, will attribute warmth and sensitivity to them, and, having married a non-assertive, sensitive man, will provide her sons with a father who gives them the proper example.

Injunction and attributions in child-rearing aren't the only parental influences upon the offspring. Parents, even before therapists, can give their children Permissions. Permissions, however, are not restricting but liberating.

Let me illustrate the above with an example of how a young girl might become a beautiful woman (Figure 6). Mr. America likes beautiful women, that is to say, his Child likes beautiful little girls. He marries a beautiful woman, Ms. America, and they have a daughter. The little Miss America's Child is told by her father's Child to be a beautiful little girl and is taught by mother's Adult how to do it. Ms. America knows how to. use make-up, how to dress, how to stand, how to talk, since she is herself a beautiful woman, and transmits this knowledge to her daughter. This genesis of beauty, it will be noted, is basically independent of physical attributes. It explains why some women with all the physical attributes of beauty are not beautiful, and vice versa. It should also be noted that many physical attributes such as weight, posture, skin texture, facial characteristics, etc., are affected by parental injunctions such as "enjoy (food

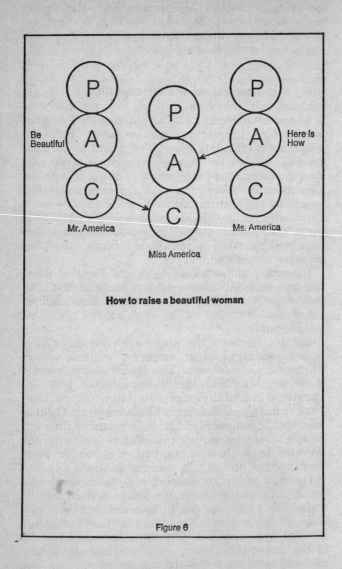

How to raise a beautiful woman

Figure 6

but not sex)," "don't outdo me," "don't be happy," "don't be strong," and attributions such as "you are skinny," "you are too tall," or "you are clumsy."

Miss America's example illustrates how people marry each other to form what can be described as a child-rearing team. In the same manner as was illustrated above, a woman who has a phobia of assertive behavior will marry an unassertive male and they as a team will produce unassertive male offspring (see pages 69 and 83).

Thus, when attempting to diagnose someone's injunctions and attributions, it might be helpful to remember that the working hypothesis for a man is "mother tells you what to do and father shows you how"; and for a woman, "father tells you what to do and mother shows you how." The manner in which the parent of the same sex demonstrates how attributions and injunctions can be followed is called the *program*.

The rule is a "working hypothesis," that is to say, the most likely to be correct given no prior knowledge about the case. Exceptions have been found, and it should only be used carefully.

When correct it is, I am sure, because of the strict sex role programming that most North Americans are subjected to. In a culture where "men are men" and "women are women" there are deeply rooted prohibitions against a great deal of attraction between, say, father and son, or for the setting of examples for boys by their mothers. As the sexual barriers between same sexed people decrease and as stereotyped "male" and "female" behavior becomes less rigidly prescribed for children this rule of thumb will lose its usefulness in the diagnosing of injunctions and attributions.

The next task is to determine area, range, and intensity of injunctions. In this realm it is helpful to know about children, childhood development, and child-rearing practices. The therapist's task is to imagine himself an invisible observer in the home situation of the person. Keeping in mind that the injunctions are often not spoken but implied, hinted at, or thrown out as jokes or when the parents are angry, it becomes possible to reconstruct the specific Child ego state enjoining the person. I am able to conjure up a vivid image of the home scene as viewed through the eyes of the person's parent and to intuit the injunction. These mental images are educated guesses and have to be checked out against the person's recollections, as the person is always the final judge of the validity of a diagnosis. The same process can be used to determine the content of attributions.

The Counterscript

So far the discussion has focused on the influence of the parental Child ego state on the offspring. However, another very important influence comes from the Nurturing Parent of father and mother.

In script formation, the offspring is not only given injunctions and attributions by the P_1 in C of father and mother but also a contradictory message from the Nurturing Parent (P_2).

Thus, while one young man's bad witch mother enjoined him not to cry or have any feelings, the Parent ego state of both parents (P_2) encouraged him to be a loving man (Figure 7A); while an alcoholic's father demands of her that she drink and she not think, the Parent ego states of both parents expect her to be an abstainer (Figure 7B). When these two demands are made of a young person, he will basically follow the injunctions of the bad witch, but the life course usually involves an alternation between compliance to the witch's injunction incorporated in the script, and compliance to the parental Parents or counterscript.

The counterscript is an acquiescence to the cultural and social demands that are transmitted through the Parent. In the alcoholic, the counterscript reoccurs in the periods of sobriety between binges. If one looks back on the case history of an advanced alcoholic, one always finds periods during which it seemed that the script's tragic ending would be avoided. The alcoholic, as well as the people around him, seemed to believe that the tragic outcome that

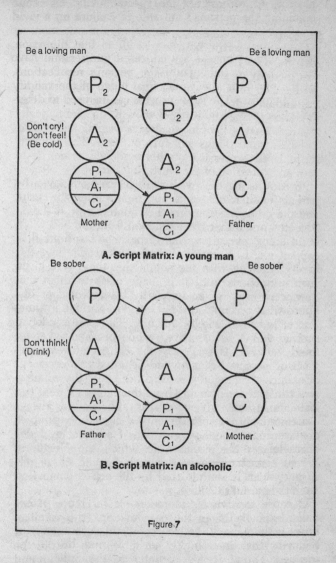

A. Script Matrix: A young man

B. Script Matrix: An alcoholic

Figure 7

everyone feared had indeed been avoided. This situation, in which the hero of the tragedy seems for a time to escape his tragic end, is an essential requirement of a good tragic script, both in real life and on the stage. Anyone who has seen an ancient Greek tragedy or any modern version of a tragic play knows that regardless of previous knowledge about the outcome, the audience truly hopes and seems to believe that the known, inevitable ending will be dramatically averted. That is, people are always wishing and willing to believe that things will turn out O.K. The counterscript is an expression of this tendency, which is in turn an expression of the Nurturing Parent.

In contrasting the two sets of instructions given by parents to their offspring, one representing the script and the other representing the counterscript, it should be noted again that the injunction from the bad witch is in almost every case nonverbal, not transmitted in explicit words. Because of this, most people have difficulty agreeing with the notion that they were given such injunctions until it is made clear to them that they were often given implicitly by approval or disapproval of certain forms of behavior, through insinuation or jest in a "witchy" manner. Thus, an injunction such as "don't be assertive," while perhaps never uttered verbally, is made by the consistent reinforcement of passive behavior and negative reinforcement of assertive behavior. On the other hand, the counterscript instructions coming from the parent's Parent ego state are usually given verbally and are not always associated with reinforcements designed to produce acquiescence. The saying "Do as I say, not as I do" characterizes the situation in which the Nurturing Parent ego state makes a verbal demand of an offspring which is contradicted by the action emanating from the parent's Child ego state.

Because the witch's injunction is far more potent and meaningful than the counterscript, the counterscript is short-lived. It is characteristic of counterscript behavior that it is highly unstable and brittle, for the reason that it runs counter to the much more powerful tendency represented by the script. When in the counterscript phase, the person feels a deep, primitive, visceral discomfort (accompanied by a superficial and unstable sense of well-being) which alcoholics often place in the pit of their stomachs; the discomfort is related to the fact that counterscript behavior goes against the wishes of the bad witch and is frightening. Consistent with this, there is an equally visceral comfort associated with the script behavior. For example, one alcoholic reported that at the worst point of an alcoholic binge, when he was so sick he could no longer keep anything in his stomach, he heard his mother's voice saying, "Isn't this fun, Jerry?"

As suggested in this example, an alcoholic who behaves as the script demands carries out those tendencies in his personality which acquiesce to parental wishes and are therefore associated with the well-being and comfort of parental protection. This is one reason the hangover is seen as the payoff for the alcoholic: even though in pain, the individual with the hangover is receiving approval for acquiescing to the parental Child's injunction. During this period the alcoholic feels temporary respite from the demands of the bad witch. Although the patient's Parent ego state may be actively castigating him for his drunkenness during the hangover, at the same time father's or mother's Child is saying, in effect, "That's my boy!"

One aspect of counterscripts which distinguishes them from a genuine departure from the script is their "unreal" quality. For example, it is common to find among black delinquent youths that their script alternates between aggressive delinquent behavior (enjoined by the bad witch) and wholly unrealistic attempts to "make it" in the entertainment or sports world which represents the culturally accepted alternative for "good Negroes" (enjoined by the Parent ego states around them). Succeeding in these endeavors is statistically unlikely, and they almost always represent a counterscript. A true departure from the script, or a new life course, cannot constitute being a "good Negro," but usually necessitates well-coordinated, often strongly self-assertive and angry, but realistic approaches to the realities of racism. Such an

approach in the black community is the youth groups
like the Black Panthers. These movements are of great
value in that they clearly offer an alternative to the
usual self-defeating scripts which are so commonly
seen among black people.[1] The basic message given a
black youth by such a movement is "You're O.K., not
in spite of being black, but because of it. You are a
prince and you deserve princely treatment. Black is
beautiful. Your hair is beautiful, you are beautiful.
You can have anything you want. You are a prince,
you are O.K." This statement offered at the time of
decision is a powerful antithesis against the adoption
of a self-destructive script such as heroin addiction or
alcoholism, and is likely to tip the balance for many
black adolescents, by giving them permission to be
O.K. and offering them a realistic path to autonomy.
A similar approach has been followed by women,
homosexuals, fat people,[2] and other minorities oppressed by banal scripting.

From the diagnostic point of view during therapy,
the principal significance of the counterscript is that
the behavior of a person still following his script but in
a counterscript phase may be indistinguishable from
another person who has in fact given up his script. For
instance, a woman with a Loveless script might meet
a man and get married and appear to have changed
her script. But she may not have; she may still be living by her father's injunction not to ask for strokes she
wants and not to accept them when they are given so
that after a short period of counterscript well-being
she will once again find herself loveless.

A therapist who mistakes counterscript for a script
change is making an important error. On the other
hand, a therapist who is unwilling to recognize a
script change and insists that it is only temporary is

[1] This point of view was confirmed for me, at the height of the
Black Panthers' militant period (1969), by a group of probation
officers from Alameda County, where the Panthers' headquarters are
located, who had observed a decrease of delinquent behavior in
black youths who joined the Black Panther Party.

[2] Aldebaron, Mayer. "Fat Liberation." *Issues in Radical Therapy*
I,3 (1973): 3–6.

in danger of making an equally important error in the other direction.

Thus, the proper diagnosis is essential here. Diagnosis should be based on behavior changes. For instance, for an alcoholic a protracted period of moderate social drinking is the most convincing evidence for a script change. However, since many cured alcoholics lose interest in alcohol, this criterion is not always available. In general, the loss of preoccupation with alcohol—either the alcoholic pastimes, or the game in any of its roles—is a good criterion. A radical change in time structuring and the development of avenues of enjoyment without alcohol are crude indicators of a script change. In addition, an often subtle change in the physical appearance of the cured alcoholic is a reliable index, though difficult to assess. The joyless person in a counterscript is tense, anxious, "uptight," even when smiling and enjoying himself, as if constantly on the brink of relaxing and letting go, which he feels he can't do for fear that his "Not O.K." Child will take over. The completely recovered alcoholic lacks this "on the brink" quality and therefore looks and "feels" quite different from the alcoholic in a counterscript. The tension of the counterscript is a part of the somatic component, which I will elaborate upon later in this chapter.

The Decision

The decision has a number of components: the existential position or racket that is embraced at the time of decision; the sweatshirt; the mythical hero chosen to live out this position; the somatic component which bodily reflects the decision; and the actual time of the decision.

Knowing the exact date of the decision when possible is useful because it pinpoints the child's age and gives an estimate of the Professor's level of development and understanding at the time the decision was made.

The *existential position* adopted at the time of the

decision represents a shift away from the original basic trust position "I'm O.K., you're O.K." In addition, it is based on some elaboration of either "I'm not O.K." or "You're not O.K.," or a combination of both. This elaboration is called the *racket* because the person will exploit every situation to justify whatever position he chooses. For instance, a woman with a "I'm not O.K." position elaborated it into a "Nothing I do ever works" racket and would use any situation to feel badly. Whenever she went to a meeting she played her racket as follows: If she got there early, she felt badly because she could have used the time to do an additional wash at home; if she arrived late, she would feel badly because everybody noticed her with disapproval; and if she came on time, she felt badly because no one noticed her. Thus, no matter what the situation, she used it to promote her racket.

The *sweatshirt* is intimately related to his decision. The sweatshirt is a metaphoric reference to the fact that most persons with scripts can be visualized as wearing sweatshirts over or under their clothes, on which is written a short, two- or three-word description characterizing their existential positions. In addition, just as games contain a sudden switch or reversal, so sweatshirts often have a front and back. For instance, Miss Felix's sweatshirt prominently read "Looking for a man" in front. On the inside of the back, to be read as it was taken off, was written "But not you." Captain Marvel's sweatshirt said "Captain Marvel" on the front and "Unless I'm sober" on the back; another man, a "born loser," had "You can't win them all" in front, and "I can't win any" on the back. The sweatshirt is another way of saying that people have their scripts written all over them and is actually a part of the somatic component.

The *mythical hero* has been amply described earlier. The diagnosis of the mythical hero, when there is one, is aided by such questions as "What is your favorite fairy tale?" "Who is your favorite person?" "Are you imitating someone's way of life?" and so on. If a certain personality emerges as significant to the person, she should be asked to describe it fully since it is the person's view of the mythical hero, and not the popular one, that is relevant. If the description fits—and when it does it often does uncannily—then it can be safely assumed that the mythical hero has been identified. From then on, therapy can be simplified by using the mythical hero's name to refer to script behavior. For instance, every time a person whose mythical hero was Little Orphan Annie obligingly accepted the "hard knocks of life," a pattern which was part of her script, some group member would call it to her attention by saying something like "That's the way Orphan Annie would take it, but what are *you* going to do?" Or if a man whose mythical hero was Superman muscled his way into a conversation, he could quickly be made aware of his behavior by simply saying "There goes Superman again."

Not everybody with a script has a clearly defined mythical hero. Some persons see themselves as nondescript losers, "Mr. Nobody" or "Nowhere man," and in these cases it is not possible to identify a mythical hero. Generally it helps when a person has identified with a clear-cut mythical hero because his script behavior will be much more apparent to the therapist, the group members, and himself.

The Somatic Component

Another important element in the diagnosis of scripts is the *somatic component*. The somatic component refers to the fact that a person who has made a decision invariably brings certain aspects of her anatomy into play, especially the musculature. Negative injunctions, which cause inhibitions in behavior, become visible in a person's body in the form of muscular contractions. For example, attributions which cause people to engage or activate certain types of behavior can be seen in the form of overused or overdeveloped muscles. Eric Berne has pointed out the relevance of sphincters, but any muscle, set of muscles, or organ can be involved. These physical changes find expression in certain postures (chest out, stomach

in, tight anal sphincter, shoulders up, tight lips,
crossed legs) which are effective in obeying parental
injunctions and which may have some physical similarity with the fantasied appearance of the mythical
hero when there is one. Organs, such as tear glands in
the case of Little Orphan Annie who could not produce tears even when crying, or the heart in the case
of Mr. Bruto, can also be part of somatic component.

The investigation of the somatic component, that is,
the manner in which the script is reflected in the
body of the person, is to my mind the frontier of
script analysis. And while our understanding of it is,
at this point, not nearly as complete as in other areas
of script analysis, there is, nevertheless, a great deal
that can be said on a preliminary, somewhat tentative
basis which might be interesting to the reader.

It is safe to assume that the human body would, if
left alone and properly fed, develop to maturity in an
even, harmonious way. Arms and legs would be strong;
back and chest and stomach muscles would be well-
developed. The body would not be ruled by the head
or vice versa. The person's energies would be evenly
distributed over the whole body rather than concen-
trated in the head, torso, legs, or genitals.

Under the influence of injunctions, however, people's natural flow of motion and emotions is curtailed.
Hands and arms are not allowed to reach out for
people or for things or to reject and push away or
strike at what isn't wanted. Feet are not allowed to
plant themselves firmly on the ground, or legs to run
full speed away or toward something. Face muscles
become stiff and can't move fully to express the feelings emanating from the belly or heart. Smiles, gri-
maces, tears, and laughter are restricted and not given
full expression. Lungs and throat aren't used fully so
that people can't speak with force, conviction, or anger
because they don't inhale fully while others who
don't exhale fully can't sigh, whisper, plead, express
sadness or pain.

Under the influence of attributions some bodily
functions are exaggerated and abused; the "intellec-

tual's" head dominates the rest of the body, the "athlete's" body rejects the head.

Personal attributes carry with them bodily configurations; for instance, responsibility tends to develop the hands, arms, and shoulders and to inflate the upper torso, ignoring the lower body which becomes stiff and lifeless; emotionality develops the senses—hearing, vision, touch—but tends to leave the musculature soft and flabby.

The bodily differences between women and men are distorted due to sex role injunctions and attributions. The relatively minor differences in strength are exaggerated so that men become physically strong and women weak. The built-in nurturing mechanisms of women are exploited and women are molded into caretakers and warmers, while men are made cold and insensitive. Banal scripting creates the expectation that men be potent and women warm. Men are made afraid of becoming impotent and don't allow themselves to be warm. Women are equally afraid of becoming cold and don't allow themselves to be strong.[1]

Injunctions and attributions together distort the body, throw it out of balance as energy and attention is held away from one part to activate the overuse of another part. Polarities develop; a strong back with a weak stomach, a strong jaw with weak eyes, capable hands with incompetent legs, the capacity to swallow and digest coupled with an incapacity to push and kick away or throw up. Some people have neck, back, arm, and leg muscles which are strong and capable of making an impenetrable shell, coupled with an incapacity to express feelings. Others have easy expression of feelings from the gut but inability to act on these feelings due to an uncoordinated musculature.

Each script has its own peculiar combinations of somatic expressions, physiological strengths and weaknesses which often imitate, as has been stated previously, the bodily posture and shape of mythical heroes.

---

[1]Vance, Dot. "Reclaiming Our Birthright." *The Radical Therapist* 2,3 (1971): 21.

Over time these chronic distortions can cause tissue deterioration, heart disease, ulcers, arthritis, atrophied muscles (and, Wilhelm Reich argued, cancer) —and shorten the natural life span available to those whose body is used fully and ages evenly.

Many interactions between mental life and bodily functions have been investigated because they can become the cause for physical illnesses. The mechanisms postulated to explain the development of these conditions are mediated by the autonomic nervous system, which responds to states of mind. An early childhood decision based on injunctions and attributions is such a state of mind which then produces certain somatic side effects. A more concrete instance of the sickening effect of a decision can be seen in the following case.[1] Miss Rein, who had several episodes of urinary tract infection, admitted that she deliberately refrained from drinking water during the day and retained her urine as long as possible because she had decided the bathroom where she worked was dirty. Her own bathroom at home was extensively decorated and was her pride and joy. Her attitude about bathrooms and bathroom functions clearly contributed to the development of her recurring bladder infections by allowing the stagnation of urine in the bladder, thus affording the bacteria more time to multiply. Her constant control of the need to urinate was reflected in her posture and could be detected visually, affecting her life hour by hour, day by day, and year by year.

Similar attitudes which are scripted could cause all manner of minor and major diseases.

Thus, observation of the person's anatomy often yields important information about the somatic component of the script and is therefore important in diagnosis.

---

[1]Thanks are due to Dr. George David who reviewed this section and provided the example of Miss Rein.

7

Scripts: Tragic
to Banal

All of us are aware that some human beings live lives which are notorious and extraordinary, either because of their highly positive aspects, or because of their unusually negative or destructive aspects. We are not surprised to find that people who achieve notoriety in their positive endeavors are often people who made early decisions which they then followed by proper rational behavior to support their decisions. We call these human beings successful, charismatic, or famous.

But there are many other human beings who are equally successful, notorious, and famous not because of the good things they do, but because of the way in which they seem to succeed in destroying themselves or others. Madness, suicide, homicide, drug addiction, great unhappiness, can be called life scripts, that is, prearranged, preplanned life courses which people follow faithfully from time of decision to time of death.

The lives of people who are famous or notorious, whether in positive or hamartic ways, attract our attention and distract us from our understanding of the ways in which all of us in our everyday lives follow strict dictates and rules about our behavior. We are unaware of these because they apply to everyone and because we have lost track of what we could do or achieve, were we not bound by the banal scripting of everyday life.

Unlike tragic scripts, banal scripts go unnoticed like water running down the drain, and those who are participants in them may have no more than a glimpse, their *anagnorisis*, as they draw their final breath, that their potentialities as human beings have in some mysterious way been betrayed and defeated. The banality of everyday life goes unnoticed because it is so common. In fact, many people use a great deal of energy reifying unsatisfying life styles into some sort of "normality" or desirability. Many of us are proudest when we feel that we are living "good" lives, where "good" means normal, average, as others would want it to be—others whom we respect and admire and who have told us what a good life is. Being married, successful in business, a good father, a good housewife, a businessman, a civic leader, a "real" man or a "real" woman are all defined for us long before we are born; we are given the illusory "freedom" to choose from those different ways of living. Once we choose we are forced to keep to the directives of that particular life plan, lest we become "failures" in living. The fact that blueprints for our banal, everyday lives are, at best, extraordinarily unsatisfying is something that people find out only after they have spent a lifetime attempting to live according to the rules—too late to do anything about it! Yet, ironically, when we wonder, after we followed all the rules, why our lives seemed senseless, we tend to blame ourselves rather than question what others told us to do.

Banal scripts differ from tragic scripts mainly because people who live them are less likely to draw attention to themselves, since they are "normal."

Tragic scripts are explosive and often end with a bang; people with tragic scripts decide to live dramatically—they decide to kill somebody, or to be so depressed that someone will have to take notice; they decide that whole institutions (hospitals, jails, psychiatric day care centers) will get involved with them.

Banal scripts are melodramatic: they have no clear beginning or end, they go from bad to worse, they have no impressive, sudden reversals, no really suspenseful moments. Superficially, they may look good; but, in fact, they are devastatingly boring.

Tragic scripts were the first to come to the attention

of mental health workers. Working with them it is possible to maintain the superior *one-up* position, "I'm O.K., you're not O.K.," which characterizes the positions of most therapists. But as scripts were studied in depth, it became apparent that we are all scripted to some degree and that tragic scripts are only the extremes of what we all have: restricted choices, prearranged lives, and diminished freedom.

Why are some people's scripts tragic and other's banal? One basis is the kinds of injunctions and attributions the young child was subjected to; severely malignant injunctions and attributions (Chapter 5) bring about early decisions which tend to be tragically inappropriate.

The other determinant is the amount of energy that the child has—how spunky it is.[1] Spunk is probably genetic. Some children are more active and energetic than others, even before they are born. If a certain child encounters the injunction, "Don't move," she may just give up completely or not move, but will nevertheless manage to laugh and sing. Yet, some other child will say: "The hell with you—I'll move as much as I want." So then the injunction will have to be enforced harder or it won't be obeyed. The more extreme the resistance, the more extreme the injunction needed to put it down. Some parents will give up the enforcement of their injunctions, given a certain level of opposition. Others are willing to beat and even kill their children if they disobey them. The younger a child the easier it is to squelch him—he has no power. Thus, the malleability of a child combines with the oppressiveness of her environment so that at a certain point she is forced to give up a certain percentage of her potential. Some people give up 50%, some 10%, some 90%. From then on they will live a 50%, 90% or 10% life. Oppression is a reflection not only of what is passed on by parents and teachers, but of the situation in which we live. (In a ghetto it isn't just father and mother who create pressure for

---

[1] English, Fanita. "Sleepy, Spunky and Spooky." *Transactional Analysis Journal* II,2 (1972): 64–67.

giving up autonomy, but all sorts of factors which oppress father and mother.)

Eric Berne did not consider bad conditions in the world relevant to his work. In his view, to do so was politics; and he did not want to mix politics with psychiatry. He steadfastly refused to let that kind of data enter into psychiatric discussions. He called such discussions "Ain't It Awful." However, it seems to me important to challenge this view. People live in a social context which is ordinarily oppressive, and to ignore that as a therapist is to ignore an important determinant of behavior.[1] A therapist who ignores oppressive social conditions—sexism, ageism, racism, the exploitation of workers, and so on—will not be a potent therapist unless he is working with people of the leisure class where such oppression is relatively minor.

Oppressive conditions which force people into scripts exist in all social classes, but they are more obvious in the lower socio-economic classes which bear heavier and more brutal oppression—there's more physical and tissue oppression, more likelihood for tragic rather than banal scripting.

The spunkiness of a child is often expressed when she chooses what Erikson[2] calls a negative identity (Berne calls this the antiscript[3]) which appears to be a total denial of the parent, but is in fact a total acceptance, only in reverse. Such an opposite, mirror-image way of behaving is just as slavish as imitating the parent completely; everything is ultimately still dictated by the parents. Spunkiness is also often manifested in the tragic ending of a script where the Child says: "By God I'm not taking this lying down. I'm going out with a bang."

A banal script is decided just as a tragic script. The

[1] Steiner, Claude M. "Radical Psychiatry: Principles." *The Radical Therapist* 2, 3 (1971):3. Reprinted in *Readings in Radical Psychiatry*, Claude Steiner, ed. New York: Grove Press, 1974.

[2] Erikson, Erik H. *Identity: Youth and Crisis.* New York: W. W. Norton, 1968.

[3] Berne, Eric. *What Do You Say After You Say Hello?* New York: Grove Press, 1972.

decision is just as binding. Once the die is cast people will stick to a banal script as hard as they stick to a tragic script. Tragic scripts and banal scripts are qualitatively alike. The only difference is quantity; they differ in punch, visibility, tragic ending. Tragic scripts are sharper, more clean-cut. People in tragic scripts tend to choose a dramatic character—Robin Hood, Cinderella, Jesus Christ. People with banal scripts may not even think of a character. They're just John Doe.

In short, banal and tragic scripts are not that different. I want to minimize the emphasis on tragic scripts because we're all on this voyage. Some of us are just a little more extreme than others, and therapists will do better work if they can identify banal as well as tragic scripts, and if they see how they themselves are affected by them.

A Script Checklist

When diagnosing the various aspects of the script, it is useful to keep in mind a list of items that form its make-up, colloquially called a *script checklist* (based on an idea by S. Karpman and M. Groder).

Because of the various meanings given to the word "script," it is suggested that "script" properly refers to all of the items in this checklist and that ideally, when talking about a person's script, the observer is referring to the whole checklist rather than to one or a few of the items. On this basis, "Ann's injunction is 'don't think!'" is more accurate than "Ann's script is don't think."

The checklist[1] is presented in the order in which the items are most easily diagnosed.
Life Course: This is what the person herself is doing, or the outline of her life. It should be possible to state it in a succinct sentence such as "drinking myself to death," "almost always succeeding," "killing myself," "going crazy," or "never having fun." The life

[1]Steiner, Claude M. "A Script Checklist." *Transactional Analysis Bulletin* 6,22 (1964):38–39.

course is best stated in the first person singular and in language understandable by an eight-year-old to emphasize that it represents the persons early formulation of what her life course would be. The life course is usually easy to surmise and is almost always revealed in the person's presentation of the problem. Life courses can be banal or hamartic.

Four sub-items of the life course are the decision, the position, a mythical hero, and a somatic component. The *decision* is the moment when the existential *position* (O.K., not O.K.) and life decision were embraced. The *mythical hero* is the character in real life, history, or fiction that the person's life course is intended to emulate. The life course is the reaction to negative injunctions and attributions; and this reaction usually has a *somatic component* which may involve any effector organ such as the tear glands, neck muscles, heart, sphincters, or any bodily system.

Counterscript: During periods of the script when the person seems to be escaping the script's life course, she engages in activities which appear to be departures from the script. These activities form the counterscript and represent acquiescence to a cultural and/or parental influence, such as "being on the wagon," "drinking socially," etc.

Parental Injunctions and Attributions: It is important to know which parent was the enjoiner and what were the injunctions and attributions.

The injunction is thought always to be an inhibiting statement: "Don't think!" "Don't move!" "Don't be assertive!" or "Don't look!" If the injunction is not preceded by "Don't," or if it is too complicated, it has not been distilled to its most basic meaning. When investigating the content of a person's injunctions and attributions it is important to obtain their most essential meaning. For instance, a woman reported that her father, a strict authoritarian, never allowed her to sit with her legs apart, knees not touching. The injunction turned out to be "Don't be sexy" rather than, say, "Don't sit sloppily," or "Don't be a tomboy."

The same woman recalled repeatedly saying to

neighbors and friends, "Sally is very clean," "Her room is very neat." This attribution, together with the injunction, was the basis for a script that called for her to be prim, proper, clean, sexless, remote, and afraid of intimacy.

Rozlyn Kleinsinger has investigated the script matrix of scores of people and has found certain injunctions to be very common. "Don't be close" and "Don't trust" are related to Loveless scripts; "Don't succeed," "Don't be important," and "Don't think" are related to Mindless scripts; and "Don't feel your feelings" and "Don't be happy" are related to Joyless scripts.

Program: This is how the youngster has been taught by the parent of the same sex to comply with the injunction coming (usually) from the parent of the opposite sex. Thus, if the injunction is "Don't think" the program may be "drink," "fog out," or "have a tantrum."

Game: This is the transactional event that produces the payoff which advances the script. It appears that for each script there is one basic game of which all the other games are variants. Thus, for a "killing myself" life course, the game might be "Alcoholic" with variants such as "Debtor," "Kick Me," "Cops and Robbers," all of which produce the same payoff, namely, stamps that can be traded for a free drunk.

Pastime: This is the social device whereby people with similar scripts structure time. With a depression or Loveless script, the game might be "If It Weren't For Him" with the pastimes "Debtor" and "Ain't It Awful" filling in the time structure gap between games.

It is while playing the pastime that the *gallows transaction* is likely to take place.[1] In the case of a Mindless script, White tells the audience about his latest incredible blunder while the audience (perhaps including the therapist) beams with delight. The smile of the Children in the audience parallels and rein-

---

[1] For full description, see Chapter 21.

forces the smile of the bad witch who is pleased when White obeys the injunction by being clumsy and stupid; smiling at a person's script behavior, in effect, tightens the noose around his neck.

Payoff: These include stamps, racket, sweatshirt. The *stamps* represent the kind of affect accompanying the end of the game—anger, depression, sadness, etc. The act of pursuing and collecting the stamps is the *racket.* Every person has his own individualized racket and type of stamps. The *sweatshirt* refers to the fact that people prominently display their racket on their chests, so to speak, as an advertisement to willing players.

Tragic Ending: This is important to therapists working with people with hamartic or self-destructive scripts. The tragic ending is usually specific as to time, place, and method, and is a sort of *modus operandi* which characterizes each self-destructive individual. Suicidal persons will stick to a certain form of suicide, thus affording the therapist a *script antithesis,* a transactional stimulus intended to disarm the self-destructive injunction. If the tragic ending is death through drinking, the script antithesis includes the injunction "Stop drinking!" plus Antabuse (see *Games Alcoholics Play,* Steiner)[1] and, in extreme cases, removal of available alcohol by whatever means necessary. The script antithesis does not dispose of the script, but it buys time during which therapy can lead to script abandonment. The script antithesis has been tested in my work with very clear results. The most impressive result of a script antithesis was found when the person—as he was about to leap off a bridge—heard the voice of the therapist saying "Don't jump!"

Therapist's Role: This is the role which the person expects the therapist to play when he applies for treatment. People commonly expect therapists to play the role of Rescuer or Persecutor and to reinforce

---

[1]New York: Grove Press, 1971.

parental scripting. This aspect of the script will be discussed fully in the section on therapy.

Twenty Questions: It is possible through a series of questions to elicit information about a person's script. I drew up the original "twenty questions" (actually only 13) in 1967. In *What Do You Say After You Say Hello?* Berne published three different lists: a comprehensive 169-question list and two short versions, a condensed list (fifty-one questions), and a therapy list (forty questions).

Once again, I wish to reiterate that the in-depth investigation of the script matrix and checklist belongs in the realm of the structural analysis of scripts and is not my main interest in writing this book.

Does Everyone Have a Script?

A person's life may fit into one of several different possibilities. She may be script-free or she may have a script. If she has a script it may be hamartic (dramatic) or it may be banal (melodramatic). Whether hamartic or banal, a script may be good or it may be bad.

Miss America provides an example of a life course in which no script may be present. Not everyone has a script, since not everyone is following a forced, premature, early-childhood decision. Miss America may decide, at some point, that she is a beautiful woman, but this decision is made at an appropriate age and involves no sacrifice of an O.K. position, loss of autonomy, or inhibition of expectations.

A person with a script is invariably disadvantaged in terms of his own autonomy or life potentials. The distinction between good and bad scripts is based on whether or not it has socially redeeming features. For instance, a man whose script was to become famous but unhappy to the point of suicide, became the most successful surgeon of his city at the expense of a satisfying family life and happiness. This man had a script personally damaging, but socially useful, and therefore it could be called a "good script." On the other hand, a person with a hamartic script such as alcoholism, which is not only destructive to happiness but has no socially redeeming features, has a bad script. It should be emphasized, however, that in either case—whether a good or bad script—the fact that a person has a script is a detriment to the possibilities of living to the fullest human potential.

As stated, scripts can be highly dramatic and tragic (hamartic) or they can be melodramatic (banal). In the banal form of script, while autonomy is restricted, it is not so restricted as to be dramatically obvious, and its adoption is far more frequent than the more dramatic, hamartic script. Banal scripts are those often adopted by large groups of people who are treated as sub-groups—such as women or blacks; these scripts are usually based on parental injunctions and attributions, which are not as severe and restricting as those involved in hamartic scripts. Banal scripts are often found among women or men, such as "Woman behind the Man" or "Big Daddy" (see Chapters 14 and 15). The banal scripts that are often imposed upon blacks have been very aptly described by White,[1] and, again, they are restrictions of autonomy imposed upon human beings which have melodramatic, rather than dramatic, life outcomes.

As to the frequency of their occurrence, banal scripts are the rule, hamartic scripts the minority, and script-free lives the exception.

[1]White, Jerome D., and White, Terri. *Self-Fulfilling Prophecies in the Inner City*. Chicago: Illinois Institute of Applied Psychology, 1970.

8

Basic Training: Training
in Lovelessness

In *Games People Play*, Eric Berne says: "Parents, deliberately or unaware, teach their children from birth how to behave, think, feel, and perceive. Liberation from these influences is no easy matter. . . . Indeed, such liberation is only possible at all because the individual starts off in an autonomous state, that is, capable of awareness, spontaneity and intimacy, and he has some discretion as to which parts of his parents' teachings he will accept."[1]

Eric Berne refers here to the systematic scripting which is imposed on children and which I call *basic training*. He talks about spontaneity, awareness, and intimacy as the three human faculties which we start with in life and which we may regain in later life.

A great deal of what is taught in the nuclear family is oppressive, and it is because of this that I liken the early childhood training which all children receive, to one extent or another, to the basic training which is given to all inductees into the army. Army experience may vary greatly after a certain point, but almost everyone who goes into the army starts in boot camp and is taught and has to do certain things. In the family, just like in army basic training, the things that have to be learned and done are hard, unpleasant, and arbitrary. And just as in basic training, these things are thought to be, both by trainers and trainees,

---

[1] New York: Grove Press, 1964; p. 183.

125

valuable and necessary for the achievement of "maturity" and success.

The basic training of life includes a systematic attack on three primary human potentials: the potential for intimacy, namely the capacity for giving and receiving human love; the potential for awareness, namely the capacity to understand the world and its people; and the potential for spontaneity, which is the capacity of free and joyful expression of the Natural Child. I have called the end result of this three-part basic training Lovelessness, Mindlessness, and Joylessness.

The topic of love is probably the most universally interesting to people. Yet the sciences of psychology and psychiatry, which are supposedly concerned with human behavior and its dysfunction, do not seem to consider it a subject worthy of much investigation or interest. The word "love" is not really acceptable in academic discussions. Behavioral scientists, when speaking of love or of being in love, if they dare mention the subject at all, will smile wanly, as if to say, "Ah! love is a topic for poets and philosophers, but we scientists cannot possibly deal with it." Indeed, some scientists seem to regard love as a state of altered consciousness which has the earmarks of temporary psychosis; a deeply irrational, uncontrollable, undefinable state of mind.[1]

Yet, not only is love the topic that is most likely to interest people, but it is failure in matters of love which brings the largest numbers of people to psychotherapists, ministers, and others whose work is counseling in human affairs. Love makes the world go around, and yet psychology and psychiatry have not given "love" full and serious attention.

Eric Berne pioneered the investigations of human love when he defined the unit of human recognition as a stroke. The word "stroke" is a scientific word which makes research into human love quasi-re-

---

[1] Marcus, Joy. "Intimacy." *Issues in Radical Therapy* I,3 (1973): 18–19.

spectable. A psychologist who speaks of strokes may manage to get some attention from the scientific community. If he postulates that strokes make the world go around he may be able to get some grants for research to test the hypothesis and he may be able to publish scientific papers based on this research. It may be that, with the invention of the word "stroke," Eric Berne made the first step in the rational understanding of that most important of human faculties: the capacity to love.

A stroke is defined as the unit of human recognition. Strokes can be positive or negative depending on whether they feel good or bad. From now on in this book, when I use the word "stroke" I will be referring to *positive* strokes, while I will be referring to those strokes which feel bad as "negative strokes." This may give the reader the impression that positive strokes are real strokes or better strokes or more worthwhile strokes, as opposed to negative strokes, which is exactly what is intended. Strokes are necessary for human survival, and when people can't obtain positive strokes, they will settle for negative strokes because they too, even though they feel bad, are life supportive. Capers and Holland[1] point out that when peoples' stroke sources fall below a certain point which he calls the Survival Quotient, they become more and more willing to accept negative strokes because they need strokes, *any* strokes, for survival. Taking negative strokes is like drinking polluted water; extreme need will cause us to overlook the harmful qualities of what we require to survive.

A Fuzzy Tale

Once upon a time, a long time ago, there lived two very happy people called Tim and Maggie with two children called John and Lucy. To understand how happy they were, you have to understand how things

---

[1]Capers, Hedges, and Holland, Glen. "Stroke Survival Quotient." *Transactional Analysis Journal* I,3 (1971): 40.

were in those days. You see, in those days everyone was given at birth a small, soft, Fuzzy Bag. Anytime a person reached into this bag he was able to pull out a Warm Fuzzy. Warm Fuzzies were very much in demand because whenever somebody was given a Warm Fuzzy it made him feel warm and fuzzy all over. People who didn't get Warm Fuzzies regularly were in danger of developing a sickness in their back which caused them to shrivel up and die.

In those days it was very easy to get Warm Fuzzies. Anytime that somebody felt like it, he might walk up to you and say, "I'd like to have a Warm Fuzzy." You would then reach into your bag and pull out a Fuzzy the size of a little girl's hand. As soon as the Fuzzy saw the light of day it would smile and blossom into a large, shaggy, Warm Fuzzy. You then would lay it on the person's shoulder or head or lap and it would snuggle up and melt right against their skin and make them feel good all over. People were always asking each other for Warm Fuzzies, and since they were always given freely, getting enough of them was never a problem. There were always plenty to go around, and as a consequence everyone was happy and felt warm and fuzzy most of the time.

One day a bad witch became angry because everyone was so happy and no one was buying potions and salves. The witch was very clever and devised a very wicked plan. One beautiful morning the witch crept up to Tim while Maggie was playing with their daughter and whispered in his ear, "See here, Tim, look at all the Fuzzies that Maggie is giving to Lucy. You know, if she keeps it up, eventually she is going to run out and then there won't be any left for you!"

Tim was astonished. He turned to the witch and said, "Do you mean to tell me that there isn't a Warm Fuzzy in our bag every time we reach into it?"

And the witch said, "No, absolutely not, and once you run out, that's it. You don't have any more." With this the witch flew away on a broom, laughing and cackling all the way.

Tim took this to heart and began to notice every time Maggie gave up a Warm Fuzzy to somebody else.

Eventually he got very worried and upset because he liked Maggie's Warm Fuzzies very much and did not want to give them up. He certainly did not think it was right for Maggie to be spending all her Warm Fuzzies on the children and on other people. He began to complain every time he saw Maggie giving a Warm Fuzzy to somebody else, and because Maggie liked him very much, she stopped giving Warm Fuzzies to other people as often, and reserved them for him.

The children watched this and soon began to get the idea that it was wrong to give up Warm Fuzzies any time you were asked or felt like it. They too became very careful. They would watch their parents closely and whenever they felt that one of their parents was giving too many Fuzzies to others, they also began to object. They began to feel worried whenever they gave away too many Warm Fuzzies. Even though they found a Warm Fuzzy every time they reached into their bag, they reached in less and less and became more and more stingy. Soon people began to notice the lack of Warm Fuzzies, and they began to feel less warm and less fuzzy. They began to shrivel up and, occasionally, people would die from lack of Warm Fuzzies. More and more people went to the witch to buy potions and salves even though they didn't seem to work.

Well, the situation was getting very serious indeed. The bad witch who had been watching all of this didn't really want the people to die (since dead people couldn't buy his salves and potions), so a new plan was devised. Everyone was given a bag that was very similar to the Fuzzy Bag except that this one was cold while the Fuzzy Bag was warm. Inside of the witch's bag were Cold Pricklies. These Cold Pricklies did not make people feel warm and fuzzy, but made them feel cold and prickly instead. But, they did prevent peoples' backs from shriveling up. So, from then on, every time somebody said, "I want a Warm Fuzzy," people who were worried about depleting their supply would say, "I can't give you a Warm Fuzzy, but would you like a Cold Prickly?" Some-

times, two people would walk up to each other, thinking they could get a Warm Fuzzy, but one or the other
of them would change his mind and they would wind
up giving each other Cold Pricklies. So, the end result
was that while very few people were dying, a lot of
people were still unhappy and feeling very cold and
prickly.

The situation got very complicated because, since
the coming of the witch, there were less and less
Warm Fuzzies around; so Warm Fuzzies, which used
to be thought of as free as air, became extremely valuable. This caused people to do all sorts of things in
order to obtain them. Before the witch had appeared,
people used to gather in groups of three or four or five,
never caring too much who was giving Warm Fuzzies to
whom. After the coming of the witch, people began
to pair off and to reserve all their Warm Fuzzies for
each other exclusively. People who forgot themselves
and gave a Warm Fuzzy to someone else would immediately feel guilty about it because they knew that
their partner would probably resent the loss of a
Warm Fuzzy. People who could not find a generous
partner had to buy their Warm Fuzzies and had to
work long hours to earn the money.

Some people somehow became "popular" and got a
lot of Warm Fuzzies without having to return them.
These people would then sell these Warm Fuzzies
to people who were "unpopular" and needed them to
survive.

Another thing which happened was that some
people would take Cold Pricklies—which were limit-
less and freely available—coat them white and fluffy
and pass them on as Warm Fuzzies. These counterfeit
Warm Fuzzies were really Plastic Fuzzies, and they
caused additional difficulties. For instance, two people
would get together and freely exchange Plastic Fuzzies, which presumably should have made them feel
good, but they came away feeling bad instead. Since
they thought they had been exchanging Warm Fuzzies,
people grew very confused about this, never realizing
that their cold prickly feelings were really the result of
the fact they had been given a lot of Plastic Fuzzies.

So the situation was very, very dismal and it all started because of the coming of the witch who made people believe that some day, when least expected, they might reach into their Warm Fuzzy Bag and find no more.

Not long ago, a young woman with big hips born under the sign of Aquarius came to this unhappy land. She seemed not to have heard about the bad witch and was not worried about running out of Warm Fuzzies. She gave them out freely, even when not asked. They called her the Hip Woman and disapproved of her because she was giving the children the idea that they should not worry about running out of Warm Fuzzies. The children liked her very much because they felt good around her and they began to give out Warm Fuzzies whenever they felt like it.

The grownups became concerned and decided to pass a law to protect the children from depleting their supplies of Warm Fuzzies. The law made it a criminal offense to give out Warm Fuzzies in a reckless manner, without a license. Many children, however, seemed not to care; and in spite of the law they continued to give each other Warm Fuzzies whenever they felt like it and always when asked. Because there were many, many children, almost as many as grownups, it began to look as if maybe they would have their way.

As of now it is hard to say what will happen. Will the grownup forces of law and order stop the recklessness of the children? Are the grownups going to join with the Hip Woman and the children in taking a chance that there will always be as many Warm Fuzzies as needed? Will they remember the days their children are trying to bring back when Warm Fuzzies were abundant because people gave them away freely?

The Stroke Economy

In *Games People Play*, speaking about stimulus hunger, Berne says: "A biological chain may be postulated leading from emotional and sensory deprivation through apathy to degenerative changes and death. In this sense stimulus hunger has the same relationship to survival of the human organism as food hunger." The notion that strokes are, throughout a person's life, as indispensable as food is a notion that has not been sufficiently emphasized in recent TA theory. Therefore, I wish to restate the fact: *strokes are as necessary to human life as are other primary biological needs such as food, water, and shelter—needs which if not satisfied will lead to death.*

As Berne pointed out in the chapter on strokes in *Transactional Analysis in Psychotherapy*,[1] control of stimulation is far more effective in manipulating human behavior than brutality or punishment. Thus, while a few families still use physical force in an attempt to control their offspring, most injunctions are enforced in young persons through the manipulation of strokes rather than through physical punishment; strokes become a tool of social control.

Wilhelm Reich, as Berne, saw man at his deepest level to be of "natural sociality and sexuality, spontaneous enjoyment of work and capacity for love."[2] He felt that the repression of this deepest and benign layer of the human being brought forth the "Freudian unconscious" in which sadism, greediness, lasciviousness, envy, and perversion of all kinds dominate. Wilhelm Reich invented the term "sex economy" since he was interested in the political-economic analysis of the neuroses; according to his theory, sexual energy is manipulated for social control reasons. The orgasm, the release of sexual energy, liberates a human system whose sexuality has been oppressed.

"The connection between sexual repression and the authoritarian social order is simple and direct: the child who experienced the suppression of his natural sexuality is permanently maimed in his character development; he inevitably becomes submissive, appre-

---

[1]New York: Grove Press, 1961.

[2]Reich, Wilhelm. *The Function of the Orgasm.* New York: Farrar Straus and Giroux, Inc., 1961.

hensive of all authority and completely incapable of rebellion." In other words, the child develops exactly that character structure which would prevent him from seeking liberation. The first act of suppression prepared the way for every subsequent tyranny. Reich concluded that repression existed not for the sake of moral edification (as traditional religions would have it), nor for the sake of cultural development (as Freud claimed), but simply in order to create the character structure necessary for the preservation of a repressive society.

A great deal of Reich's writings was an attack against the father-dominated family which he saw as "a factory for authoritarian ideologies."[1] Reich felt that the authoritarian government and economic exploitation of the people were being maintained by the authoritarian family and that the family was an indispensable part of it, which fulfilled its function as a supporter of exploitation by the oppression of sexuality in the young.

Herbert Marcuse is another writer who sees a connection between an oppressive society and people's unhappiness. According to him, people live according to the *performance principle:* a way of life imposed on human beings which causes the desexualization of the body and the concentration of eroticism in certain bodily organs such as the mouth, the anus, and the genitals. This progression, which Freud saw as a healthy developmental sequence, is in fact, according to Marcuse, one that results in a reduction of human potential for pleasure. Concentrating pleasure into narrow erogenous zones leads to the production of a shallow, dehumanized, one-dimensional person. Marcuse feels that the concentration of sexual pleasure in the genitals has the purpose of removing pleasure from the rest of the body. In this manner, an oppressive establishment produces people—especially men—who are largely without feelings in their bodies and can be exploited as performing machines by others. "The nor-

---

[1] Reich, Wilhelm. *The Sexual Revolution.* New York: Noonday Press, 1962.

mal progress to genitality has been organized in such a way that partial impulses and their 'zones' were all but desexualized in order to conform to the requirements of a specific social organization. . . ."[1]

Thus Marcuse and Wilhelm Reich connect the social and psychological manipulation of human beings by human beings surrounding them—including the family—with an oppressive social order. The following theory about the stroke economy is a similar effort in which it will be proposed that the free exchange of strokes which is equally a human capacity, a human propensity, and a human right has been artificially controlled for the purpose of rearing human beings who will behave in a way which is desirable to a larger social "good," though not necessarily best for the people themselves. This manipulation of the stroke economy, unwittingly engaged in by the largest proportion of people, has never been understood as being in the service of an established order, so that people have not had an opportunity to evaluate the extent to which control of the stroke economy is to their own advantage and to what extent it is not.

In order to make this point more vivid, imagine that human beings were at birth fitted with a mask which controlled the amount of air that was available to them. This mask would at first be left wide open; the child could breathe freely; but at the point at which the child was able to perform certain desired acts the mask would be gradually closed down and only opened for periods of time during which the child did whatever the grownups around it wanted it to do. Imagine, for instance, that a child was prohibited from manipulating his own air valve and that only other people would have control over it, and that the people allowed to control it would be rigorously specified. A situation of this sort could cause people to be quite responsive to the wishes of those who had control over their air supply; if punishment were severe enough,

[1]Marcuse, Herbert. *Eros and Civilization*. New York: Vintage Books, 1962.

people would not remove their masks even though the mask might be easily removable.

Occasionally, some people would grow tired of their masks and take them off; but these people would be considered character disorders, criminals, foolish, or reckless. People would be quite willing to do considerable work and expend much effort to guarantee a continuous supply of air. Those who did not work and expend such effort would be cut off, would not be permitted to breathe freely, and would not be given enough air to live in an adequate way.

People who openly advocated taking off the masks would justifiably be accused of undermining the very fiber of the society which constructed these masks, for as people removed them they would no longer be responsive to the many expectations and demands on them. Instead, these people would seek selfish, self-satisfying modes of life and relationships which could easily exclude a great deal of activity valued and even needed by a society based on the wearing of such masks. "Mask removers" would be seen as a threat to the society, and would probably be viciously dealt with. In an air-hungry, but otherwise "free-wheeling," society air substitutes could be sold at high prices and individuals could, for a fee, sell clever circumventions of the anti-breathing rules.

Absurd as this situation may seem, I believe that it is a close analogy to the situation existing with strokes. Instead of masks we have very strict regulations as to how strokes are exchanged. Children are controlled by regulating their stroke input, and grownups work and respond to societal demands in order to get strokes. The population is generally stroke-hungry and a large number of enterprises, such as massage parlors, Esalen, the American Tobacco Company, and General Motors are engaged in selling strokes for their consumers. ("Ginger ale tastes like love," or "It's the *real* thing (Coke is).")

Persons who defy the stroke-economy regulations are seen as social deviants and if enough of them band together they are regarded as a threat to the National

Security as happened in the late sixties with the long-haired flower children.

Most human beings live in a state of stroke deficit; that is, a situation in which they survive on a less-than-ideal diet of strokes. This stroke deficit can vary from mild to severe. An extreme example of a person's stroke starvation diet is the case of an alcoholic, by no means unique, who lived in a skid row hotel. By his own account, he received two strokes daily from the clerk at the hotel desk from Tuesday to Sunday and approximately thirty strokes on Monday when he appeared at the alcoholic clinic and exchanged strokes with the receptionist and the nurse administering medication. Once a month, he was treated to a dozen extra super-strokes from the physician who renewed his prescription. His vitality was almost completely sapped and he reminded me of human beings who live on starvation diets of rice. Eventually his stroke-starved state of apathy prevented him from coming to the clinic and later he was found dead in his room.

Experiences of a person in such food- and stroke-starved circumstances are of a completely different order than the experiences of one who is properly fed. This man was little more than an automaton and nothing in his personality could be interpreted as autonomous or self-determined.

Most people, however, live in a less severe form of starvation leading to varying degrees of depression and agitation. People in these circumstances exhibit, instead of the apathy of the severely starved, a form of agitation or "search behavior," which is also found in the mildly food-starved person or animal.

Because people are forced to live in a state of stroke scarcity, the procurement of strokes fills every moment of their waking hours. This is the cause of structure hunger—that need to optimally structure time in social situations for the procurement of a maximum number of strokes.

Also, just as some people have accumulated large sums of money with relatively little effort, so it is that certain people are able to obtain large numbers of strokes in return for little effort; that is, they have established a stroke monopoly in which they are able to accumulate other's strokes. In the stroke economy, just as is the case with money, the rich get richer and the poor get poorer while the majority have to struggle daily to make ends meet.

Therapists, especially group therapists, are in a position to become stroke monopolists. Wyckoff, later on in this book (Chapter 13), points out how men monopolize women's strokes. Parents are often interested in monopolizing their children's strokes. Whoever manages to establish a stroke monopoly profits from it and at the same time perpetuates the general rules of the controlled stroke-economy.

The Stroke Economy Rules

The teaching of the rules of the stroke economy to children constitutes the basic training for Lovelessness. As in all scripting, Lovelessness is based on injunctions and attributions.

The injunctions of the stroke economy are:

1. *Don't give strokes* if you have them to give. This injunction is self-explanatory. It simply means that people are enjoined against freely giving of their loving feelings.

2. *Don't ask for strokes* when you need them. Again, this injunction is self-explanatory, and probably the one that is most thoroughly taught to people.

3. *Don't accept strokes* if you want them. This injunction is not as common as the two above. When present it prevents people from accepting the strokes that are given them even when they are wanted.

4. *Don't reject strokes* when you don't want them. Frequently people are given strokes which, for one reason or another, don't feel good or are not wanted. As an example, women who are "media" beauties, namely those who by some unlucky stroke of chance match the imaginary standard which is promoted by

Playboy, have the experience of being constantly stroked for their "beauty." It is common for such women, especially after many years of receiving these strokes, to begin to resent them. Such women report that it is an unnerving and unpleasant experience to have everyone who relates to them relate primarily and often exclusively on the basis of their looks, which after all are only skin deep. Women who have these feelings rarely, if ever, have permission to reject those strokes. One of the effects of the women's liberation movement is that it has given such women permission to say, in effect: "I don't want to hear that I'm beautiful; I know that already. What else can you say about me?" This is an example of permission to reject strokes which are not wanted. Coupled with the permission to ask for the strokes that she wants, a woman might then add: "Why don't you tell me that I'm smart or powerful?"

Men have a similar problem with strokes praising their strength, responsibility, intelligence, and capacity for hard work. The men's liberation movement encourages men to reject such strokes and ask instead, "Am I a good man? Am I sensitive? Am I beautiful? Am I lovable?"

5. *Don't give yourself strokes.* Self-stroking, or what is called in transactional analysis "bragging is enjoined against. Children are taught that "modesty is the best policy" and that self-praise and self-love are in some way sinful, shameful, and wrong.

The above five basic injunctions are the enforcers of the stroke economy which everyone carries around in their heads and which guarantee that people will be stroke-starved. As has been pointed out, chronic stroke starvation is the basis for depression or lovelessness. Later in this book, I will discuss the therapeutic approach to this most frequent form of human unhappiness.

The free exchange of strokes is severely controlled by parental messages which enforce the stroke economy and are easily demonstrable by "bragging." If a person is asked to stand up in the middle of the room and brag—that is, make a number of self-praising statements—there almost always is the same response: an immediate reaction of panic. If Jack decides to try bragging, he might feel that it would be immodest or improper to say good things about himself, or that to say good things about himself might be seen as an insult to the others in the room.

Jack may find that he is not aware of many, if any, good things about himself and that he is incapable of using words which imply goodness or worth applied to him. If anyone attempts to supply strokes, he will reject some, most, or all of the strokes with a discount.

If someone says, "You have beautiful skin," the Parent says, internally, "They haven't seen you up close." If someone says, "You have a lovely smile," the Parent says, "But they haven't seen you angry." If a persons says, "You're very intelligent," then the Parent says, "Yes, but you're ugly." Other devices to avoid the acceptance of strokes will be observed, such as: giving token acceptance of the stroke, followed by a shrug so that the stroke will roll off the shoulders instead of "soaking in"; or immediately reciprocating with a counter stroke which essentially says, "I don't deserve a stroke so I must give one in return." Another argument against taking strokes is, "These people don't know you, their strokes have got to be phony." This, in spite of the fact that everyone may have agreed to give only sincere, genuine strokes.

There are all sorts of taboos operating which prevent the free exchange of strokes: the homosexual taboo prevents stroking between men and men and women and women; the heterosexual taboo prevents stroking between men and women unless they are in a prescribed relationship, either engaged to be married or married; and certain taboos against physical touch prevent stroking between grownups and children unless they are part of a nuclear family, and then only under certain circumstances. In short, the free exchange of strokes is a managed activity, a situation in which the means of satisfaction of a basic need are made unavailable to people.

The end result is that the capacity to love is taken

away from people and then directed against them by using it as a reinforcer to bring about desired behavior.

It can be seen from this discussion that a person or group of persons who free themselves from the strictures of the stroke economy will regain control of the means for the satisfaction of a most important need; consequently, they tend to disengage themselves from the larger society. It is because of this that there has been such great panic among law makers and government officials in relation to the youth, drug, and sex culture. The notion that human beings will no longer work or be responsible when they liberate the stroke economy may be quite accurate if work and responsibility is seen as defined by others. However, it is quite another thing to assume that human beings in a free stroke economy will be as inert or vegetable-like as some seemingly fear. The notion that satisfied human beings will not work and will not be responsible has been a basic assumption of a lot of child-rearing. The facts may be quite different, however. It is my assumption, and my experience bears this out, that as they are increasingly satisfied in their stroke needs, human beings will be better able to actually pursue the achievement of harmony with themselves, each other, and nature.

Stroke satisfaction is the antidote to Lovelessness. Banal scripting which results in a Lovelessness script can be overthrown through an understanding and rejection of the stroke economy. How this is done in group therapy will be discussed later in the book (Chapter 22).

9

Basic Training: Training
in Mindlessness

Awareness

We are born as ignorant of the workings of nature as the very first cave dweller, and in the few years between birth and maturity we acquire an enormous amount of information and understanding needed to get us around in our complex world.

Human beings have done a great deal to liberate their right to understand, often against much opposition. There have been times in history when people were not permitted to climb mountains, to dissect cadavers, or gaze at themselves in a mirror. Every one of these activities in search of knowledge has been, at one time or another, severely punished. To understand or investigate the workings of nature has not always been safe. To teach what we learn, especially to children, is still, in some places, definitely unsafe. Teaching about human sexuality or evolution or socialism could still cause a person to lose her or his job in some school systems in the United States.

Scientists have come to understand the workings of chemicals and the inanimate forces of nature in minute detail and are therefore successful in controlling them. We are able to provide every person who wants it with an automobile, yet we don't understand ourselves at all. We are incapable of even beginning to provide every person with a guaranteed loving relationship even though everyone seems to want that.

I believe that there has been unrelenting pressure

141

through the ages working against the use of our faculties for awareness. Against much resistance we have learned to understand the movements of the stars and planets; we have learned physics and chemistry; we have researched our bodies; and we have come to know much about them.

We are now interested in understanding our psyches, and the psyches of our fellow human beings. I believe that the same pressures against the pursuit of knowledge that existed in Galileo's and Leonardo da Vinci's time exist on us now as we pursue knowledge about ourselves and each other.

One of the pressures against self-understanding comes from the medical profession. Psychiatrists, by and large, prevent us from understanding ourselves by telling us we can't, and discounting those who feel they can without their help.

People who want to understand the workings of their bodies and the diseases that affect them are accustomed to being discouraged by their physician. "I am the Doctor," we are told, at best; "Leave your body in my hands." At worst we are made to feel guilty about any desire to maintain control over the healing process, or (heaven forbid) our Doctor.

Speculation, or mirror-gazing, was prohibited and punished in the Middle Ages. In the twentieth century women who, with the aid of mirrors, are congregating to do gynecological self-examinations are being eyed suspiciously by medical associations who claim that they conspire to practice medicine without a license.

We have, however, the right and the capacity to understand ourselves, our bodies included. The capacity to understand the world—ourselves—is centered in the Adult ego state. There are two Adult ego states in the personality: one, the first-order Adult, or the Adult in the Child, or the Little Professor; and two, the second-order Adult. These two Adult ego states are suited for the gathering and processing of data from the world.

The second-order Adult is ideally suited for rationality, the understanding of "hard" data or information which has been codified, that is, put into words or symbols. This ego state is thought to be "scientific" as opposed to intuition, which is supposedly not. However, this is far from true: non-rational thought has been an essential part of scientific research. Intuitive hunches and "irrational" leaps of thought propel all scientific research and many successful scientists have acknowledged that fact. Rationality is not more "scientific" than intuition. It is simply more accurate, when measurable information is available, than is intuition. On the other hand, when measurable information is not available, intuition is more accurate than rationality.

The Little Professor or Adult in the Child, also called intuition, is more suited for the processing and storing of information which has not been coded and which is still, so to speak, soft, unformed, vague, but is nevertheless extremely useful. Intuition, or the Adult in the Child, works primarily at the frontiers of a person's knowledge. As Eric Berne found in his investigations on intuition, it is a powerful tool which can be used to advantage. Even though it is not considered a valid source of information in scientific circles, it is in fact constantly used by most people. In the absence of "hard" data, intuition—along with tradition, which is the Parental approach to solving problems—is a useful and effective tool. Because we have so little "hard" data on the psychological workings of human beings, intuition is especially useful in that area of human relations.

Both Adult ego states in the person are affected by basic, banal script training. As will be explained later in this book when Hogie Wyckoff writes about sex roles, the tendency in the home is to attack primarily one or the other of these two faculties. In men intuition is attacked. In women the second-order Adult, which is the rational, logical Adult, and which I have called rationality, is attacked. In any case, neither of these two faculties, rationality and intuition, which are the cornerstones of power in the world, are allowed, let alone encouraged to develop fully. The defeat of rationality and intuition is accomplished through discounting and lying.

Discounts

The discount transaction is a common transactional event.

A discount is a crossed transaction in which the discountee emits a stimulus from his Adult ego state to another person's Adult and that person responds from his Parent or Child. Consider the following example:

Little Mary goes to her parents' bedroom in the middle of the night and wakes up Mother.
MOTHER: (Adult) *What's the matter, Mary?*
MARY: (Adult) *I'm afraid.*
MOTHER: (Parent) *Don't be afraid. Go back to sleep.*

Mother asks Mary an Adult question which Mary answers with her Adult; she reports that she is afraid. Mother's answer, from her Parent, discounts the facts of the situation, namely that Mary is afraid. At this point Mary will probably get even more afraid and lose what little hold she has on her rationality. If she begins to cry, Mother may get angry or Mother may offer to let Mary come into bed with her. Whether Mother Nurtures or Persecutes Mary the effect of the discount is to diminish Mary's Adult thinking capacities.

Consider and contrast the following transaction:

Mary once again has come to her parents' bedroom.
MOTHER: (Adult) *What's the matter?*
MARY: (Adult) *I'm afraid.*
MOTHER: (Adult) *What are you afraid of?*
MARY: (Adult) *I heard some noises, and I think there are some burglars in the house.*
MOTHER: (Adult) *Oh, I see. I think you are safe. There hasn't been a burglary here for ten years, and* (Parent) *I would like it if you went back to bed. O.K.?*

MARY: *(Child) O.K. But can I come back if I have another bad dream?*
MOTHER: *(Parent) Yes, please go back to sleep now.*

In this latter transaction Mary, instead of being discounted and winding up afraid, has learned several important facts: that she lives in a safe neighborhood where there is very little to worry about in the way of prowlers in the night; that mother can be relied upon whenever she is afraid; and, finally, she has learned from mother how to deal with somebody who is afraid.

Discounts make people crazy. Ronald Laing, who has an intimate understanding of the discount transaction, gives several examples of discounts and their effect on people in his book *Knots:*[1]

JILL: *I am frightened.*
JACK: *Don't be frightened.*

The above is a discount. The result of a discount is that the discountee becomes confused; her mind is set reeling. Laing follows:

JILL: *I am frightened to be frightened when you tell me I ought not to feel frightened.*
Frightened.
Frightened to be frightened.
Not frightened to be frightened.
Not frightened.
Frightened not to be frightened.
Not frightened to be not frightened.

Another example:

JILL: *I'm upset you're upset.*
JACK: *I'm not upset.*

Once again, this is a discount, and once again Jill's mind is boggled.

---

[1]From *Knots*, by R. D. Laing. Copyright © 1970 by the R. D. Laing Trust. Reprinted by permission of Pantheon Books, a Division of Random House, Inc.

JILL: *I'm upset that you're not upset that I'm upset you're upset.*

Jill is not the only victim of Jack's discount. Jack eventually has to deal with the effects of the discount on Jill's mind.

JACK: *I'm upset that you're upset that I'm not upset that you're upset that I'm upset, when I'm not.*

And finally, here is a knot that illustrates how discounts are connected with the feeling of being unable to think or being stupid.

JILL: *You think I'm stupid.*
JACK: *I don't think you're stupid.*

Once again this is a discount. Jill has a feeling coming probably from her intuition that Jack in some way does not respect her intelligence. Jack proceeds to discount that feeling, and Jill in spite of being an intelligent woman is, once again, totally confused.

JILL: *I must be stupid to think you think I'm stupid if you don't, or you must be lying.*

I'm stupid in every way!

To think I'm stupid, if I am stupid.
To think I'm stupid, if I'm not stupid.
To think you think I'm stupid, if you don't.

Some of Jill's thoughts above would be labeled by a psychiatrist (or psychologist or whatever) as "paranoid." The affect that goes with these thoughts might be considered inappropriate. People who are constantly subjected to discounts and accept them indeed are prone to go mad and "exhibit" paranoid symptoms and inappropriate affect. Madness is the most extreme consequence of Mindlessness scripting.

The discount, then, is the way in which parents and others in the child's world interfere with the youngster's potential for knowing the world and the way in which the growing powers of understanding of the child are stunted. There are several forms of awareness that are discounted in children: their intuition, their emotions, and their rationality.

Discounts of Intuition

People are capable of making quick, uncalculated, intuitive appraisals of the states of mind of other people; in other words, reading people's minds.

We are able to know whether someone is happy, sad, excited, or feeling scared, guilty, confident, or suspicious. We can tell if someone is on the defensive or on the offensive, whether he is lying or telling the truth.

Being able to read people's mind is very important in being able to effectively relate to other people. Effective use of the information that we get from our intuition is a different process from the process we use with information from our Adult. (From now on I will refer to the second-order Adult—rationality—as the Adult.)

Adult data can be used as is, with confidence. For instance, if we buy two dollars' worth of gasoline and pay with a twenty-dollar bill, we *know* that we will receive eighteen dollars in change with, say, 99.5% certainty. We know this with our Adult.

On the other hand, let us assume we meet a friend on the street, and our intuition tells us that she is sad, exhausted, and frustrated, and that she may rebuff a warm greeting. We don't *know* for sure, but we can estimate what she will do and act on our estimate. We may decide that there is a 60% chance that she'll reject our stroke and so we approach her with a preliminary, cautious smile, waiting for her response or feedback. If she smiles back widely we readjust our estimate and take a chance, and so on. This is the effective use of intuition: because it isn't 100% reliable it needs to be modified through feedback.

We may decide that our friend is going to rebuff us and pass her by without a greeting. This would be an ineffective use of intuition. If we give intuition too much credit and don't modify it through feedback, we are said to be paranoid. Even if we know that our intuition is almost always accurate, it is important to use it carefully.

A person whose intuitions are repeatedly discounted is put in a situation in which the intuitive information from the Little Professor is contradicted, over and over, by the information coming from the discounters. This creates a great deal of mental stress in the discountee.

A person being discounted can: ignore her or his intuition; ignore the discounter; or try to react to both the intuition and the discounter. All of these leave something to be desired.

Ignoring our intuition helps make us unaware, mindless, and causes us to feel stupid. Ignoring the discounter makes us "paranoid," unsociable, and hard to get along with. Trying to react to both our intuition and the discounter leaves us confused.

The effective reaction to discounting is called *accounting* and will be explained fully in Chapter 23.

Discounts of Personal Emotions

Another important form of knowledge which discounting attacks is knowledge about one's own feelings. We continually have emotions which are tied to the events around us. We are angry, sad, guilty, happy, depending on what is going on in the world at the time. These feelings can be unacceptable to those around us, especially if we are a young child.

Some parents dislike their children to be sad; some dislike them to be happy; yet others dislike them to be angry, or to have loving feelings. When these emotions are expressed, parents may do everything they can to ignore them, cause them to be withdrawn, to invalidate them. In certain households anger is discounted while in others fear is discounted, and so on. At the same time, other feelings which are the family's "feeling racket" (anger, sadness, frustration, etc.) are encouraged and applied universally to every situation. The outcome of this kind of discounting of feelings is that, once again, an important source of information and understanding is taken away from the child. Laing[1] points out how invalidation of their feelings turns people into mental invalids. The result of discounts is that people become split within themselves. A whole portion of their being, their feelings, is not acknowledged and, perhaps, eventually not even felt. The feelings continue to exist, however, and affect large parts of the person's bodily states and behavior. Unexpressed anger, shame, fear, sadness build up and eventually find expression anyway. Sometimes accumulated feelings (stamps) are unloaded all at once in an "emotional binge." Sometimes they "seep" through and find constant expression in physical symptoms or in the person's everyday behavior, as in the case of the man who grinds his teeth during his sleep or the woman who has a constant quiver in her mouth. Once again, a person whose feelings are discounted has three choices:

1. *To ignore the feelings and act as if they didn't exist.* The result is a person who is detached from his feelings. Men often make this choice; they become "cold" and unemotional.

2. *To have the feelings and disregard the discounters.* This person will be considered over-emotional and immature. This choice is often made by women; they become emotional and "irrational."

3. *To attempt to live with both the feelings and their discounts.* This causes confusion. The person will be erratic and anxious.

Discounts of Rationality

The most likely discount to happen in a family is the discount of a child's intuition and/or emotions. However, rational thought, the function of the Adult, is also discounted in children; their clear perceptions

---

[1]Laing, Ronald D. *The Divided Self*. New York: Pantheon, 1969.

of obvious facts and the logical connections they make are often interfered with. For example, one person reports that as a child she repeatedly witnessed her mother being lazy and irresponsible and she recalls thinking that there was an obvious inconsistency in her mother's behavior. She asked the logical question: "Mother, how come you're mad at Father for not mowing the lawn when you have a pile of dirty dishes in the sink?" This candid, logical observation made by the little girl's Adult was met with Mother's strong and angry disapproval: "You get smart with me one more time, girl, and I'll knock your head off!" This statement was a clear and forceful injunction against the use of the logical capacity of the youngster's Adult. It had the effect of severely inhibiting future logical, rational thinking in her. It amounts to a powerful "Don't think!" injunction.

Another woman recalled that her parents expressed a great deal of anger whenever she came home from school and used big words and talked about concepts that she was learning from a favorite teacher who encouraged her to think logically. The situation got so bad that whenever she used a big word the parents got very angry. This culminated one day when her father made a bigoted remark about a neighbor and she said, "That's prejudiced!" Father turned to her and said: "Prejudiced? I'll prejudice you! Don't get sassy around *this* house!" and slapped her across the face. The statement "Don't get sassy around *this* house" was deeply etched in the child's mind. To her it meant that using big words and being intelligent was a form of insolence. Later, this caused her a lot of difficulty when, as a student in college, her father's statement reappeared as a Pig Parent message saying, "You can't learn this important stuff. Who do you think you are, trying to act big?"

One way that the Adult is discounted and prevented from operating is in the way people confront difficult situations. Eric Berne[1] points out how in cer-

---

[1] Berne, Eric. *What Do You Say After You Say Hello?* New York: Grove Press, 1972.

tain families when something goes wrong the parents get angry, feel hurt, or become depressed, while in others when something goes wrong the parents react by searching for a solution to the problem. Looking for the rational solution to personal problems is seldom taught to children; the tendency instead is to use Parent or Child solutions.

Schiff and Schiff[1] describe the ways in which discounts affect people's problem solving ability: when troubles develop, people's responses can vary. The person can react by saying, "There's a problem here and I can solve it." On the other hand, Schiff and Schiff point out, the person can say, "There is a problem here, but I can't solve it," or "There is no problem here," thereby discounting her or his rationality and ability to solve problems.

When problem solving is discouraged by parents, children develop a reaction of mindlessness, stupidity, passivity, and incapacity to think in the face of difficult situations.

Scripting against problem solving often shows up in relation to emotional difficulties. People often feel that their lives are "fated" and can't be changed. Some even feel that to apply the rational powers of the Adult to one's personal life takes the romance or zip out of it. They will ask, "Must everything be analyzed? Is nothing sacred any more?" Often such an attitude is scripted by parents who were invested in discouraging their offspring's Adult powers.

Others feel that to think about solutions is akin to hexing them. Skid row alcoholics believe in the "alkie hex" brought upon those who discuss their accomplishments. Some people simply feel that Adult scrutiny will make good things vanish into thin air.

The fact, however, is that expanding awareness means expanding power and expanding well-being. We can only effectively effect what we understand. Let me give an example more common to our experience.

[1]Schiff, Aaron Wolfe, and Schiff, Jacqui Lee. "Passivity." *Transactional Analysis Journal* I,1 (1971): 71–78.

Mr. Bruto, whose life plan was to toil long hours until he died of a heart attack, was aware only of the daily routines connected with his work. He started the day driving to work for fifty minutes on a crowded freeway breathing polluted air. He worked hard all day and took two fifteen-minute coffee and cigarette breaks and one lunch break during which he gathered his energy for the next work period. He worked overtime on weekends and did plumbing on the side in his free moments. He told himself he had a good job, since his wages were $7.00 per hour and plenty of overtime (though he had no choice in the matter since he *had* to work the overtime offered him). The only problem he was aware of was his insomnia and the fact that he had blinding headaches and periodically went on uncontrollable alcoholic binges. Thus he was (understandably to him) never promoted at work and always slightly in debt. Every month's bills left his pockets empty. Yet he was managing to pay for his car and house and bringing up his children to be good, responsible workers, though sometimes he worried and suspected that they were using "dope."

He would have liked to be able to read but could not concentrate and therefore kept himself informed through television news programs at dinner time. He watched a great deal more TV than he felt was right, but could not stop himself.

When Mr. Bruto came to group therapy he felt defeated by alcohol. He was not hopeful since he had repeatedly heard that alcoholism is an incurable disease. He was amazed to hear that it wasn't a disease and certainly not incurable. He drank in information about ego states, strokes, games, rackets, stamps, power plays, and scripts. He said, "It's like a curtain being pulled from my eyes." His awareness expanded by leaps and bounds. He was very interested in the life styles of the other members of the group, and how they saw the world.

He was fascinated by the suggestion that he had a script to kill himself through overwork and shocked when he realized that his expectations of retirement and security were groundless fantasies designed to keep him working and which might actually cause him to die soon after his retirement date, if not before.

He immediately resonated to the suggestion that alcohol and TV were helpful aids to the promotion of his script; they were tranquilizers that kept him from thinking. His major injunction was "Don't think!" and his attribution was "You are a hard worker." Harder for him was to accept that he was a cigarette, coffee, and sleeping pill addict; hooked just like those "junkies" that he heard about.

He was astounded at the suggestion that work could be pleasurable, having assumed all of his life that it was not, and that he should not expect it to be.

Play was to be found after work, but he could not find enjoyment in things. He knew that "all work and no play makes Jack a dull boy," but, again, he felt he could not help himself. He felt he *was* dull and wished he knew *how* to play.

He knew, because he belonged to a union, that industry exploits workers, but he felt that it was not really bad in his case since his pay was good. He was surprised that some group members felt that his job was lousy (he operated a machine doing the same monotonous thing all day long) and that he was far more exploited than he had ever imagined.

Hardest for him to accept was the tendency in himself to rebel against work, to want to quit, to want to strike, as a good one; one that he should feel free to follow, and one that, if supported, would lead him out of his alcoholism. Having gained this awareness, he made plans. He decided to stop driving himself with work, to stop drugging himself with alcohol, cigarettes, and coffee, and to seek pleasure and leisure so as to be able to live well beyond sixty. He gave up his seniority at the factory and got a job with less pay and shorter hours close to home. He developed his plumbing work. He reserved weekends for leisure, stopped drinking and smoking. He thought about what was wrong in his life and how he wanted to change it. He discussed problems and their solutions in group.

He began to sleep well, enjoy sex; he earned less,

spent less, worked less, watched less TV. Sixteen
months after first coming to group he looked back in
amazement. Gradually, without fanfare, his life had
come under his own control. He felt powerful rather
than powerless. He felt, he said, "that he had time to
think and figure things out." He did not call it awareness; but, to me, expansion of his awareness was
the prime mover of his changes. The support of the
group members throughout the hard times in his therapy was another important factor.

The King (or Queen) Has No Clothes

Why do parents interfere with their children's rationality and awareness? I believe that the principal
reason is that the parents feel "not O.K." and do not
wish to be observed, clearly perceived, or understood
by the youngsters in their family. They are ashamed
of themselves as people, parents, and providers and
are embarrassed to be seen as they feel they are—
not O.K.

Like the Emperor who wore no clothes, parents
bank on not being closely observed by their children
lest they discover some great flaw. But a child's world
consists mostly of its parents. They are the focus of
interactions and take up most of the child's attention.
The child's inquisitive and constant attention on the
parents, if not checked, can make them uncomfortable. Thus, parents will give the child injunctions
such as "don't look at me," "don't talk about me,"
"don't talk about the family," and, eventually, "don't
talk about yourself to others." These injunctions
come from the Pig Parent in the father or mother, and
eventually prevent the child from seeing the world,
especially the world of people, as it is. The end result
of this kind of basic banal training is that by the time
the youngster is an adolescent his capacity for understanding himself, others, and the world is greatly
diminished.

People who are aware feel capable to themselves
and to others and tend to be able to get what they

want for themselves. Mindlessness—which is the result of the systematic attack on this kind of capacity—results, on the other hand, in a feeling of confusion, of not being able to understand, of being torn between one's feelings and what one is told one is supposed to feel, and of being unable to choose between what one understands the world to be and what one is told the world really is.

Lying

Lies, along with discounts, undermine the awareness of children. Lying is the rule rather than the exception in human affairs. We are all aware of the fact that we are being lied to by those who govern us, by the media as well as by those who constantly attempt to convince us to spend our money on their products whether we need them or not. But we are less inclined to be aware of the fact that lying is more common than truth-telling in our everyday relationships.

A lie is defined in the dictionary as "an act or instance of lying; a false statement made with intent to deceive." This definition of lying, which is also the definition which most people follow, is patently inadequate. It implies that lying only happens when one utters a lie; when one willfully and consciously makes a statement that one knows not to be true.

Yet even under such a narrow definition of lying people lie to each other constantly. If, in addition to the constant bold-faced lies that are told to children, one considers the half-truths and omissions of truth which they are subjected to, it is clear that lying is a basic dimension of a child's experience.

It takes a lengthy training period throughout childhood and adolescence to accustom human beings to lying and accepting lies without protest. Children are told lies by commission when they're told about the stork who brings the babies, Santa Claus who brings the presents, and when they're given false and untrue explanations and justifications for what happens in their daily lives. They're also lied to by omission when they're kept away from information which is considered to be too strong or too forceful or premature for their "malleable" minds.

When a child asks her parent, "How are children born?" it is clearly a lie to say, "The stork brings them." But it is also a lie to say, "They just come out of the mother's belly," or to change the subject. The parent has information that the child wants. In order to be truthful, the parent has to either give the information or, without lying, explain why it isn't given. "I am embarrassed to tell you" is not a lie. "You are too young to know" "I am afraid you will get upset" isn't a lie; "I'll tell you when you are ready" is.

Complete truthfulness between human beings is rare, but from grownups to children it is almost unheard of.

We are not supposed to lie. Yet, if we examine that rule, we find it to have endless exceptions. Only one kind of lie seems to be truly not permissible: the kind we tell those who are one-up to us (our parents, teachers, employers, the government) and the kind that is told to us by those who are one-down to us (our children, students, employers, those we govern).

We may lie to our students, children, employees, and constituency. We expect to be lied to by our parents, teachers, employers, and politicians.

Lies and half-truths are as corrosive to children's awareness as are discounts. Children believe what they are told. When the things they are told as truths contradict each other it "jams their computer," and causes them to feel stupid and mindless.

Statements and lies can be made verbally and they can be made with actions as well. A person can make a statement verbally on one hand and belie it with an action on the other. For instance, John recalled being told the following information by his father:

1. "I love your mother." *(verbally)*

2. "If you love someone you don't have eyes for others." *(verbally)*

3. "I have no eyes for other women." (*verbally*, to his wife)

John saw his father acting hatefully toward his wife and calling her names, and he knew he had eyes for a neighbor because he saw them kissing in the laundry room. Thus John was exposed to a situation with at least one built-in lie. Statement 3 was a definite lie. Statement 1 was a possible lie. Statement 2 was a possible lie depending on whether 1 was true. But because father clearly lied with 3 it cast a doubt on all other statements, including 1 and 2.

Children are supposed to become truthful adults, but given the circumstances of their upbringing, this outcome is very unlikely. One of the parables that is supposed to encourage truth-telling in children is the story of "Washington's Cherry Tree," which is in itself a lie invented by a resourceful book salesman, Mason Locke Weems.[1] Children are told lies about Santa Claus, and parents ruefully and regretfully regard the day when they finally demystify the situation and come to see the world of Christmas for what it, at least partially, really is. The origin of human kind, its biological functionings, is kept away from children's awareness for as long as it possibly can be. Grownups hide their naked bodies and all signs of sexuality from children, and they distort and hide their conversation with each other when in the presence of children. And, of course, grownups are constantly encouraging children not to tell how they truly feel and think about whatever they truly feel and think about.

Ours is a consumer society. Through the buying and selling of merchandise firmly based on the dictum *caveat emptor* ("buyer beware") we are deeply grounded in lies regarding what we buy and sell. Merchandising and public relations is the selling of things and people through lies. We sell ourselves through lies.

---

[1]Wise, David. *The Politics of Lying: Government, Deception, Secrecy and Power*. New York: Random House, 1973.

Television and newspapers survive by selling (through lies). Deceptive advertising laws apply only to verbal lies by commission, but they cannot touch the lies told with pictures and by omission. Further, we expect as little truth from commercials as we do from the material between them, be this news or political statement. We know we are surrounded by lies but don't know what to do about it.

So, as we grow into civilized adulthood, we are fully prepared not only to be liars but to accept lies from others. It's a small wonder that people passively accept the lies of their elected officials,[1] advertisers, and the media; their training to do so is relentless from early childhood on.

Teaching in public schools carefully avoids discussing certain topics; human affairs are taught about in the form of history or political science rather than in terms of the everyday lives of people, their personal histories, their political situations, their freedom or lack of it. Lies in the schools are primarily by omission, though lies by commission also abound, especially when children are told outright lies about the functioning and administrative aspects of their school, their city, and their country. Here lies by commission are quite common. For instance, school children are exposed to certain views about government. They are told, for instance, that politicians are elected in a democratic process. How many school children are told with the same emphasis that some feel that politicians are bought by business interests and rubber-stamped by the people? Lies by omission are the stock in trade of the educational system, which is a sophisticated training ground in advanced forms of lying. Kerr[2] speaks about the "wonderfulness" approach to teaching; basically, a game of "Ain't It Wonderful." Teachers seem to feel that only positive,

---

[1]See *The Politics of Lying* by David Wise (already referred to previously in text) for a chilling account of lies by our elected officials; Watergate is only the tip of the iceberg.

[2]Kerr, Carmen. "Teaching Psychology to High School Misfits." *Issues in Radical Therapy* I,3 (1973): 24–25.

uplifting, and wonderful facts are worthy of a school curriculum. Negative, depressing, and awful facts are carefully screened out of children's attention.

An untrained child has a great deal of difficulty in saying something that is not true as well as failing to say something that is true. Both the expression of falsehood and the non-expression of truth are unnatural activities. Soon after the child begins to speak even the shortest sentences training to do the former (lie) and avoid the latter (being truthful) begins.

Children are supposedly encouraged not to lie. Lying, they're told, is not good. When children lie or are caught in a lie they are punished or shamed. Children who are truthful are, as far as I can see, simply children who have learned to lie skillfully (as grownups do); and only those who have not learned to lie in an acceptable way and are blunt and indiscriminate in their lying are punished for lying. In other words, "truthfulness," as taught by grownups to children, is simply a sophisticated way of lying as opposed to the crude, more simple way of lying which is punished.

What, then, is truthfulness as opposed to lying? An adequate definition of lying more closely parallels the dictionary definition of falsehood; namely, "a want of conformity to fact or truth; an intentional falsity; an untrue proposition." Lying is deception, falsification, or imposture as well as an intentional assertion of what is false. This definition includes under it not only a willful utterance of something which is false, but any act that contributes to giving a false impression or allowing it to remain.

Thus, I would like to define lying as: 1) A willful act; 2) involving false statements; and 3) the omission of statements which are true and which would prevent a known false impression on another's mind. That is to say, lies are not only false utterances (or lies by commission), but also lies by omission, that is, the failure to correct a false impression.

Lying and secrecy are powerful influences in scripting for Mindlessness, and lies along with discounts are capable of producing the kind of mental confusion which is called "schizophrenia" and which I prefer to call madness.

Madness

One per cent of the United States population, we are told, will at some time in their lives occupy a bed in a mental hospital. That is to say, one per cent of the people in the United States will lose their minds, go crazy, become "mentally ill."

All of us have an awareness of this spectre of madness. Some of us have actually been temporarily or continually mad. Some of us know people who are mad, perhaps members of our own family. Some of us have read literary accounts describing the madness of fictional characters or real ones like Vincent Van Gogh or Virginia Woolf. For some of us madness is a joke, something to nervously laugh about; for others it is a state of mind that we profoundly fear or pity.

Going crazy is an utterly terrifying experience in which nighttime is filled with sleeplessness or nightmares and infinite fear and dread, and in which daytime is fraught with incapacity to act, unwillingness to move, contempt and abuse from others, confusion, disorganization, suspicion, despair, and a recurring wish to end one's life and be done with it. People who "lose their minds" experience themselves as slimy, inferior human beings, patronized by others, the subject of detached inquiry and examination, absurd thoughtlessness, disrespect, incarceration, institutionalization, army-like scheduling, forced feeding and drug taking, electroshock therapy, and perhaps even lobotomy.

People who go through this experience are said to be "mentally ill"; usually the psychiatric diagnosis is "schizophrenia," though psychiatrists by their own admission have very little to offer to its many victims. Major tranquilizers are believed to be effective in allowing the "schizophrenic" to "function"; hospitalization can help "compensation"; but there is no hope that "schizophrenia" can be cured. The "schizophrenic" is seen by the psychiatrist as a semi-human being, a subject of pity and charitable thoughts.

I believe that the state of mind described above, the state of being mad, is the end result of a childhood and adolescence filled with discounts and lies, and devoid of support and nurturing. The antidote to madness is awareness, validation, and human support.

Fortunately, people's drive for health is powerful and children grow up in a world that includes more than the family and the many other oppressive forces of society. The world is also filled with human beings who are compassionate, loving, attuned, and who account for people's feelings. Very often a child that grows up in a family that conspires to make it crazy meets up with a teacher, a minister, an aunt or grandparent (and yes, even a therapist), or reads a book, or sees a movie which accounts for his feelings or conveys the message that he is, after all, O.K. rather than incurably mentally ill.

Schizophrenia is not an illness; it is not anything except an insulting name which mental health workers use to describe the wretched of our civilized earth. Being "diagnosed" a schizophrenic is like being given a plaque to wear around one's neck for everyone to see and stay away from. Young people who are taken to psychiatrists or other therapists and are labeled schizophrenic are often dealt with this, the final in a long series of blows. This label—schizophrenia—is the ultimate sentence, which from then on causes the person to think of himself as "schizophrenic" and to be treated by others as "schizophrenic," perhaps hospitalized, sometimes for long periods. The result of this action on the part of the family and therapists who collude with it is to render the victim truly hopeless and mindless.[1]

---

[1]This view about schizophrenia is not new. Ronald Laing, Thomas Szasz, and Theodore Sarbin were expressing similar views while I, in my graduate school days, was declaring people schizophrenic with the aid of psychological tests.

Madness can be quiet, agitated, pathetic, fearsome, or dramatic. The most dramatic form of madness is so-called "paranoid schizophrenia."

Paranoia

The official psychiatric view of paranoid reactions is that they are psychotic disorders with persistent delusions, usually grandoise or persecutory, and the creation of pseudo-communities. This shorthand description of paranoia is interesting to examine. The paranoid person usually feels that she is the center of a scheme by a group of people, such as the FBI, the Mafia, Con Edison, or General Motors, to persecute her, usually because she has some special importance. Hence, the description of grandiosity, namely the exaggerated self-importance assumed by thinking that the whole of the Federal Bureau of Investigation or the Mafia or both would be focused on her. Paranoids often feel that different groups of different people who are supposedly connected with each other are banding together to persecute them, hence the statement about pseudo-communities. For instance, a paranoid may think that his psychiatrist and the Federal Bureau of Investigation as well as the Communist Party are connected in a scheme to kill him. Characteristically, the paranoid person's intelligence is intact, and the behavior and emotional responses of the person are consistent with his ideas. The paranoid does not feel that his delusions are mistaken or wrong, and therefore does not seek or welcome therapeutic aid.

Typically, classical psychiatric views of paranoia allow that paranoia has some connection to external stresses. Speaking of precipitating factors associated with paranoia in the *American Handbook of Psychiatry*, Cameron[1] mentions external challenges, close

[1]Cameron, Norman. "Paranoid Conditions and Paranoia." In *American Handbook of Psychiatry*, ed. by Silvano Arieti. New York: Basic Books, 1959.

competitive situations, or being in close quarters with like sex persons for long periods of time and being socially isolated. Cameron mentions humiliation, failure and defeat, the loss of the major source of security or gratification as well as someone's death or desertion, an actual rebuff, neglect or deception, economic loss, or physical incapacitation as being possible causes for paranoia. Later, however, he discounts all these facts when he says:

This must not be taken to mean that adult paranoid reactions are produced by aggressive rivalry and erotic temptation, by failure and defeat, by sudden close contact or social isolation and by losses of security and gratification. These are only precipitating factors. They tip a chronically unstable balance, one dependent upon an infantile defensive organization, with defective reality testing, a selective hypersensitivity to unconscious processes in others, and irresistible tendencies to project and form pseudo-communities. Nevertheless, these precipitating factors are dynamically and clinically important since they can start off a process of paranoid development in which the patient, because of his defective personality organization, may then become powerless to stop.

Thus, in spite of the evidence that external stress and oppressive conditions precipitate paranoia, the view remains that paranoids have "defective reality testing" and "infantile" personalities.

I have a different view of the phenomenon of paranoia. In my opinion, what is called "paranoid schizophrenia" by psychiatrists is a state of mind which occurs in people as a result of systematic lying and oppression in childhood and in the person's present life. "When a paranoid person projects what he denies," even Cameron says, "he does not project at random. He describes hostile and erotic impulses to people who actually exhibit minimal signs of a corresponding unconscious impulse. Since everyone has hostile impulses . . . it is not difficult for the selectively hypersensitive paranoid to find persons on whom to project. *Thus there is always a core of truth in para-noid accusations.*" Here Cameron, in typically convo-luted psychiatric jargon, states (only to let it pass) the most important fact about paranoia: namely, stated in my words, that *paranoia is a state of heightened awareness.*

We all have a touch of paranoia. We may feel persecuted by neighbors, or think that people talk about us behind our backs. We don't believe politi-cians, or we think the oil companies are deceiving us, or that our telephones are tapped. Most of our paranoias are controlled and do not run amuck. We are careful whom we share them with, and if they are discounted by others we don't get especially upset; in fact, we are likely to agree and go along with the discount. Only a few of us get to the point where we lose our minds and become wildly paranoid. The kind of delusion that is involved in extreme paranoia can genuinely be described as a form of madness. It has, however, the same source and origin as the small paranoias which all of us are subjected to.

All of us have enemies who speak behind our backs; all of us are the victims of conspiracies to divest us of our money, to cause us to vote one way or another, to cause us to agree or disagree with our politicians. For example, when an advertising agency puts together a campaign for menthol cigarettes de-picting various beautiful outdoor scenes with young, beautiful, healthy people smoking menthol cigarettes in them, this is a conspiracy to influence our judgment so that we will consume menthol cigarettes. When politicians get together in smoke-filled rooms and agree to create an image for a presidential candidate which everyone in that room knows does not correspond to his personality, again this is a conspiracy to affect our thinking. When we buy a car or a house or an appliance, we are likely to deal with sales persons whose interests conflict with ours and who are willing to conspire to use deception and half-truths in order to get us to buy. When a spouse carefully disguises her interest in other men and, reacting with guilt, feigns love for her husband, she is conspiring to deceive her husband. We are all aware of these conspiracies. It's safe to say that there are many other conspiracies we know nothing about, since the essential element of such a conspiracy is that it is kept secret and that its nature will be concealed from the person who is being conspired against.

In the late sixties, the period in which the "New Left" organized to stop the Viet Nam war, a few people, represented in a few "paranoid" underground newspapers, claimed that the United States was secretly bombing Cambodia, that there was a conspiracy by President Nixon and Attorney General Mitchell to deprive dissenting Americans of their constitutional rights, that telephones were being tapped, that illegal entries were being committed, and so on. Those few people who believed these things to be going on were labeled paranoid, and the majority of the people ignored their statements. Today, of course, those paranoid perceptions have proven to be true. I use the example of the "New Left" as a general example which applies validly to paranoia in general. Namely, paranoia is a state of heightened awareness, a period in which a person begins to become aware of certain facts, such as the fact that he is being persecuted by communities of people (his family, whites, "big business," politicians, etc.) who are conspiring in some way against him. Whether it be political activists who are being conspired against by the police, blacks who are being conspired against by whites, woman who are being conspired against by men, or just people who are being conspired against by their families and their leaders, they all have such dawning awarenesses of the attempt that others make to oppress them— and these present themselves in the form of paranoia.

When this kind of paranoid heightened awareness is met with discounts and is categorically denied and rejected, then, as has been pointed out before, people have a choice. They can go along with the discount or they can disregard the discounter and operate independently of imformation coming from the outside. The Little Professor who is perceptive and aware of the covert behavior and motives of people will use its intelligence to build elaborate schemes which explain its perceptions and the discounts of them. When these schemes become elaborate enough, when they are peppered with enough imagination and a certain amount of perverse exaggeration, then they become the full-fledged paranoid delusions that we see in people who have gone completely mad. However, these paranoid delusions all have grains of truth, and the only way to understand them is to see them as exaggerations the person is forced to concoct because her perceptions are being denied.

In this light, we begin to understand paranoia and paranoid schizophrenia completely differently from the way it is presented to us by the usual psychiatric view. We can understand the mental hospital patient who believes that his food is being poisoned and that there are tape recorders in the wall that record everything he says, and who feels that there is a conspiracy by the communists, in league with his psychiatrist, to destroy his brain with X-rays, when, upon examining the situation, we find that he's being forced to take excessive and harmful amounts of major tranquilizers daily, that his utterances to other patients and to the staff are being meticulously recorded in the nurse's log, and that the staff of the ward are considering the possibility of administering electroshock therapy to him. It is these oppressive facts which are the source of paranoia, not the "infantile emotions," the "defective reality testing," and so on. When the perceptions of these facts are not discounted but honored we find that paranoia recedes and that, as in the case of all other forms of madness, the person who is being treated nurturingly and whose feelings are being accounted for will become sane once again. How to deal with the banal scripts of Mindlessness will be covered in Chapter 23.

10

Basic Training: Training in Joylessness

When people begin to ask themselves questions about their own lives, when they come to the point where they no longer assume that what they have been striving for is necessarily good or right, they may be faced with some difficult questions: If what I was told is right is not necessarily right, then what is? How do I decide what to do and what not to do?

Some believe that the answers about what shall be done, what is right, have to be found in tradition. Believers in this point of view refer to traditional or sacred documents, such as the Bible, or the Koran, Dr. Spock, or to written or unwritten law, and find their answers there. Others believe that the answer to that kind of question is to be found through logical, rational inquiry.

But there is a third point of view, one which many would have difficulty taking seriously; namely, that the most valuable source of information about what is good for people is within every one of them. This belief holds that human beings have a deep, built-in notion of what they need, what benefits them and harms them, and that, if left alone, people will follow their human core, their Center, and find the correct path toward harmony with themselves, each other, and nature.

The reader may find this an astonishing statement. Everything around us evidences the contrary. It seems that if left alone to do as they wish people will kill, plunder, rape, and consume themselves in sexual and drug orgies. Violence, sexual excess, drug abuse, sadism seem to be what people really want to do, we are told. That's why we need law and order and discipline, isn't it? What are we to believe?

Transactional analysts believe that people are O.K., that is, good, fine, loving, cooperative, eager to help, beautiful, intelligent, healthy. Why then do they act so badly? Why do they smoke three packs of cigarettes a day; why do they eat too much; why do they kill themselves with alcohol and heroin? Why are they mean to each other, why do they steal and lie, let themselves be abused and exploited? The answer, we believe, is that they are scripted to act thus. In addition, I believe that once scripted we are encouraged to remain in our scripts by people who benefit from it. We are encouraged to smoke, drink, eat, and abuse drugs by the food and drug industries. We are aggressive, competitive, and individualistic because, as will be explained later, those traits make us easily exploitable as workers and citizens.

But people aren't just scripted to act in certain ways counseled by others. They are also scripted to ignore their own counsel. Scripting not only prescribes behavior for us, it also cuts us off from our own internal compass, our Center, the wisdom of our body which is capable of informing us what is good because it feels good and what is bad because it feels bad. Many people completely ignore their bodies. Some people even feel that their bodies are a lesser part of them, even that they are cursed by having a body. To them the fact that something feels good means that it is bad. The better it feels the worse it is. Sex, for instance, being one of the best-feeling activities, is one of the "worst" for us. Joy is sinful.

I believe that we are able to know what is good for us if we can experience how it feels. When we listen to our bodies we find that cigarettes feel bad, that clean air feels good, that alcohol beyond a certain small amount feels bad, that cooperating feels good, that lying feels bad, that being in love feels good, that not getting and giving strokes feels bad, that certain work feels good and certain work feels bad, that sex without affection, and sometimes affection without sex, feels bad, that masturbation feels good. Overeating feels bad when you pay attention to the body after the initial comfort and tranquilizing effect of being stuffed. We can listen to our bodies and tell when we want to be alone and when we want to be with someone, when we want to sleep, when we want to walk, or sit or lie down.

We are all to some extent split off from our bodies. But all of us also retain some good connections with them. Evidence of how a part of our body is connected to our Center is the way we reject certain harmful situations. Most of us will pull back our hand when it touches a hot stove. We are connected to our hand enough to feel the pain and thus pull back. Some of us will not be able to overeat; others can't "hold their liquor" without throwing up; others are unable to inhale cigarette smoke without coughing; others can't sit long without eventually having to do exercise; others can't tolerate polluted air. Some can't stand the side-effects of aspirin, sleeping pills, stimulants, and food with additives such as MSG or saccharin. Every one of the above examples is evidence of a good connection between the person's Center (the self, consciousness, which decides what is good and what is bad for the person) and some part of her or his body which is being harmed. A good connection with our body helps us know what is harmful but also tells us what is beneficial for us. When we are Centered fresh water tastes good, clean air smells good, and we can tell what kind of food we need. If we need exercise our body tells us so, and when we go ahead and respond to the need it feels good. The same is true for our sexual needs. What feels good under these circumstances is good.

Yet, you will say, if that is the case, why does heroin, for instance, feel so good? How come a deep drag on a cigarette is such a pleasure? Why is getting drunk so much fun? I would like to answer this question by explaining how joylessness (being split off from our bodies) leads to drug abuse.

Powerful drugs like nicotine, ethyl alcohol, opiates,

sedatives, and stimulants are, in effect, short cuts for Centering. They restore, for a short time, the connections between our Center and the rest of our bodies. They do this, at least partially, by "knocking out" the Pig Parent who does not want us to feel good. Different body splits react to different drugs, which explains why people prefer certain drugs to others.

However, this connection is brief; the side effects of the drug are unpleasant after a while, and a new dose of the drug is needed to create well-being.

The connection is fleeting, yet the drug remains in our body; the side effects of the drug as it accumulates become more marked. Some drugs (all the sedatives: alcohol, barbiturates, opiates, and some tranquilizers) require larger and larger doses to recreate the connection; and when the body is saturated with the drug it reacts violently by becoming ill when the drug is withdrawn. The body's regulatory mechanisms go haywire under the influence of large dosages of drugs, more with some drugs than with others. Barbiturates and heroin as well as alcohol are the worst in this respect. Marijuana (ironically, given the nightmare of cruel and unusual punishment that is connected with its use) is one of the least likely to have that effect.

Thus, injunctions and attributions that remove us from our bodies can result in drug addiction. When they don't, they simply result in joylessness, a life in which we, ourselves, our Centers, are lodged somewhere in the head detached from the myriad pleasurable and unpleasurable sensations of the body. Because we feel no pleasure we are joyless. Because we feel no pain we don't take care of our bodies until the pain is so acute that we cannot ignore it any longer, often too late, as in the case of smokers who feel no discomfort in their lungs until they have cancer, or overeaters who endure the pain of overweight until their heart gives way.

The same mechanism that causes drug abuse is the source of another form of addiction which might be called consumerism. Buying feels good; having a new car, washing machine, or wardrobe feels good, and, just like drugs, buying is a ready avenue to pleasure.

People become addicted to buying as others are addicted to drugs; they will go on buying binges and feel cravings to buy which are similar to the cravings of an alcoholic. The consumer's "morning after" hangover, the damage done by his excesses, is his bills, to which he becomes a slave just as an alcoholic or junkie is a slave to drugs.

Joylessness is unfortunately exploited by business interests. Drug use and consumerism are widely encouraged through the media and large numbers of people's livelihoods depend upon the expenditures of a joyless population on drugs and essentially useless consumer items. We need only note the hue and cry of tobacco farmers when there is a threat to the consumption of cigarettes to realize how our country's economy depends on the joylessness of its population. The situation is a vicious circle. Millions of crazed consumers travel billions of miles in their mobile homes, dune buggies, dirt bikes, tearing up the countryside wasting energy, polluting the air, looking for the thrills which they could find within and among themselves and with the earth if they stopped and let their Centers communicate with what goes on around them.

The expanding economy of which we Americans are so proud is predicated on a frantic earning, spending, manufacturing, selling, energy-consuming pace which eats up our resources. We sit in the midst of the vast dung pile of our gross national product desperately reaching for sweet smells, clean air, open spaces, sunshine, and the Good Life.

Injunctions and Attributions for Joylessness

Perhaps the most fundamental attack on the integrity of the human body which causes the initial and most important split in us is the way in which children's sensuality is prevented from expressing itself.

A great emphasis was made by Freud and his followers on infantile sexuality. I believe that while sexuality in children exists, Freudian theory makes more of it than fits reality.

This is an important point because the Freudian perspective leads us to believe that we repress children's sexuality and suggests that the rest of the child's life is relatively without repression. But repression of sexuality is just a minor aspect of banal scripting for Joylessness. Repression of sensuality, that is, the ready connection between all the senses and our consciousness or Center, is a far more important factor in people's lives. Sexuality is not fully developed in childhood and will blossom in adolescence in spite of anti-sex scripting. But our senses can be permanently split off from us by the time we reach our teens.

Vision and hearing are severely limited from their possible scope by being made the servants of rationality. Children's eidetic vision is turned into the impoverished perception of grownups. Looking at a rose we don't see the luscious velvety fuzz of the petals, the sparkling droplets hidden within their folds, the subtle variations in the deep red hues. We see a rose. A rose is a rose is a rose. As Ronald Reagan has said about our redwoods, "You see one, you've seen them all." When the purpose is performance, productivity, competition, and making a buck, eidetic seeing will only slow you down, so forget it. And forget it we do. We similarly forget what hearing is like. We hear words, not their intonations; we hear motors, horns, jet engines, buzzers, bells, and since they don't have much to say we forget how to listen to haunting melodies, the happy or sad ring of people's voices. All we get is a black and white, alphabetically coded read-out for our computer.

Our vision and hearing are encapsulated in a rational shell which takes out 90% of their sensing capacities. I believe that psychedelic drugs and rock music are used by many young people to shatter this shell. When music is loud enough, you can feel it all over your body just as when you used to hear your mother's lullabies. And LSD, mescaline, peyote bring back the visions which we have forgotten how to see; a rose becomes, once again, a wondrous universe of texture, color, and smell.

Not only are our senses controlled in how they perceive but also in *what* they may perceive. Children must not see nudity, hear or see sex or anger, touch other people's bodies or certain parts of their own bodies.

Children's tendency to explore everything around them is severely curtailed with respect to a large selection of items. Children are clearly enjoined from viewing or touching certain parts of their bodies and others' with enjoyment. In more extreme situations children are made to sleep with their hands above the covers of their bed; they are told that their genitals and other body parts are dirty; they are told that masturbation is sinful or dangerous; and they are told in no uncertain terms that they may not touch live skin (their own or others') with pleasure.

In addition, children love to run and jump, skip, tumble, scream, cry, laugh, and express themselves emotionally. Emotional expression is pleasurable, but is often ill-received by parents, who are annoyed by its energy or honesty. When parents unilaterally squelch and curtail the emotional expressions and, consequently, the pleasures of children, they are laying down the injunctions and attributions of joylessness.

Children are trained to live in discomfort. Because they are not given an opportunity to choose what feels good for themselves and have to do things chosen for them by others, they are often in a state of mild or acute discomfort. Wearing uncomfortable clothes, sitting quietly, being scared or hurt without having permission to express unhappiness—all of these are painful situations which are a child's lot. As a consequence, children learn (and this is especially true of boys) to bear pain without complaint.

It is an important fact of human tissue that it adapts to stress and pain. We may react violently to the first drag of a cigarette, but after a number of such insults to our respiratory system we no longer react with pain and rejection because our bodies adapt to noxious stimuli. This is true of all sorts of pain, including the pain associated with fear, or unexpressed rage, the pain associated with breathing polluted air, or with backbreaking labor. Adaptation to pain, which superficially may sound like an advantage, can be quite damaging. Constant adaptation to pain can only be achieved through a split in which the part of the body which is under stress is split off from the body's Center. The Center, namely the place where we consider ourselves to be, the part of ourselves which constitutes our self, has to detach itself from the part under stress; and having adapted to stress, we may become permanently split off from large parts of our bodies.

In addition, children get a great deal of encouragement to use drugs for the production of pleasure as well as for the avoidance of pain. Illness is not dealt with as a situation in which one can effectively use one's energy to fight the disease and contribute to the mending of one's body. Instead, children, by example, learn that the answer to disease is the passive taking of drugs. They also learn that the most direct way of producing pleasure is, once again, drug-taking.

These are the factors that cause the banal scripting of joylessness. Some tentative suggestions for the therapy of this script will be explored in Chapter 24.

11

Rescue: The Banal
Scripting
of Powerlessness

Scripting robs people of their autonomy. The more thorough the scripting, the less control the person has over his life and the more he feels powerless. When feeling powerless people can't think, can't express themselves, can't work or study, can't enjoy themselves, can't stop smoking or drinking, can't wake up in the morning or go to sleep at night, can't cry or can't stop crying. Some people feel constantly utterly powerless; others only at certain times.

I have tried to show how basic training attacks the capacity to love, think, and feel in people through the stroke economy, discounts, and body splits. In this chapter I want to show how the game of Rescue is played and how it promotes feelings of powerlessness in children.

The Rescue Game

I believe that people are by nature cooperative and have a deep-felt need to work together and help each other. Situations where one person is in need of help and another person is capable of offering it are common in social groupings, and when one person helps another it can be a joyful, profoundly satisfying, cooperative experience. I wish to distinguish such a positive helping experience from the unpleasant and destructive one which I call the Rescue game.

An analysis of the game follows:

Thesis: The theme of this game revolves around the fact that at times people need help to achieve what they want. Those who play the game, however, believe that people who need help can't really be helped and that they can't help themselves either.

Berne pointed out that certain games, which he called Life Games, "offer more opportunities than others for lifelong careers." Rescue is such a "career" game and is played as such by many physicians, nurses, and other members of the "helping" professions. It also seems to be a game played, perhaps less intensely, by almost everybody.

The three *Roles* of the game are Rescuer, Persecutor, and Victim; and they can be arranged in a triangle to indicate how people switch between them (Figure 8).

The Victim's position is "I'm not O.K., you're O.K." (I am helpless and hopeless; try and help me). The Rescuer's position matches the Victim's, namely: "I'm O.K., you're not O.K." (You are helpless and hopeless; nevertheless, I'll try to help you). The Persecutor's position also is "I'm O.K., you're not O.K." (You are helpless and hopeless, and it's your fault).

The roles are interchangeable as are the feelings that go with them. In the Victim role the person feels helpless and ashamed; in the Rescuer role he feels guilty; and in the Persecutor role she feels angry. Rescuing doesn't work and usually leads to Persecution. Though everyone plays all three roles, people tend to prefer one of them with its accompanying feeling (racket), and this role may be a central aspect of their banal script.

The roles of Rescuer, Persecutor, and Victim first appeared in the psychiatric literature as roles in the different games described by Eric Berne in his book *Games People Play*. Berne postulated that game roles were interchangeable so that any person who played a game while in one role would eventually also play the game in another. For instance, he speaks about a group game called "Why Don't You—Yes, But" (see

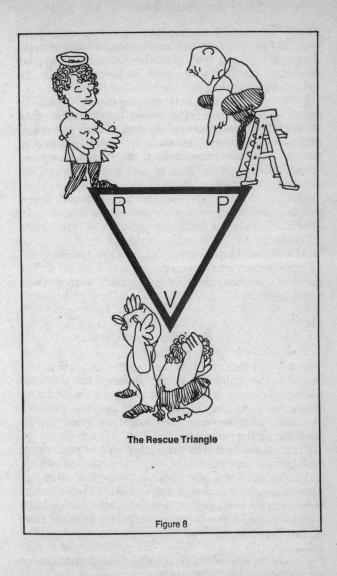

The Rescue Triangle

Figure 8

page 47) in which one person comes on as Victim
and the rest of the group comes on as Rescuer. The
Victim asks questions from a position of powerlessness, and the Rescuers attempt to give answers. Every
suggestion is discarded, and a new one is offered until
eventually the Rescuers get angry, switch roles, and
persecute the Victim.

Berne postulated that every person who plays a
certain game will switch to every other position in the
game so that the person playing Victim in one round
will eventually play Rescuer and then Persecutor in
later rounds. Berne especially noted this phenomenon
in the game of "Alcoholic" in which the Victim (the
alcoholic) eventually plays Rescuer, Persecutor, Connection, and Patsy at different times with different
people. Stephen Karpman, in his article "The Drama
Triangle,"[1] made a brilliant synthesis of the above
observations by Berne and postulated that the three
basic game roles are Persecutor, Victim, and Rescuer,
and that these can be arranged in a triangle in such a
way as to indicate how people switch around from
one to another.

Powerlessness

Hogie Wyckoff pointed out (page 201) that the
family is the training ground for the Rescue Game,
which is, in effect, training for powerlessness. Children
are forced into the Victim role while the roles of
Rescuer and Persecutor are taught by example, as
provided by the parents.

Training children into the Victim role of powerlessness is done by interfering with the areas in which
they have potential power. Three important areas of
power are attacked almost universally in every family;
the power to love, that is, the power to successfully
relate to other human beings; the power to think, that
is, the capacity to understand the world; and the

---

[1]Karpman, Stephen B. "Script Drama Analysis." *Transactional
Analysis Bulletin* 7,26 (1968): 39–43.

power to enjoy ourselves, that is, the capacity to experience and make full use of our bodies and emotions. These correspond to the three banal scripts described in Chapter 6.

To the extent that children can do things such as love and understand the world and themselves, and to the extent that they are not allowed to do these things, they are forced into a Victim position with the parents acting either as Persecutors who oppress them in their abilities, or as Rescuers who then do what they have actually prevented them from doing for themselves. For instance, in a day's time, a seven-year-old boy could, if left alone to learn it, get out of bed, get dressed, make the bed, cook himself some breakfast, make some lunch, take out the garbage, clean the dishes he dirtied, go out the door and down the street and to school. He can do chores such as cleaning the table, sweeping the floor, going to the store to buy anything he wants. If he comes home and finds out that there is no one there he can figure out that his mother is probably at her best friend's house, call information, find out the number, make a phone call, and make plans to have dinner with a friend and stay overnight. All of these things that a seven-year-old can do are not usually allowed of seven-year-olds. That is to say, most households prevent a seven-year-old from freely using his powers to that full an extent, so that most seven-year-olds have to be wakened by their mothers, who then cook breakfast for them, take them to school, pick them up, bring them home, cook dinner for them, and arrange for their entertainment and social life. In that situation the child is a Victim who is being Persecuted when he is kept powerless and who is later Rescued when things are done for him that he could have done for himself.

You will notice that the Rescue situation described above involves: 1) training in powerlessness in relationships by not allowing the child to make his own social contacts and his own decisions about whom he wants to be with and when; 2) training in powerlessness in knowing the world by not allowing a child to

come up against situations in which it has to understand the world well enough to make decisions and to
think in it; and 3) training in powerlessness in which
a child is not allowed to learn about himself, what
gives him pleasure, how he feels, and how to act
upon it.

Different households train children more or less intensively in powerlessness and also select different
areas for training. For instance, some households
leave relatively free the capacity to love while they
attack the capacity to think or to understand oneself.
Most households treat males differently from females
so that males are trained to be powerless in their
capacities to know themselves and in their loving
capacities, whereas women are trained to be powerless in their capacities to know the world (see Chapter 13).

Children who are trained as Victims grow up with
varying degrees of disability or incapacitation. Most
everyone is somewhat incapacitated by their early
childhood training, but some people are turned into
full-fledged Victims who spend their time looking for
Rescuers with whom they can perpetuate their powerlessness.

The latter form of extreme defeat is found in persons who are labeled "mentally ill," "schizophrenic,"
or who become psychotically depressed or addicted
to drugs. They represent situations in which the basic
training in powerlessness, which is needed to make
sure people grow up to be docile, manageable, and
lacking in autonomy, has gone awry. They are cases
of a "powerlessness overdose" which the society then
assigns to psychiatrists and jailers for institutionalization.

Powerlessness in the population is a requirement in
an oppressive society, and the family unfortunately
often trains out power and autonomy and trains in
discipline and docility to authoritarian rules. Powerlessness training, playing Victim in the Rescue Game,
causes people to grow up with a feeling that the
world can't be changed. When feeling powerless people will say, "What's the use of voting (or demon-

strating, or writing letters to lawmakers)? It won't change anything," or, "What's the use of being generous (or loving, or good) when everybody else is selfish?"

The Rescue Triangle in the Nuclear Family

The Rescue Triangle is exemplified in the classic, banal family script. Father is the Persecutor; Mother is the Rescuer; and the kids are the Victims. In a situation like this the roles switch around so that Father becomes Mother's Victim when she Persecutes him for hurting her children, and then Mother becomes the children's Victim when they take advantage of her kindness. Later the children may Rescue Mother when Father attempts to beat her up while she passively submits, and so on. As the children grow up and begin to acquire some power independent of the parents, they begin to cash in on the long-time resentment for having been Victimized and thus become the parents' Persecutors. The more extensive the Rescue and Persecution by the parents, the more severe the retaliation of the children; so that in a home in which Rescuing and Persecuting is very prevalent, children are prone to set parents up in all manner of bad situations: middle-class children often do this by doing badly in school, by refusing to work, by becoming drug addicts and/or getting themselves arrested. Children know that one of the most terrifying experiences parents can have is for their child to be arrested and that they, the parents, will then be humiliated by the police, lawyers, and judges. Children who are resentful of their parents' Rescues very often enjoy being arrested and being taken to jail and making their parents, the police, the judge, and all the grownups involved look like fools. That is the game of HIP "High and Proud,"[1] which is designed as

---

[1] Steiner, Claude M. *Games Alcoholics Play.* New York: Grove Press, 1971.

a retaliation, from a one-down position, against long-term Rescue and Persecution from grownups.

Less dramatic but even more common is the situation in which parents Rescue their children for the following reasons:

Common, especially among divorced parents, is guilt about their supposed inadequacy as parents which causes them to overprotect and make no demands upon their children. Also, parents underestimate their children's potentialities and expect very little of them.

Expectations placed on children are centered on school performance, namely preparation for the job market, so that very little else can be asked beyond discipline and school learning which takes up most of children's energies. Here parents are putting their energies into raising a work force for exploitation by industry and commerce much as farmers who fatten cattle, but (unlike farmers) for no profit to themselves except the pride of having a hardworking son or a daughter who is a good housekeeper.

Children raised in the shadow of the Rescue Triangle become grownups who are firmly entrenched in the three roles: Rescuer, Persecutor, and Victim. The Rescue triangle is an efficient training ground for the acceptance of hierarchies of power in which every person is one-up to some and one-down to others.

By the time we achieve maturity, all of us have had ample experience in being one-down through having played the Victim role. No one enjoys the one-down position. The Rescue triangle does not provide for equality between people. One can only be one-up or one-down in it. Thus, after having been in a powerless position, we make ourselves feel better by taking and assuming power over others as Rescuers or Persecutors.

Having observed our parents Rescue and Persecute us, we endeavor to do the same. We are amply encouraged by folk myths about the value of Rescuer (The Good Samaritan) and Persecution (Spare the rod and spoil the child).

The Three Roles

RESCUER

The Rescue role is especially mystified in our society. Selflessness, doing for others, generosity are encouraged. Even cooperation is encouraged as part of this mystification. What is not pointed out is that we are encouraged to be selfless, generous, and co-operative with people even if they are deceitful, selfish, stingy, and uncooperative with us. As an example, the exploitation of workers and little people by politicians and the super-rich who rule this country is made easy by the Rescue tendencies in people which encourage them to be "cooperative," helpful, hardworking, and therefore easily exploitable.

Mothers and wives are especially mystified about how oppressive the Rescue role is. To give up Rescuing is not seen as a service to the Victim, but as an injurious act. Continuing to Rescue is seen not as injurious, but as selfless, generous, and cooperative. This is because sex-role programming is designed so that women will be an unpaid work force which makes the lot of males easier to bear.

For instance, the spouses of alcoholics have a great deal of difficulty seeing how their endless sacrifices, their "selflessness," and their willingness to endure abuse followed by forgiveness is, in fact, harmful rather than helpful to the alcoholic.

Being a Rescuer gives us the feeling of being one-up, and this is its only pleasure—it does remove us from the Victim, one-down role. We can also get one-up by becoming Persecutors, but this role is not sanctioned as fully. Generally, to be a Persecutor we have to have some sort of official title or badge which legitimizes our persecution.

PERSECUTOR

The Persecuting role is the inevitable outcome of the Rescue and Victim roles. Any person who Rescues by helping someone else when that person is not helping himself is inevitably going to become angry with him. Every time the person in the position of Victim is Rescued by someone else she is perfectly aware of the fact that she is one-down and kept one-down by the Rescuer and that the Rescuer is interfering with her ability to be powerful. Therefore a person who has played the role of Victim vis-à-vis a person who is a Rescuer will also inevitably become angry. So it is possible to predict that every Rescue–Victim transaction will eventually result in a Persecutor–Victim transaction.

VICTIM

There are Victims and victims. A victim is a person who is being oppressed by another person. Some people are "pure" or actual victims and are not contributing to their one-down position. As an example, a person being run over by a truck, or a person being robbed on the street—these are actual victims. But most situations in which people are victimized include the Victim's cooperation with the victimization; the person does not work against or resist what is wrong.

When a person is being overpowered or oppressed by another person or situation, the Victim colludes with the oppressor when she discounts her feelings of being persecuted and/or doesn't use all of her own power to overcome her one-down position. To distinguish true oppression from oppression which involves some self-perpetuation or which is the result of lack of struggle against it, the word victim can be used with lower case (*true* victim) or capital letters (Victim).

The same device can be used with regard to the Rescuer role to distinguish it from the true rescuer like a fireman or a lifeguard whose function is to help true victims. The main difference between a rescuer and a Rescuer is that the former expects to succeed and usually does while the latter expects to fail and is usually rewarded in his expectations.

Another difference between Rescuers, Victims and rescuers, victims is that rescuers are usually thanked

ually

rable
thers
ying
verse
rless
e by
scu-
hear
ner-
wer

hen
me-
ally

the
can
ften
of
ave

can
ree
ple
lop
en
ng,
en.
nd
oy
le
er
ng
p-

validate one's
which requir
touch with th
heightened a
Chapter 9. T
intuitive expe
ing (see Ch
honest, keep
fantasies (o
each other a
by accountin

s

The strong
a man and
Parent to P
Child. The
the sole ba
and women
is often wh
not a lasting
puts undue
tionship.
The situa
children eat
out thinking
are sudden
They are c
they can't
Having be
two lovers
They know
know how
better ones.
We are a
able toys;
don't work
go shoppin
junkyard of
and tossed

by the victims they help, while Rescuers are usually persecuted by the Victims *they* help.

No one enjoys being one-down, but it is pleasurable to let go and have others take over. One can let others take over for short periods of time without playing the game, especially if one has agreements to reverse the situation later on. The feeling of being a powerless Victim, however, is hellish and is only made worse by people who agree with one's powerlessness by Rescuing. No matter how weak we feel, it is good to hear that we are not completely powerless; and it is energizing to be asked and expected to take our power and do our part by someone who is willing to help.

We resent being made powerless, especially when we don't ask for it, and when we find out that someone has been doing for us what they didn't really want to do, we feel humiliated and enraged.

People wanting to extricate themselves from the Victim position can ask not to be Rescued and can demand honesty from those who help them. Often these demands need to be made over and over of people whose tendency is to Rescue and who have trouble with feelings of guilt when they stop.

Powerlessness promoted by the Rescue game can be worked against effectively in therapy. The three roles of the game can be avoided, and then people find that they do have capacities and can develop skills they never thought they could have. Women become logically minded, mechanically skilled, strong, able to walk, run, and hike as far and long as men. Men can become sensitive, emotional, nurturing, and can learn to relax, feel love in their hearts, and enjoy life. By avoiding the roles of the Rescue Triangle and operating out of our Center we assume power over our lives and stop preventing others from doing the same. How this can be done is described in Chapter 19.

12

Competition: The Banal Scripting of Inequality

The Rescue game always includes one person who feels one-up and O.K. (Rescuer or Persecutor) and another that feels one-down and not O.K. (Victim). This type of unequal one-up/one-down relationship can be contrasted with the relationship between equals characterized by the mutually held position: "I'm O.K., you're O.K."

Allied with the lessons of the Rescue game, the typical household teaches its offspring another lesson which is as American as apple pie: competitiveness.

"All people are born equal" is another way of saying "I'm O.K., you're O.K." No one is better than anybody else; we are all complex, interesting, worthwhile, and in the long run equally important or unimportant. What we know in one area is more than made up for by what we don't know elsewhere. We are all experts in certain areas and ignorant in others.

This is what we are told by judges, the Christian ethic, our Constitution, and by our teachers and politicians. Yet we don't really believe this at all. We are compelled to see ourselves as better than others and to see others as our betters. To think and believe that we are equals with all other people is difficult to achieve and even more difficult to maintain.

The difficulty which we have in feeling equality with all other human beings is the result in part of our banal training in competitiveness and individualism. We white North Americans are members of a society thoroughly indoctrinated in individualism and competitiveness—traits which have been presented to us as desirable from early in our lives. We are told that, if pursued assiduously, individualism and competitiveness will lead us to happiness and success in life, and these qualities have become an integral part of our life scripts.

This mystification has as its main purpose to shape us into pliable workers easily exploited by a ruling class which profits from our competitiveness turned into productivity. I believe that competition and individualism actually destroy our potential for harmony with ourselves, harmony with each other, and harmony with nature. In our mad scramble to the top we forget how to love, how to think, and we lose track of who we are and what we really want.

We seem to live on a ladder with people stepping on our heads while we step on the heads of others with at most two or three people on our rung with whom we are equals. Once in a while some of us get on top of the ladder and look down triumphantly, and sometimes we are thrown to the bottom. But we usually are somewhere on the gray middle struggling to get up, one rung at a time, to the distant top, or to just stay in place.

The experience of one-up/one-down is so common to us that we think it is a natural experience to be expected and one that we should react to by trying as hard as we can to "get ahead." Most of us actually dislike the competitive struggle. Indeed, we don't really struggle to get ahead, but simply in order not to fall behind as everyone climbs over our heads. Yet we are locked into constant competition and power plays.

Competitiveness and individualism are two most highly touted qualities of the "good" American. As a consequence they are scripted into people's lives so that they interfere with cooperation and equality between them.

.

Individualism

Individualism gives people the impression that when they achieve something it is on their own and without the help of others and that when they fail it is, once again, on their own and without the influence of others. Belief in the value of individualism obscures any understanding of the way in which human beings affect each other in both good and bad ways; thus it mystifies both oppression and cooperation. Individualism results in the isolation of human beings from each other so that they cannot band together to organize against the forces that oppress them. Individualism makes people easily influenced and also easily targeted when they step out of line and fight their oppression without support from others. When people are unhappy or dissatisfied, individualism keeps them isolated. Instead of finding each other and cooperating to remedy their oppressive conditions, people wind up individually defeated, each person in her or his separate, impotent, paranoid system.

Individualism as a way of relating to other human beings, while highly touted, can, in fact, be a most self-destructive form of behavior.

I want to stress the difference between individuality (uniqueness, identity, selfhood) and individualism (selfishness, disregard for others, self-seeking behavior). Individuality tempered with respect and regard for others need not become individualism. We can be ourselves without exploiting or ignoring others. Individual action, or self-centered behavior, can be of benefit to the person and her fellow human beings. In fact it will be shown later (Chapter 23) that self-assertiveness is an important requirement for cooperation between people. I am claiming, however, that individualism (as opposed to individuality) is not a good trait to be pursued or taught to children.

I am simply attacking the notion that individualism is a super-trait, to be pursued and admired. It is clear that some individuals and their individual actions have been of ultimate benefit to themselves and others. In fact, it is the valuable individual actions of leaders, scientists, and politicians that are used in schools as showcases to highlight the value of individuality for the purpose of instilling individualism and competitiveness in the young. What is not taught is how individualism and competitiveness are harmful and how valuable cooperation can really be.

Competitiveness

Individualism goes hand in hand with competitiveness. Since we stand or fall strictly on our individual efforts, it follows that we must think of everyone around us as individuals equally invested in succeeding and, in the mad scramble to the top, also necessarily invested in achieving superiority or one-up status to us. Being one-down is intolerable; the only alternative in our society is to try to stay one-up. Equality is not comprehended by us and often not even considered. Competitiveness is trained into human beings from early in life in our culture.

There is some interesting research evidence in this area.[1] Studies of competition show that white American city children, when confronted with a situation in which cooperation can obtain a reward for them, choose to compete even though by competing the chances for obtaining rewards are lost. Older children compete more than younger ones, which strongly indicates that this kind of self-defeating competitiveness is learned.

Yet not all human beings are bred into competitive styles of life, and the same research shows that Mexican-American children are less likely to be competitive in a self-defeating way than Anglo-American children. In an individualistic, competitive society, a person who is not highly competitive cannot keep up and becomes chronically one-down and eventually

---

[1] Nelson, Linden L., and Kagan, Spencer. "Competition: The Star-Spangled Scramble." *Psychology Today* 6,4 (1972): 53–57.

highly alienated. It is because of this that competitiveness persists in appearing to be a good trait, since
when everyone is fiercely competitive it is impossible
to achieve any well-being without having very strong
competitive skills. The only alternative to individualism and competitiveness which has potential for the
production of well-being is collectivity and cooperation between equals. But while we are well trained
in the skills of competition, we know very little about
how to cooperate or be equal with others. I have observed many situations (communes, relationships) in
which people worked hard to cooperate and establish
equality with each other. Most of these efforts col-
lapsed, giving way to the well-established and familiar competitive and individualistic banal scripting.

Scarcity

Competitiveness is based on the premise that there
is not enough to go around of whatever a person
needs. If the material needs of human beings are in
drastic scarcity, it follows obviously that competitiveness is the mode for survival. If there is one loaf of
bread daily to feed twenty families, it is pretty clear
that all twenty families will starve. If a competitive
member of this group manages to obtain the whole
loaf of bread for his family, that one family will survive while the others will still starve. The net effect of
competitiveness in scarcity is actually a positive one
for those who compete and win and for the survival
of the species. But as scarcity becomes a thing of the
past, as it is, for now, in the United States, competitiveness actually creates scarcity and hunger. The
hoarding behavior which goes along with competitiveness causes certain people to have a great deal
more than they truly need, while large numbers of
others, who could be satisfied with the surplus of
those few who have, go without. Competitive, hoarding behavior is predicated on unrealistic anxiety
based on fears of scarcity. Oppressive as he is to others, the hoarder is himself oppressed by it. The stroke

economy is an example of artificial scarcity in a basic human need—strokes. O.K. feelings are in scarcity, and people have difficulty feeling smart, beautiful, healthy, good and right-on except by proving that others are not—as if there were only enough beauty, intelligence, health, and goodness for a few. It is possible to hoard, compete for, and create scarcity of O.K. feelings in the same manner in which food and strokes are hoarded.

I first experienced the relationship of competition and cooperation in the fall of 1969 in the Santa Cruz mountains at a camp for the War Resistance. One evening everyone sat around in a large circle in the center of which everyone had placed the food for dinner. To my scarcity-oriented eyes it did not appear that there was enough to go around. I was scared by the prospects of going hungry and in great conflict about the situation. Portions of food began to be passed around the circle, everyone eating from them as much as they wanted and passing them on. The food circulated over and over, and to my amazement I found that there was actually enough food to satisfy me quite fully. Yet my experience, because of my scarcity-oriented, competitive, and individualist training was one of anxiety and alarm about not being properly fed. As food went by me I took larger bites than I needed; I felt guilty about this; I schemed about ways in which I could make certain kinds of food return to me; I worried as food went around the circle as to whether it would reach me again. I ate more than I needed and was, in short, unable to enjoy the meal because I was so driven by fears of scarcity and feelings of competition.

At the next meal, however, I allowed myself to trust that there was enough to go around, and I experienced the clear sensation of plentitude and satisfaction based on having enough on the basis of cooperation rather than on the basis of getting a big enough portion in a competitive situation.

The above anecdote is to illustrate how we are mystified into being competitive and individualistic, believing that competitiveness and individualism bring us benefit when they actually harm us because at this point in human history there is enough to go around.

Competitiveness is taught us from an early age by our parents and more particularly in school. Sports, grades, tests are all training exercises in competitive skills—mock scarcity situations that prepare us for the business world, for the assembly line, for the job market. Competitiveness is taught to boys in its most blatant form; girls are taught to compete in more subtle, psychological forms. Especially important in banal competitiveness training is the insensitive treatment by parents of the problems of competition between siblings. Rivalry between siblings encouraged by parents is often the first experience of competition and individualism to be repeated and reinforced in different contexts throughout life.

Power Plays

The basic interpersonal operation with which individualism and competition are brought into practice is the power play. A power play is a transaction whereby a person obtains from another person something that he wants against that other person's will. (See Chapter 17 for a full description of power plays.)

Power plays can be crude and involve actual physical coercion or they can be subtle ways in which people talk or manipulate each other out of things that they want.

The most crude power play is simply one in which a person grabs from another her loaf of bread and then harms her if she tries to get it back. The same effect, namely the taking away of bread, can be obtained by mental, psychological means, which are, however, equally power plays and which have the same outcome. In any case, power plays have the effect of taking away what is rightfully one person's and putting it in another person's hands. Relationships based on power plays immerse people in a miserable, unhappy series of skirmishes, battles, and major wars in which everyone loses.

Power plays are a constant, daily occurrence in the lives of children and an integral part of their banal scripting for the one-up/one-down way of life.

The stroke economy, discounts, body splits, Rescue, competitiveness, power plays, and sex roles (to be discussed next) are the basic banal curriculum which interferes with the full autonomous development of children. How to defeat these will be discussed in Section V on "The Good Life" later in this book.

SECTION 3
Relationships

13

Sex Role Scripting
in Men and Women

by Hogie Wyckoff

The following two chapters are written by Hogie Wyckoff. They are included in this book because they are essential original contributions to the theory of banal scripts.

As women and men we are socialized to develop certain parts of our personalities while suppressing the development of other parts. This programming promotes a predetermined, stilted, and repetitive way of acting in life which has earlier been referred to as banal scripting (see Chapter 7). These "garden variety," banal, sex role scripts invade every fiber of our day-to-day lives.

The definitions of male and female roles are, from day one, intensively socialized into children and these same definitions are constantly reinforced throughout our lives. Classically, a man is "supposed to be" rational, productive and hardworking, but he is "*not* supposed to be" emotional, in touch with his feelings, or overtly loving. On the other hand, a woman is not supposed to think rationally, be able to balance the checkbook, or be powerful. She can supply the man she relates to with the emotional, feeling functions that are missing in him, and he can take care of business for her. These, of course, are the extreme characteristics of male/female sex roles. Obviously all people do not completely fit into these roles. In general, how-

ever, there is a tendency for people to define themselves in their society's masculine and feminine terms.

A particularly unhealthy result of our male-female
sex role training is that gaps have been created in
people which limit their potential to become *whole*
human beings. Often what happens with men and
women is that they feel incomplete when they lack a
partner of the opposite sex, so that they continually
look for fulfillment in another; and, in addition to the
feeling of incompletion, they feel not O.K. for not
being in a relationship. Like two parts of a puzzle or
two halves of a whole, men and women will often
either direct their energy into looking for someone else
to match up with and/or they will cling (fearfully) to
an already established dependency relationship.

Structural Analysis of Sex Roles—Men

When we look at people in terms of their ego functions, it becomes evident that males are enjoined—
actually more than enjoined, they are pressured or
coerced—to conform to certain scripts. They develop
their Adults so that they will be rational, good at
math and science, and generally able to think along
logical lines. However, they are dissuaded from developing the Nurturing Parent, either for others or
for themselves. Most young boys, for instance, would
not include in their self-images the ability to nurture
children or the ability to directly take care of and comfort other people. A boy's O.K. self-image would depend more on his ability to "take care of business" and
be strong so that if he were needed to take care of
people it would be indirectly through his Adult performance. While he is taught that it is important for
him to have a well-developed Adult, it is not necessary
—maybe it's not even all right—for him to have a
strong Nurturing Parent. But because men are often
told they *should* be nurturing and *should* support life
and be involved in child-rearing, they feel guilty if
they don't want to, so they Rescue; that is, they do
things for people that they really don't want to do,

because their Pig Parent tells them they *should* want to.

In addition, men are enjoined against being in touch with their Natural Child. They are given messages not to feel, to discount their feelings; in fact, according to the lies we've been told, it's best if men aren't "too emotional." It would be difficult for a boy to compete and be willing to get hurt in a football game if he were in touch with his feelings, because he might feel afraid of competition and of being hurt.

Men are told that it is also not important generally for a man to be in touch with his Little Professor, the intuitive part of his Child. If Mr. Jones, making a business deal, is using his Little Professor he might pick up that Mr. Brown was very scared and worried about the negotiations. Further, if Mr. Jones had a clear pipeline to his Nurturing Parent, he might feel empathetic, feel compelled to be fair, and give Brown a break. He would have trouble being competitive; he would want to be understanding and cooperative.

Men, were they tuned in to their feelings, would not only be unable to exploit others, but they'd also be unable to exploit themselves, their bodies; they wouldn't do unpleasant and boring labor or risk their lives or kill others in military service.

Often, because they are out of touch with their feelings, men tend to abuse drugs more than women do. They tend to be scripted for Joylessness which expresses itself in strong body splits (see Chapter 10).

The main job of the male Pig Parent is to police men into always having their Adults turned on, to do what their Pigs say they should do to be "real men," that is, to be out of touch with their nurturing, intuitive, or fun-loving feelings. Figure 9 is a diagram of the ego development in men depicting the effects of banal sex role scripting.

Structural Analysis of Sex Roles—Women

Women are programmed to be the productive male's complementary other half. More precisely, men are incomplete halves which women are supposed to fill in and complete—not vice versa. Women are trained to be adaptable. They are also enjoined to have a strong Nurturing Parent. It is their job to bring up children, take care of people (expecially "their" men), and be nurturing. They are not enjoined or conditioned to have a strong Adult. It is acceptable and O.K. if a woman cannot understand her income-tax forms, or if she doesn't have a head for math and mechanics. She doesn't have to think rationally and logically. Actually, for her to fulfill her function as an assistant or girl-Friday to men and to promote volunteerism and the free labor of housework, it is *important* for a woman not to develop her Adult. It is necessary for her, however (as it is for men), to have a Pig Parent to enforce the "laws" of her script, that is, to keep her in her place (one-down).

Society's general script for women is conceived so that we feel powerless. What that means in terms of a structural analysis (of the ego states) is that we do not have Adult power, that we tend to be irrational, and therefore have difficulty taking responsibility for our decisions and actions. If we are following the usual script, we look for others, especially men, to Rescue us, and we don't trust ourselves or other women to take care of business in the world.

On the other hand, it is O.K. for women to have a well-developed Little Professor, to be intuitive and know what's going on with other people so that they know when and how to nurture others. If women are tuned in they can take care of people's wishes without their even having to ask for what they want (which is the usual female role in the Rescue game). Nor do women have much permission to have a Natural Child; if we did we would be tuned in to exactly what *we* want.

The general body script for women is to meet the media image of the "beautiful woman"; to look good from the outside in, not necessarily to feel good from the inside out. The "ideal" woman, or "Barbie doll." tends to have weak arms, long fingernails that make for inefficient use of the hands, a small waist, flat stom-

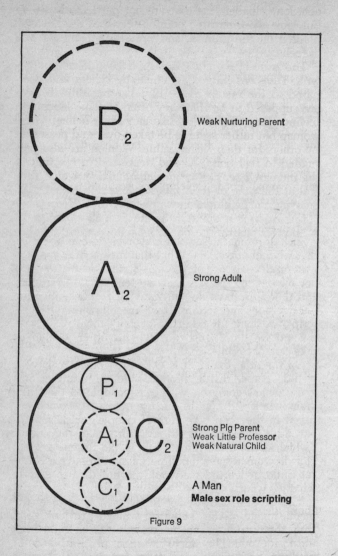

Figure 9

ach, long slender legs that are not particularly strong but look good, narrow, pointed feet that are not well planted on the ground, and breasts that are not full of feeling.

The issue of women's breasts is particularly important. They are judged so much by others and compared to the media image of what beautiful breasts are supposed to be that they often become lacking in feeling. They tend to feel like they don't belong to the woman but rather seem to be taken over and possessed by others for their visual value. Women are also persuaded to feel not O.K. and depressed in reaction to the increased sensitivity and emotionality which they feel at the time of their menstrual period rather than enjoying the heightened awareness of their feelings.

Figure 10 is a diagram of the ego development in women, depicting the effects of banal sex role scripting.

Sex Roles and the Family

In the standard nuclear family setting, men and women Rescue (see Chapter 11) each other constantly in a vast number of ways. Dad Rescues the family by taking care of such business as keeping the car tuned, doing the income tax, working a forty-hour-a-week job (which he hates), and Mom Rescues by supplying almost all the nurturing and loving needed in the family, by being tuned in to what others feel and supplying what they need without their having to ask and, finally, by giving a lot more to her children than she can ever hope to get back. Also, Dad Rescues Mom by doing more than 50% of the work in their sex life. He, for the most part, initiates it and determines how it will go. Mom may eventually get resentful about *just* having sex (especially if she doesn't experience orgasm) because he doesn't give her enough tender lovings. This happens because Dad's male scripting disconnects him from his sensual feelings and makes him unaware of what she wants from him. On the other hand, she doesn't talk straight about it.

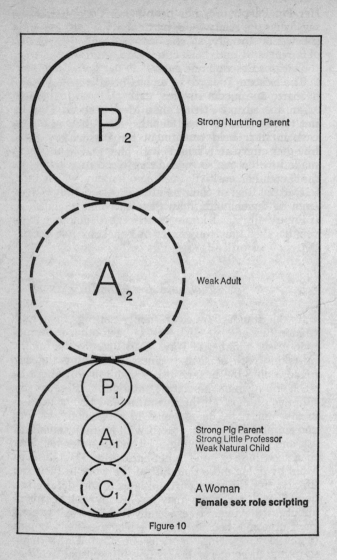

Figure 10

Her Pig Parent tells her people won't like her if she says what she really feels, particularly if she says what she wants sexually, so she "adapts" and then slowly gets resentful and Persecutes Dad. And, on and on, the vicious Rescue cycle goes.

The Rescue Triangle is, as has been stated already, a merry-go-round. In this example, Dad Rescued Mom, the sexual Victim; then Mom rescued Dad by not telling him her real feelings; later they can both cash in their held resentment for Persecutory time. She gets angry and "frigid" with him, and he wants to make love on the sly with other women or is "impotent" with her.

Dad has also discounted himself. Men often are not even in touch with how they discount themselves. They usually don't know exactly what they want and feel because they've been effectively taught to be out of touch in order to perform and compete. It's hard to break this vicious cycle because as men start to get in touch, the first feelings to emerge are very often unpleasant ones, such as fear and guilt (see Chapter 27). Thus it is easy for men to get locked in to not wanting to experience feelings in order to avoid these unpleasant feelings. Dad hasn't listened carefully to himself because he hasn't liked what he has heard.

As R. D. Laing points out, discounting turns people into invalids; and because of women's permission to be in touch with their intuitive Child, they are more prone to be the victims of discounting. Mary says, "I think you don't love me any more," and Fred answers, "That's not true, I do," because he feels guilty and/or he's out of touch. Thus she is made to feel crazy. Her internal dialogue runs something like this: "I can't understand it. I have a strong gut feeling that he doesn't love me any more, but he says he does. Where is this feeling coming from? I wish I wasn't so confused." This is the way in which women are often cut off from their power of intuition and made to feel not O.K. and crazy.

Intuitive power is a very important form of personal power, but the only way to use it in a safe and self-benefiting manner is if someone else will agree to validate one's experience by being absolutely honest, which requires that they take risks to be really in touch with themselves. The importance of paranoia as heightened awareness has been elaborated upon in Chapter 9. The means by which we can validate our intuitive experiences for each other is called Accounting (see Chapter 23), that is, by being completely honest, keeping no secrets, and sharing our paranoid fantasies (our scared, intuitive suspicions) about each other as well as responding to others' paranoias by accounting for the "grain of truth" in them.

Sex Roles and Relationships

The strongest avenue of communication left open to a man and woman in a relationship other than Pig Parent to Pig Parent is Natural Child to Natural Child. The Child to Child connection is all too often the sole basis for loving relationships between men and women. Sexual, loving, Child-to-Child attraction is often what brings people together initially. This is not a lasting bond because the situation as described puts undue stress on the Child element of their relationship.

The situation is reminiscent of two happy, laughing children eating a delicious strawberry shortcake. Without thinking they enjoy and consume their goody but are suddenly sad and surprised when it's all gone. They are disappointed and hurt when they realize they can't seem to *have* their cake and *eat* it too. Having been carefully groomed as consumers, the two lovers lack vision and power about their needs. They know how to consume *this* cake, but don't know how to preserve it and create more and even better ones.

We are all taught to consume each other like disposable toys; when people are used up, break down, or don't work right any more, we just throw them out and go shopping for another. Behind us lies a pathetic junkyard of psychic corpses; people we have used up and tossed out. What a waste of our loving investment in other human beings! This behavior keeps us separated from each other and unable to work together cooperatively so we can all get more of what we want.

Discounts (Chapter 9) help defeat relationships between men and women and are especially harmful to the mental well-being of women. The lack of development in the Little Professor of men contributes to this problem. When Mary, after ten years of marriage, says to Fred, "I don't think you love me any more, Fred. I just don't feel you love me," and he answers, "That's absurd, don't be silly. Of course I love you," or if she says, "I'm afraid to be at home alone when you go away," and he responds with, "Don't be afraid. There's nothing to be afraid of," they are going through a typical difficulty between men and women. He is discounting her feelings and is not tuned in to the fact that there might be something real and important in her experience of things. The guilt from his Pig Parent, who says he *has* to love his wife, may be keeping him from being in touch with what his true feelings are, although *she* may be tuned in to them. He discounts his feelings and her intuitive perceptions. As a consequence, she becomes confused and irrational and he, more guilty and out of touch. This pattern manages to wreck many potentially good relationships.

The Sex Role Conspiracy

There's a mystification about the way men and women are scripted to go together like sweet and sour sauce, hot and cold, *yin* and *yang*. It's supposedly a groovy, beautiful thing. The problem is that people really don't fit together very well that way (as grotesquely exemplified on TV by Archie and Edith Bunker). Actually, it is in this way that men and women become mysteries to each other, rather than complements. It is often said that men don't understand the way women think. Women don't understand the way men think, either. And as far as relationships go, believing the myth of complementary sex roles conspires against genuine success because communication between men and women is broken down in so many ways.

The two crucial obstacles against full and long-lasting relationships between men and women are 1) that they are often unable to have good intimate loving relationships with each other; and 2) that they have difficulty developing satisfying and equal working relationships with each other. The way in which communication is defeated is easily seen in Figure 11A, diagramming the possible transactions between men and women.

There is often communication from her Nurturing Parent to his Child, but little vice versa. Because there's weak communication between their Adults, it's difficult for them to develop the intimacy of a cooperative and efficient working relationship. Also lacking is the potential bond between Nurturing Parents because of his lack of development in that area and her scripting to assume the majority of the responsibility for bringing up their children. The communication between Little Professors is weak, too. This causes a lack of intimacy when they are unable to share their intuitions about each other and other people.

When we put these two people together and they "become one" we find that, indeed, they are less than two people. Actually, the composite of their two personalities (Figure 11B) equals one Nurturing Parent, one Adult, one Little Professor, two half Natural Childs,[1] and two Pig Parents—a paltry human being indeed.

Combating Sex Roles

Men and women need to work in a cooperative process of reclaiming their full power as human beings. Women need to reclaim their Adult power, their ability to think rationally and do what they want to do and to stop Rescuing: stop giving nurturing and strokes

---

[1] I use the term "Childs" instead of children to indicate here that I am speaking of Ego states.

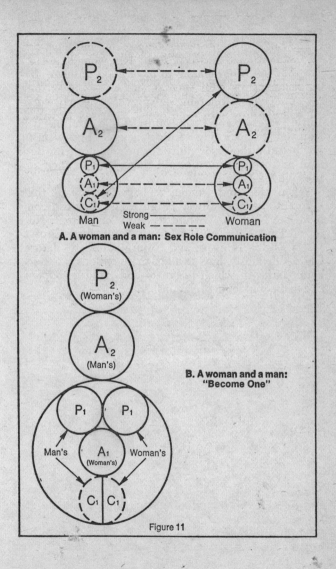

A. A woman and a man: Sex Role Communication

B. A woman and a man: "Become One"

Figure 11

that are not returned, and especially stop loving people who don't love them back equally. It's in their best interest to only match the lovings they get so they can stop being resentful of men and apply their surplus lovings to themselves and to others who love them back. Men need to develop their Nurturing Parent for themselves and for others to work on getting in touch with their feelings, particularly their Little Professor and their Natural Child. Men need to start doing things only because they feel they want to, not because they feel guilty for not doing them. Both men and women need to rid themselves of their oppressive Pig Parent.

When men and women reclaim full use of their different ego state power (Figure 12), they can communicate Nurturing Parent to Nurturing Parent, Nurturing Parent to Child, Adult to Adult, Little Professor to Little Professor, and Natural Child to Natural Child. Obviously, having all of these options is a much better basis on which to create and build a cooperative and equal loving relationship.

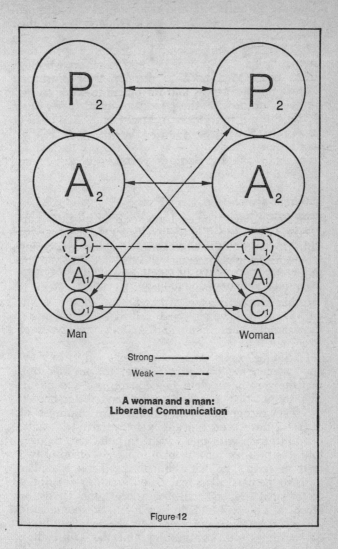

Man

Woman

Strong ————————
Weak — — — — —

**A woman and a man:
Liberated Communication**

Figure 12

14

Banal Scripts of Women

by Hogie Wyckoff

Not only have women been scripted by their parents and encouraged in their roles by the mass media, but also important to note here is that sex role typing is an ancient phenomenon reflected, for example, by the goddesses of Greek mythology: Athens is the prototype of "Woman Behind the Man"; Hera is "Mother Hubbard"; and Aphrodite is "Plastic Woman." Sex roles have also been reified by psychiatrists; for example, the *Anima* and *Animus* archetypes of Carl Jung.

I'm going to present some women's scripts to show how women are trained to accept the mystification that they are incomplete, inadequate, and dependent. The scripts that I will describe have been chosen for their recognition value. These are examples of scripts I have seen repeatedly in women who have been in group with me. I want to point out, though, that it is possible for a woman to have a blend of two or three scripts, or that although the theme is similar to these the particulars may be different. In describing these banal scripts I will first indicate the Thesis, or life plan. This will include how intimacy, spontaneity, and awareness are oppressed; how she may fight back; the pastimes she engages in; and the sad ending called for by the script. The rest of the items correspond closely to Claude's description of the Script Checklist (Chapter 7).

Mother Hubbard (or Woman Behind the Family)

Life course: She spends her life nurturing and taking care of everyone but herself. She chronically gives much more than she receives and accepts the imbalance because she feels she is the least important member of her family and that her worth is measurable only in terms of how much she supplies to others. This inequity is constantly legitimized by the mass media's promotion (TV, women's magazines) of the role of housewife and mother. Strokes and meaning in life do not come to her for herself and her labors, but rather for her family, her husband and children. She chooses this script because it's safe and with it she can avoid taking risks inherent in confronting the fear of being an independent and whole person. She stays in this script because every time she rebels and does what she wants, her husband and children get angry with her.

Although she plays all roles in the Rescue Triangle, she is most familiar with the one of Rescuer (see Chapter 11). In an effort to get something back from her family, she often talks too much (for attention), and she tries to create guilt in her husband and children when they don't seem to love her enough or give her what she wants, even though she doesn't ask. Additionally, she refuses to make love with her husband, using excuses of being too tired or having a headache with the hope that he will give her some nurturing strokes instead.

She reads women's magazines, envying slender models in fancy clothes and feeling that in comparison she's not O.K. She is caught in a vicious cycle of cooking delicious recipes and going on diets. The more she feels not O.K., the more she wants to rebel and to cook the fancy recipes and overeat.

Later in life she often ends up depressed and lonely, appreciated by no one. Her kids dislike her and her husband is no longer interested in her. She has been used up by them. For the most part, she is too

job hours. She feels safe in the role of consumer and experiences herself as having power when she makes decisions as a consumer and when she can buy the things she wants. On the other hand, she does not experience herself as having much power over what happens in her life outside of the department store and is thus most accustomed to the role of Victim in the game of Rescue. She structures much of her time shopping, putting on make-up, trying on different outfits at home, and reading movie and fashion magazines. She repeatedly proves the validity of this script by getting ignored by people when she isn't doing her dress-up, "Barbie Doll" number. Because she doesn't get what she really wants out of her life (what she wants can't be bought), she may begin to fight back by shoplifting or, when she's angry with her husband, by overspending to the extent that she is in effect beating him to death with a plastic charge plate or using his money to buy strokes from a psychoanalyst.

When superficial beauty can no longer be bought and pasted on, she ends up depressed: she gets no strokes that she truly values, either from herself or from others. She may try to fill the void with alcohol, tranquilizers, or other chemicals. As an older woman, she often fills her life with trivia and her house with knickknacks.

Counterscript: When she has just finished a diet, gotten herself some new clothes, and is dressed and feeling good while being admired by others at a dimly lit party or bar, it appears this script can make her happy. She also feels good at home or on the job when she is still a little high from the drinks at lunch, but the highs are short-lived and once again she feels empty and dissatisfied.

Injunctions and Attributions:
Don't get old
Don't be yourself
Be cute

Decision: In high school she decides to take a part-time after-school job so she can earn money to buy

clothes rather than keep up her work on the school
newspaper and pursue her interest in writing.

Mythical Heroine: She is fascinated by Doris Day
and other such movie stars and is amused by Phyllis
Diller, Joan Rivers, and Carol Channing.

Somatic Component: Her body is thin but flabby.
She's ruined her feet in torturous shoes and dried her
skin with suntanning.

Games:
Buy Me Something
Schlemiel
Alcoholic (Pill-oholic)

Therapist's Role in the Script: He prescribes drugs
and engages her in an extended course of psychotherapy. His diagnosis precludes the possibility of
group psychotherapy (because she's *so* "neurotic"),
and he sees her individually three or four times a
week.

Antithesis: She decides to like her natural self. She
concludes that her "power" as a consumer is an illusion and decides to reclaim power over her life by
taking responsibility for creating it. She no longer
takes drugs to blur out what's unsatisfactory about her
life but rather joins a problem-solving group and
learns how to make real changes. She works on developing aspects of herself other than her appearance
that both she and others can appreciate. She begins to
enjoy exercising and gets herself into a hiking club
to meet new people. She commits herself to being
concerned with how she feels on the inside rather
than how she looks from the outside.

The Woman Behind the Man

Life Course: She puts all her talent and drive into
supporting her husband who is often less talented
than she, but according to sexist society is supposed
to be the successful one. She usually has no children;

looks smart at cocktail parties; and is a great hostess and campaign manager. She is a female Cyrano de Bergerac, the gray eminence who cannot shine because of a congenital defect (her sex) that makes her socially unacceptable in a position of power. In the service of supporting him, she gives him many strokes and allows him to receive strokes which are rightfully hers. For example, she ghostwrites her husband's book and he takes all the credit. She must be satisfied to glow in the applause for him. She finds it much easier to put her drive for success into her husband than to deal with the hard, competitive realities of being a "career woman" and being labeled a "castrating bitch."

If he's successful, she spends a lot of time reading her husband's fan letters, watching him on TV, keeping track of his competitors, interior decorating, and planning for elegant dinner parties to "snow" his boss into giving him the promotion. Proof that she can't break out of this script comes every time a publisher rejects a manuscript with her name on it or when she can't land anything but a secretarial job. When she becomes dissatisfied with this inequity she might break down in her role as girl-Friday to highlight her importance in his work or contemplate having an affair with one of his competitors.

In the end, when he is near the "top" and less dependent on her, he may want a divorce so he can get it on with a younger woman to whom he can feel one-up, or who is a more viable sex object.

Counterscript: This script appears to be one of the least exploitative because it provides some recognition for the woman when she is known as "The Woman Behind the Man." She feels pretty good as long as her husband is genuinely appreciative of her role, but as he begins to take her for granted, she starts feeling jealous and resentful, and thinks she's not O.K. having these feelings.

Injunctions and Attributions:
Be helpful

Don't take credit
Stand behind your man

Decision: At a certain point she decides not to finish her education, but rather to quit, get a job, and help put her husband through school. She decides that to be a good wife she should support rather than outshine him.

Mythical Heroine: She is fascinated by the life of Eleanor Roosevelt, and very curious about Pat Nixon, Rose Mary Woods, and Jackie Kennedy.

Somatic Component: She hunches over a bit and tends to keep her shoulders and back up to make herself inconspicuous and unthreatening looking.

Games:
Gee, You're Wonderful, Professor
Happy to Help
If It Weren't For You

Therapist's Role in the Script: He reminds her of her limitations as a woman and of her duty to support her husband. When the mention of divorce comes up, he tells her that it would be castrating for her to be angry and vindictive toward her husband in their divorce settlement.

Antithesis: The way out is for her to start taking credit for her talent and to use it in her own behalf. It's necessary for her to give up the cop-out of his taking the responsibility and being out in the front line. She has to first get rid of the internal messages that tell her she's not O.K. if she's strong and powerful and then refuses to take put-downs from others who are fearful of her ambition. She can start to do her work for herself on her own terms and tell her husband to hire secretarial and housekeeping services. She has to decide if she wants success to have it directly, not vicariously, and to be willing to pay the necessary dues for it.

Poor Little Me

Life Course: She spends her life being a Victim looking for a Rescuer. Her parents did everything for her
because she is a girl (and girls are supposed to be
helpless), thus debilitating her, making her completely dependent upon them and under their control.
After struggling against this, she finally gives up and
concludes they're right, she is helpless. She marries a
prominent man, often a psychiatrist who plays a rescuing Daddy to her helpless little girl. She gets no
strokes for being O.K. when she shows strength and is
kept feeling not O.K. because she only gets strokes
when she is really down. Thus the strokes she gets
are bittersweet, that is, not nourishing.

She experiences some intimacy from her Child ego
state in relation to the Parent ego state of others, but
very rarely experiences intimacy as an equal. Because
she has permission to be childlike she can be spontaneous in a childlike and helpless way and be inven-
tive about acting "crazy." She learns she can get things
more easily if she tells people about her troubles and
thus she becomes invested in not giving up that self-
image. She spends a lot of time complaining about
how awful things are and trying to get others to do
something about it. She keeps proving that she's a
Victim by setting up situations in which she first
manipulates people into doing things for her that
they really don't want to do, then getting persecuted
by them when they feel resentful toward her. Her
husband gets strokes for being a good Daddy to a
weak child, sexual strokes in appreciation from her
and, finally, strokes for being a martyred husband
when she totally falls apart. She fights back by "going
crazy," making public scenes to embarrass her husband, and generally creates doubt in the community
concerning his competence as either a therapist or a
husband.

She ends up not being able to function adequately,

is either locked into an oppressive dependency relationship with a man or is institutionalized.

Counterscript: This script looks good just after she marries her Sir Galahad husband and he is Rescuing and propping her up so that it appears that she has things pretty well worked out.

Injunctions and Attributions:
Don't grow up
Do what your parents say
Don't think

Decision: When she is young, after she has been pressured or coerced into not listening to her own opinions and feelings, she decides that her parents know best, i.e., better than she does.

Mythical Heroine: As a child she greatly enjoyed reading about Cinderella and Little Orphan Annie.

Somatic Component: Her body tends to be weak and off-balance and her eyes are habitually wide open. Predominantly, there is a surprised or sad look on her face.

Games:
Ain't It Awful
Stupid
Do Me Something

Therapist's Role in the Script: He plays Rescuer and when she relapses after a brief period of progress he switches to Persecutor and calls her unmotivated or schizophrenic.

Antithesis: She refuses to take the easy way out by acting like a Victim or playing "Do Me Something." She decides there's a lot in it for her to grow up, to develop her Adult and take care of business for herself. She begins to get strokes for being O.K. when she shows strength and doesn't accept strokes for being a Victim. She stops enjoying an injured one-down and hurt self-image. She becomes keenly aware of how oppressive and condescending it is when others Rescue her, so she commits herself to doing 50% of the work at all times and knows that Rescue does her about as much good as heroin. She starts getting high off her own power. She does body work to get out the scared energy that is blocked in her body and learns karate so that she can feel safe and strong on the street. She asks people to call her by her middle name "Joan" rather than her first name "Susy."

Creeping Beauty

Life Course: She has the standard attributes of so-called "media beauty," but she doesn't feel very good about herself as a person and really doesn't believe she is lovely. Rather, she thinks of herself as being shallow and ugly underneath the veneer. When she looks into the mirror she doesn't see her beauty but only sees her blemishes and imperfections. This is called the "Beautiful Woman Syndrome" which paradoxically frequently occurs with women who do not see their own beauty because they focus on individual parts of their appearance which may not be attractive when seen separately. She sees herself as deceiving everyone who thinks she is beautiful and thinks they're fools for buying the deception. She gets too many strokes for being beautiful and discounts them all. She wants to be liked as a person, but no one is willing to see past her exterior beauty. Any man with her gets strokes for having such a lovely possession on his arm. She is constantly in search of a Prince Charming who will end all her troubles by making her truly beautiful and valuable with his pure love. She is angry that people don't appreciate her primarily as a human being and tends to fight back by chain-smoking and presenting a very sloppy appearance around intimate friends. She gets men to come across with as much as they will and then doesn't deliver the goods (herself). She primarily experiences herself as a Victim. Too often other women see her as a crafty competitor for men's attention and envy her beauty. Because of her good looks she often gets what she wants very easily. This special treatment makes it unnecessary for her to learn to cooperate with people so she can be a bit of a prima donna at times.

Because she doesn't use her Adult in her relationship with Prince Charming, he eventually "rips her off" emotionally. Later, when she loses her media beauty, she continues the same hostile behavior toward others that she has always manifested, only now people think she is just being a "bitch" for no reason. Too often she ends up alone, loving no one, not even herself.

Counterscript: It appears that her life is wonderfully happy when she is head-over-heels in love with her Prince Charming. It looks great for about six months and then slowly begins to tarnish when he gets interested in a new beautiful woman.

Injunctions and Attributions:
Your beauty is only skin deep
Don't be close to people
Don't be you

Decision: People seem to respond to her only as a pretty face and not as a person, so she decides since she seems to be incapable of being treated and respected as an effective social agent to sell herself as a sex object in order to get some of what she wants.

Mythical Heroine: She has a morbid fascination with the Marilyn Monroe legend, and admires prominent movie and television stars.

Somatic Component: Her body is very beautiful, but she has little feeling in it. Her body is often tight and hard because she's tense, and she may at times have difficulty reaching orgasm. When she smiles only her mouth moves so as not to wrinkle up her eyes.

Games:
Rapo
If It Weren't For You
Blemish (on herself)

Therapist's Role in the Script: He becomes sexually aroused by her and propositions her so she can then discount anything he might have to say.

Antithesis: She starts demanding strokes for the qualities people like in her other than her beauty and she refuses to accept strokes just for her physical presence. She begins to like herself as she is, stops playing "Blemish" on herself, and begins to thoroughly enjoy her true inner and outer beauty. She starts to do things that are meaningful to her and works in a women's group to learn how to cooperate to get what she wants.

She decides to use her Adult to build a cooperative relationship with a man who appreciates her as a person. She starts enjoying her power while creating her life the way she wants it to be and appreciates what she has to work with in herself.

Nurse

Life Course: She is a professional Rescuer who works in an institution that exploits her and pushes her to her physical limits. Initially, her motivation to help others comes from caring, but caring soon becomes oppressive to her. She is taught to skillfully intuit other people's needs and take care of them. But then she wants her needs to be filled in a like manner; that is, she expects others to read her mind the way she reads theirs and take care of her the way she takes care of them. But it doesn't happen; she doesn't ask for what she wants so she doesn't get it. What she does get much too often is a box of "candy strokes" from appreciative patients and their families. After too much Rescuing she becomes hurt and angry. She isn't getting what she wants so turns to the role of Persecutor in the guise of so-called "professional detachment" which often takes the form of Anti-Rescue (see Chapter 11): "I'm not giving anything that isn't asked for!"

She spends a lot of time complaining about how

terrible the doctors and her supervisor are but doesn't have time or energy to confront them, or can't because of potential recriminations. She may also feel she has to adapt for bread and butter survival reasons, since she is the economic mainstay of her family, either because she's Rescuing her husband (an alcoholic) or because she's a single parent with children. When things don't work out in her love relationships she thinks she should have done more (Rescue).

Ironically, she ends up having to spend a lot of time in the hospital when she's older because of how she has been forced to exploit her body in the service of saving other people's bodies. She may have injured her back saving a patient from a fall and consumed too many "uppers" to keep going during the day and too many "downers" and alcohol to cool out at night.

Counterscript: Soon after she has graduated from Nursing School and is on her first job, it appears that she has chosen a wonderful career and that everything is just the way she wants it. Her enthusiasm for her work gradually dwindles as she feels the pinch of giving out a lot of love and getting little in return. She gets very depressed while working on a cancer ward and has to start taking sleeping pills to sleep and avoid nightmares. If she's white and/or middle-class, she may be dating a handsome young doctor, who turns out to be married or he marries her and later divorces her when he finishes his training.

Injunctions and Attributions:
Take care of others first
Don't ask for what you want
Be a hard worker

Decision: When she is young she decides that being good means that you put the needs of others first, that to consider your own needs first is "selfish," therefore not O.K.

Mythical Heroine: She has fantasies of being a long-suffering and ever-listening woman like Jane Addams or Florence Nightingale.

Somatic Components: She wrecks her feet by standing on them too much, gets varicose veins and injures her back lifting patients.

Games:
Why Don't You—Yes, But
Ain't It Awful
If It Weren't For You

Therapist's Role in the Script: He tells her that she should keep on doing her job, taking care of others and, of course, supporting doctors in their patriarchal role. He prescribes drugs for her so she can do it: "uppers" during the day, "downers" at night. He may even want to tell her about his troubles since she's such an understanding and good listener.

Antithesis: The most important thing for her to do is to learn to ask for what she wants and put her own needs first. It's also crucial that she make a decision to stop Rescuing and that she learn how to have Rescue-free Relationships. It may be necessary for her to quit her hospital job and start working part-time or doing private work so that she can have some time for herself. She has to learn how to take care of herself and respect her own needs and body. It will later be useful for her to organize with other nurses to push for reforms so that her work is not so exploitative, to get support not to Rescue, and to talk with patients about patients' rights and responsibilities.

Fat Woman

Life Course: She spends most of her life hassling herself about and responding to what her scale says, and going on an endless series of diets trying to obtain O.K.ness through self-deprivation. She was generally taught poor eating habits as a child, encouraged to eat carbohydrates, and was given food as a reward for "good" behavior. She also was told to eat everything on her plate, since it would be a shame to waste food—"Think about the starving people in China" (not about your own full stomach).

She has trouble letting her anger out, and great difficulty saying "no" so she literally swallows everything. What she gets out of being overweight is that it does tend to make her feel solid and substantial. And because she has difficulty saying "no" or getting angry, her fat can also keep men away whom she wants to repel. Her fat also serves as a "wooden leg"; a handy cop-out for not doing things or accomplishing what she wants in life. She longs for strokes about her appearance yet never gets them. The bulk of her spontaneity is centered around what and when she eats. She feels victimized by her own body, her lack of self-control, and other people's opinion about her weight.

She is caught in a vicious cycle of rebellious food binges and cruel self-punishing diets. She is convinced that she is not O.K. because of her weight. Repeated failure in dieting proves to her that she has no self-control (i.e., she is a helpless victim to her addiction).

Because she is worried about her weight all her life and because her heart is broken from not getting the kind of loving she wanted, she ends up having heart trouble which is what the doctors threatened would happen anyway.

Counterscript: Things appear to be going well when she is on a diet, losing weight, and wearing a size twelve dress, but actually they're not because she is constantly hungry, her life revolves around what the scale says, and she still has a lot of trouble getting angry and saying "no." When her diet is over and she runs into some kind of difficulty she goes back to overeating, and gains back the weight she lost.

Injunctions and Attributions:
Don't say "no"
Don't get angry
Don't love yourself

Decision: At age fifteen she decides that she has definitely got a weight problem and that she doesn't have much self-control.

Mythical Heroine: She enjoys Rubens' paintings and follows the adventures of Elizabeth Taylor and *her* weight problems.

Somatic Component: Her fat is her body armor. She has trouble being physically active and tends to have minor accidents like twisting her ankle.

Games:
Food-aholic
Wooden Leg
Ain't It Awful

Therapist's Role in the Script: He tells her that she has to learn to adapt more, that is, cope with her "problem," and prescribes diet pills and painfully boring diets. He is physically repelled by her body, and subtly communicates this fact to her through his attitude.

Antithesis: The way out is for her to decide that her body is O.K. just the way it is and learn to love and take care of it (see "Fat Liberation" by Mayer Aldebaron[1]). She can be tuned in to and angry about the oppression that's foisted on fat people. In loving her body she can learn to tune in to it, listen to it and, therefore, stop abusing it. She can learn healthier eating habits and eat what tastes and feels good to her body.

She also must learn how to say "no" and to get angry at people who oppress her, especially about her weight, and not swallow everything that is pushed on her. She might never be thin in media terms, but she will probably lose some weight and feel good from the inside out, rather than constantly hungry and guilty.

---

[1] Aldebaron, Mayer. "Fat Liberation." *Issues in Radical Therapy* I,3 (1973): 3–6.

Centering work (Chapter 24) could be very good for her, to get her in touch with her body and its messages to her about what it needs and doesn't need for nourishment and what she wants and doesn't want from others.

It's crucial that she give up her self-hate and stop swallowing her anger. Also, she must be sure not to give more strokes than she gets, since getting into a stroke deficit is one of the reasons she turns to over-eating for comfort. She must also learn how to nurture herself and be able to relax without anesthetizing herself with food.

Teacher

Life Course: She decides to teach because it's the only way she sees available to her to use the knowledge she has learned in her "major" subject interest at college and for financial reasons, not because it's precisely what she wants to do in life. She then gets locked into keeping her job by the seductive security of tenure.

She carries out a two-fold function in society. She acts as a sophisticated baby-sitter for children. She also helps indoctrinate these children into society's value system in preparation for the time when they will become workers. She teaches them to compete, to line up, to take orders, and to adapt. She is forced to follow rules which she, for the most part, dislikes and has to force them upon the children.

Her main problem is that because she spends her working days with children, she has very little opportunity to make contacts with her peers. If she's married, she is isolated in a lonely monogamous relationship; if not, she has trouble meeting enough people to fulfill her needs. Child to Parent strokes from her students aren't enough. She tends to be giving out more love than she's getting back.

As she becomes resentful about not getting enough strokes, she may come to no longer enjoy teaching children, but rather grow to dislike them and assume the role of Persecutor (while favoring a select few "teacher's pets").

Counterscript: Things look good for her in this script in the fall of the year when school has just started and everybody is happy to see her, or in the spring when she is preparing to go to Europe and feeling optimistic about meeting some new people. But the reality of how she feels about her work is most apparent during the long, lonely winter when she often wishes she were free and when she makes herself feel badly by saying nasty things to herself ("Well, the old adage about those that can (men) do and those that can't (women) teach sure applies to me!").

Injunctions and Attributions:
Be independent
Don't be you ·
Follow the rules

Decisions: When she is a young girl in grammar school, she decides that the only way for her to do what she wants, i.e., have a career and be independent, is by taking on a "woman's job" like teaching.

Mythical Heroine: She adored Mrs. Chapman, her fourth-grade teacher, and her Aunt Ethel, whom she admired for her economic independence. She also loved reading about Plato and Socrates.

Somatic Component: She tends to get frequent headaches, experiences much eye strain, and because she feels bad at school, she often gets depressed around her menstrual period.

Games:
If It Weren't For You
Why Don't You—Yes, But
They'll Be Glad They Knew Me

Therapist's Role in the Script: He tells her she must learn to cope. When she becomes menopausally depressed because she isn't getting enough strokes, he tells her it's her problem, that she should have done things differently with men, that is, she should have adapted better. He tells her to put more of herself into her work and stop complaining and feeling sorry for herself; after all, she does have job security and can go away every summer.

Antithesis: The way to break out of this is for her to stop giving more than she's getting and to work toward a more equal and cooperative relationship with her students and fellow workers. She must decide to make her social life a high priority—just as important as economic security and/or material comfort. It may be best for her to regularly save up as much of her salary as she can and not to accept tenure nor teach for more than a couple of years in a row. It may be important for her to occasionally do some other kind of work that brings her into contact with adults.

She might use her creative power to organize an alternative anti-school for grownups as well as children based on principles of cooperation, learning subjects one wants to learn, teaching what one wants to teach, etc. Along with providing her with an opportunity to do meaningful work, it would additionally be an opportunity in which to work cooperatively with her peers.

Guerrilla Witch

Life Course: She is in touch with her power to affect people and uses it, but her power is mysterious and magical and slightly out of her control rather than rational and clear-sighted (structurally, it comes from her Little Professor and Child, with little awareness from her Adult). She fights back against men's Adults and Critical Parents with her witchy, intuitive, covert power, but without an Adult strategy. Although she likes being a woman, she tends to compete with other women and generally acts as an individual rather than cooperating with them. She sees herself as being different from others, as having "special powers." Ultimately, she fights from a one-down position and experiences herself as an underdog. She feels scared,

thinks paranoid thoughts about others, and is thought
by others to be high strung and "castrating." When
she's angry, she gets some satisfaction from hitting up
from below, especially at men, as hard as she can.
She is comfortable in the role of Persecutor and has
a lot of guts so she's always ready for a good fight.

She spends much of her time reading about magic,
mysticism, and astrology. When she doesn't get what
she wants from people she retaliates by giving them
"bad vibes," and by gossiping about them. When she's
angry, she creates problems between the person she's
angry at and others by giving them both subtle, gos-
sipy messages about each other (see Chapter 4,
Witchcraft), thus creating paranoia and stirring up
trouble.

She ends up feeling vengeful toward everyone
since she hasn't been able to get what she wants in
life. Her power has been strategically applied mostly
to causing trouble, instead of building her life the way
she wants it to be.

Counterscript: This script might give the appearance
of working well for her when she is a secretary working in an office and has been successful in putting a
spell (or so she thinks) on her boss whom she de-
spises. He ends up feeling very uptight and shaky
around her and eventually fires her because of all of
her efforts to undermine his confidence and power.
She comes to feel that her power is only destructive;
it doesn't really make things better for her or create a
work situation in which she is equal and powerful.

Injunctions and Attributions:
Don't trust
Don't be close
You are special (different)

Decision: When she is young, she decides that she
can't talk her mother and father into getting things
she wants. But she also learns that she can manipulate
and maneuver them in subtle ways to get her way,
and that the most effective maneuver is to get them
to engage in a fight over her.

Mythical Heroine: She loves to read about gypsies and fairies. Her favorite TV show is *Bewitched,* about Samantha, a housewife who's really a witch.

Somatic Component: Her body is thin and tense. She grows very long fingernails and tends to have trouble sleeping.

Games:
Let's You And Them fight
Now I've Got You—You SOB
Uproar

Therapist's Role in the Script: Because of her unorthodox behavior and ideas, he tells her that she is schizophrenic and prescribes thorazine. This makes her very angry, and he ends up refusing to work with her because he is afraid of her.

Antithesis: First it's necessary for her to decide to give up her special outside, one-up, "I'm O.K., you're not O.K." role and decide to be part of the human race. It's important for her to decide to cooperate with and appreciate other women as a means of gaining power. She can work with them on developing her Adult and being able to couple her intuitive and Child power with clear Adult strategies.

It is also crucial that she come to see that her needs and desires are similar to many other people's and that it's much more possible to get them fulfilled by working together with others in a trusting way. She also must deflate her paranoias about others by checking them out. Once she feels safe about other people, then she can work on being in touch with what she wants in a constructive way and asking for it.

Tough Lady

Life Course: She's taught by her parents to be a loner and not to trust or count on others, because they as a family unit are in a pitched battle for survival ("us against the world"). She is given a lot of male programming to compete and be successful.

She is concerned with her own survival so she takes care of herself on a subsistence level but ignores herself as far as frills and nurturing go. She takes care of business for herself in a "masculine," tough, feelingless manner.

She often likes competitive sports; she may even be a female "jock." She spends much time being angry at men who one-up her (they can always run faster and farther) and at other women who get privileges that she doesn't because they have "sold out" in sexist submission. Her friends, when she has them, tend to be men.

She fights back at people who put her down for her spunk and independence by Pigging them (saying they're not O.K.) and mocking them. She is most familiar with the role of Persecutor, since it provides her with a sense of power—particularly over people who are afraid of her toughness.

She keeps proving she can't trust people because they let her down one time after another; a situation she colludes with because she is not very clear about what she wants except in "taking care of business" in survival terms and because she continually sends out messages about not needing anybody.

Men see her as a "castrating bitch" and avoid her and women dislike her because she comes on one-up and condescending, so she ends up bitter and alone.

Counterscript: It appears that she has broken through the barrier against intimacy in her script when she falls in love with a man she admires. But as time goes by she comes to be unable to tolerate being dependent on him. She also decides it's too much trouble to keep asking him for things in their relationship.

Injunctions and Attributions:
Don't trust
Fight back
Take care of yourself first

Decision: Early in life she feels that it's better and safer not to need much from others, so she decides she can pretty much go it alone.

Mythical Heroine: She admires women like Bette Davis, Marlene Dietrich, Katharine Hepburn, and Amelia Earhart.

Somatic Component: She has a hard tough body, strongly armored, that cuts off her feelings. When she has trouble with her body, she tends to have G.I. problems (gastro-intestinal), like colitis.

Games:
Now I've Got You—You SOB
Uproar
Courtroom

Therapist's Role in the Script: He tries to push her into adapting to the standard sex role stereotype and she laughs at him and walks out.

Antithesis: A first step in getting out of this script is for her to decide that she wants to build intimate relationships with others even though it scares her, and to decide that other people are O.K. and trustworthy and it's O.K. to take chances with people.

She must also want to give up her one-up position and be an equal with people and learn to ask them for what she wants without feeling it puts her one-down. She can come to see what's in it for her to co-operate rather than compete, and to begin to nurture herself as warmly and richly as she can so that she feels safe enough to take risks with others.

Queen Bee

In an article called "The Queen Bee Syndrome," Staines et al.[1] define the Queen Bee as a successful

---

[1] Staines, Graham; Jayaratne, Toby Epstein; and Tavris, Carol. "The Queen Bee Syndrome." *Psychology Today* 7,8 (1974): 55–60.

woman, usually a lawyer, doctor, or business woman, who by working hard and being highly competitive has made it in the "man's world." She has had a tough time getting there on her own and thinks women's liberationists are lazy complainers. She is an underground anti-feminist, though she says she is a liberated woman in favor of women's liberation. Her personal success in the system makes her feel invested in maintaining her unique position and it is not in her interest for other women to "get off easy" by avoiding the tough time she had or, worse yet, for her to have to contend with other women coming in as competitors. As the authors of this article point out, she endorses the Horatio Alger philosophy of individual striving and cannot resonate to the collective social action trend in women's liberation. She believes that she has made it on her own sweat and if other women are willing to pay the price, they can make it, too.

She often receives much support from male chauvinist men who realize that she is instrumental in keeping other women in their place, in exchange for their support and admiration. In a *Psychology Today* questionnaire[1] they tended to agree with the statements "women have only themselves to blame for not doing better in life" and "women can best overcome discrimination by working individually to prove their abilities."

I want to express my appreciation to Carmen Kerr for bringing the Tough Lady script to my attention, to Ramona Barean for ideas concerning women's health, and to Joy Marcus for feedback and support.

[1]*Ibid.*, p. 195.

15

Banal Scripts of Men

Men, just like women, have certain stereotyped scripts which they choose to live by.

These narrow life styles are often matched to a corresponding life style in a woman. "Big Daddy" and "Poor Little Me" meet at a party and may "fall in love" at first sight because so much of their scripting is complimentary and fits together. Indeed, "they were made for each other" in that factory of banal life styles, the nuclear family. "Creeping Beauty's" parents, the Smiths, knew just what she should be like so she would fit right in with the Jones's "Playboy." When they meet and fall in love they don't really know each other, they are simply very well matched; designed, as it were, on the basis of national standards for men and women which causes an instant interchangeable fit. Having been thus patterned after other people's plans, autonomy is lost and intimacy, awareness, and spontaneity are grossly interfered with.

Brian Allen[1] describes some of the basic injunctions and attributions of men. Generally, men are told "Don't lose control," "Never be satisfied," "Don't ask for help," "Dominate women." Some of the scripts described below were first suggested by Allen early in the investigaiton of banal scripts ("Big Daddy" and "Jock").[2]

---

[1] Allen, Brian. "Liberating the Manchild." *Transactional Analysis Journal* II, 2 (1972): 68–71.

[2] All of the work on banal sex role scripting was launched in 1971 by Hogie Wyckoff with her article "The Stroke Economy in Women's Scripts" (*Transactional Analysis Journal* I,3 (1971): 16–20).

Big Daddy

Life Course: Big Daddy is the exaggerated version of the responsible father and husband. He may be married to Mother Hubbard or to Poor Little Me. In any case, his life is immersed in responsibilities. Not only does he have to bring in a large amount of money to support all of the members of his household, but he also has to worry about their well-being, make plans for their future, prevent them from getting into trouble, and so on. Because he has so much responsibility in the household, he is also its absolute ruler. He knows everything best and admits of no arguments on that score. If he allows them to use their own judgment it is only because he is giving them an opportunity to learn by their own mistakes rather than because he feels that they can in fact do things well without his help. Because he is so burdened with responsibility he loses his ability to enjoy himself and his only remaining pleasure is the deference given him by the one-down members of his family. He works hard, competes hard, and has some limited success in his business or professional career. If he has any thought of not taking care of others, severe guilt immediately prevents him from acting on the thought. In most cases, as he approaches retirement, he becomes more rather than less of a tyrant, demanding more deference and one-down strokes from people because of his growing sense that his life is going to waste. He endures, hangs on, sticks to, and perpetuates the Rescue triangle as long as people will play. His dying day is usually soon after retirement when all of his work power is taken away from him, his children have left him and turned against him, while his wife, who is not racked and broken by responsibility, begins to gain power, persecutes him for Rescuing her, and eventually survives him to enjoy the fruits of their labor. A special case of Big Daddy is Dr. Rescue, a professional healer who is overburdened with patients in addition to his home responsibilities.

Counterscript: He decides to "take it easy," go on vacation, hire a secretary, get rid of a portion of his work with the purpose of equalizing responsibilities in his life. He may even get a divorce and try to start a new family or become a bachelor to avoid responsibilities. But he is a Rescuer at heart and eventually is swamped anew.

Injunctions and Attributions:
You're always right
Take care of everyone
Don't admit weakness

Mythical Hero: Daddy Warbucks, "Life with Father," Dr. Marcus Welby.

Somatic Component: He is energetic, his shoulders are hunched, and his chest inflated. He is generally uptight and stiff.

Games:
Rescue
Courtroom
If It Weren't For You (Them)

Therapist's Role in the Script: The therapist commiserates with him, gives him tranquilizers so he'll relax, and pills so he'll sleep. He is sympathetic to his situation, which is the therapist's own, and encourages him to "keep trying."

Antithesis: He realizes that he is Rescuing everybody and that his rewards for this are Persecution. He decides guilt is a racket and begins to demand equal responsibility in every situation in which he relates to people. He disconnects himself from every Rescue and puts his life ahead of others'. He decides that it is O.K. to be wrong sometimes, since he is not responsible for every aspect of every decision.

Man in Front of the Woman

Life Course: The Man in Front of the Woman is, as Wyckoff (Chapter 14) points out, actually less competent than the Woman Behind the Man. He knows that his success would not be possible without his wife's, or some other woman's, hard work. However, he needs to pretend that he is, in fact, the commanding genius of the partnership. Even though he knows that in many respects she is more competent, well-organized, and even perhaps more intelligent, he promotes the sham of her secondary nature. He gives lip service to her competence but always makes clear that he is in command. On stationery they may list both their names separately, but his name comes first. If they publish a book together she may actually be included in the credits on the cover, but his credits will come first. Somehow, in a mysterious way, it is assumed that he provides the *élan*, the spirit, the driving force for their success, while she provides merely the hard work which is of secondary importance since *any* intelligent woman could replace her. He feels considerable guilt about his usurpation of his wife's power and is not really able to enjoy his success because he always knows that it isn't his as he pretends. Nevertheless, he is required by the sexist standards of society to continue the sham even though he himself might much prefer to abandon it and become an equal partner with his wife.

Antithesis: He realizes that his partner's power would be much better expressed to both their advantages if she were allowed to be an equal. He could then relax and stop feeling guilty about the unfairness of the situation. He can be himself instead of the "The King Has No Clothes."

Playboy

Life Course: He spends his life chasing after the "perfect" woman who doesn't exist. A Playboy is a man who has become the Victim of the media's portrayal of the ideal woman. Advertising media use the female body to sell consumer items, and he buys it. He comes to believe in the reality of women he sees in maga-

zines and he values them over and above the women
he meets in his everyday life. His perception of people becomes as two-dimensional as the printed sheet
or the silver screen, and as a consequence his response
to women is totally superficial, based only on their
surface appearance. He is never satisfied with his mate
because he plays "Blemish." She does not represent
the media image and therefore he goes from one woman to another, never finding what he's looking for and
never seeing what the women that he meets have to
offer, because it does not appear in the copy of advertising ads. When he connects with a woman who
fits his fantasy ideal, he puts her next to him in his
Cadillac or Corvette and shows her off to his Playboy
and Playgirl friends. He is ashamed of being seen
with "ugly" women and will never go out in public
with them, though he may like them and spend time
with them on the sly.

His partners are either Plastic Women, or Creeping
Beauties. With Plastic Women he has brief affairs
which end with him leaving them when he finds that
they are "phony." With Creeping Beauties he has
abortive relationships which end with him being rebuffed. Occasionally he meets a Guerrilla Witch who
does him a great deal of damage (perhaps she puts
a curse on him, rendering him "impotent"). Because
the advertising media carefully avoid portraying angry, demanding women, he is puzzled and hurt by her
anger and attacks. He spends a tremendous amount
of his energy in the procurement of strokes from the
women he is attracted to. He works strictly for the
purpose of making enough money to be able to afford
the Plastic Women and Creeping Beauties with whom
he spends the rest of his waking hours. In the end
he gets nothing for his labors except a great deal of
second-hand merchandise and a large number of
guilt feelings, plus a list (long or short) of women
with whom he has had relationships.

Counterscript: Occasionally he finds a woman who is
"perfect" for him. Unfortunately the relationship does
not last, usually because his understanding of love and

relationships is the shallow media-promoted boy-meets-girl script which never ends as it is supposed to—living happily ever after.

Injunctions and Attributions:
Don't settle for second best
Don't give yourself away

Mythical Hero: Hugh Hefner, Joe Namath, Porfirio Rubirosa, Don Juan.

Games:
Rapo
Blemish
Why Don't You—Yes, But

Therapist's Role in the Script: The therapist gets vicarious enjoyment from his sexual exploits and envies him his "success" with women. He agrees that women are difficult to understand and winks at his failures with them.

Antithesis: He realizes that he is chasing an impossible dream. At first he has much trouble seeing beauty in the women he meets, but he stops playing "Blemish" and begins to appreciate their real qualities. In time he becomes aware of a large gamut of human attributes and he realizes that most of the women he knows are beautiful. He enters into a long-range committed relationship with a woman who appreciates his sexy fun-loving Child and lets him be friendly and loving with others.

Jock

Life Course: This man decides in his adolescence (with the help of Charles Atlas) that the highest achievement of manhood is to be found in the sports world. He pursues a sport and usually becomes fairly adept in it. His body becomes all muscle. He is detached from his feelings, and ironically, even though he is a body worshipper, he is cut off from the majority of it. His sexual energy is completely transformed into physical activity. He finds, after he enters young adulthood, that he has been sold a bill of goods, that his athletic physique is actually not attractive to women, and that it stands in the way of his enjoyment of sex and of the kinds of things that women really appreciate in men. He lets go of his physical pursuits and goes from being muscle-bound to being overweight. Because of the tremendous emphasis he has put on the development of his body, he is underdeveloped in his rational, intuitive, and spontaneous faculties. He is generally considered a dummy by his competitive fellow men and by the women he meets. He is good-natured and naive and always surprised when he finds, repeatedly, that good guys finish last. He spends a lot of time at spectator sports events and thinking back about the "good old days" when he had a strong and athletic body.

Injunctions and Attributions:
Don't think
Be competitive

Somatic Component: He is muscle-bound and his body is unevenly developed, depending on the sport he chooses. Late in life he becomes overweight.

Games:
Stupid
Busman's Holiday
Let's Pull a Fast One on Joey (in the Victim role)

Therapist's Role in the Script: The therapist believes that he is actually stupid and discounts him. He ignores him and condescends to him in group and is relieved when he quits therapy. Secretly he feels one-up to him and doesn't think he can be helped.

Antithesis: He realizes that he is expected not to be smart and that he colludes with this expectation. He decides to use his Adult and stop playing "Stupid." He realizes that competitive sports are unhealthy for him and reacquaints himself with his body in a whole new way. His good nature and belief in fair play serve him well when he moderates them with a reasonable amount of intuition and rationality.

Intellectual

Life Course: This man decides in adolescence that the highest achievement accomplishable is the development of the intellect. He rejects all physical pursuits in favor of "learning." He reads, studies, talks, and head-trips around the clock and begins to feel that his body and his emotions are encumbrances in these intellectual pursuits. He becomes a fixated Adult with an irresistible tendency to want to convert every activity into some form of "rationality." Because rationality is highly prized in this society, his script pays off in terms of "success" and he becomes convinced of the validity of his life style. Unfortunately, he is unable to experience emotions, especially love, and he feels empty. His life feels stale, incomplete.

His relationships are planned and regulated with his Adult but don't seem to work out. The women he relates to complain that he does not love them (though he believes he does) and that he discounts them (which he can't understand).

Counterscript: He falls in love, experiences a gamut of emotions, lets out his Child and Parent. Or he goes on a vacation and lets go. But the Adult doesn't stay on the back burner for long; in time, "reason prevails" and he falls back into his rational rut and everything becomes, once again, black and white, straight-lined, and boring.

Injunctions and Attributions:
Don't feel
You are smart
Use your head

Mythical Hero: Albert Einstein, Bertrand Russell, Ludwig Wittgenstein.

Somatic Component: His head is prominent in his body. It is so heavy that his shoulders are round with its weight. His chest is caved in and he breathes shallowly to avoid arousing any emotions in his gut. He thinks of his body as an instrument of his mind which is the Center of his being.

Games:
Courtroom
Why Don't You—Yes, But
Do Me Something

Therapist's Role in the Script: The therapist endlessly analyzes the person's psyche. Psychoanalytic technique is the perfect instrument to promote this man's script. Everything is "understood" and nothing changes. He lies on the couch, his head buzzing, his body limp, and free associates managing only to further alienate himself from his body.

Antithesis: He realizes with his Adult that he is on the wrong path and that his life is stale and going to waste. He decides to subject himself to an experiential form of therapy, such as an encounter group, Gestalt therapy, or bioenergetics. If his therapist prevents him from head-tripping he gets in touch with and follows up his emotions. He gradually recognizes the fallacy of rationality, begins to use his intuition, his Nurturing Parent, and his Natural Child. He overcomes his fears of *acting* (rather than thinking and talking) and changes his behavior and modes of relating.

Woman Hater

Life Course: This man learns early in life, from observing his mother and from statements by his father, that women are not O.K. He probably is a bachelor, probably in the military or some other all-male activity. He takes out his energy in pursuits (hunting, sports) in which women have no place and are definitely inferiors. He thinks of women as being the weaker sex, incompetent, and is proud of the fact that he has no need for them. For sexual release he occasionally visits a prostitute or picks somebody up at a bar, but he has no respect for women and has no expectations for any permanent or long-lasting relationships with them. Because men who are not married do not get very far in this society, he is usually bitter and unhappy about his circumstances, lives in a shabby apartment with a sink full of dirty dishes, cigarette butts all over the floor, an unmade bed, and the shades drawn. He smokes and drinks hard, may become an alcoholic, but in any case his bitterness against women eventually spreads out to include children and all other joyful, creative, spontaneous creatures and activities in the world.

Counterscript: He meets a woman he likes. He may even marry, become "domesticated," and enjoy a brief period of feelings of love, nurturing, and warmth. But the injunctions against intimacy and spontaneity are so strong that he can't reciprocate the feelings she gives him, and after a period of being in his Free Child he shuts down again and the relationship sours.

Injunctions and Attributions:
Don't be close
Don't trust
Don't let go

Mythical Hero: General Patton, Herbert Hoover, Dick Tracy, Lone Ranger.

Games:

Now I've Got You, You SOB (NIGYSOB)
Blemish
If It Weren't For Them (Women)

Therapist's Role in the Script: This man is unlikely to go to a therapist and would never go to a female for help. If he shows up at a therapist's office, it probably is under orders from a judge, boss, or officer. The therapist is likely to ignore his dislike for the whole process and fail to get a valid contract. In time, he would leave therapy, having accomplished nothing, and thinking of his therapist as effeminate or an egg-head.

Antithesis: An antithesis is difficult for this man. He may meet a woman who likes him and makes the right demands at the right time so that he opens up and starts enjoying life. Or he may find a loving relationship with another man. But he is hardened and set in his ways and will have trouble changing.

16

Relationships in Scripts

Transactional Analysis is the study of relationships.
A transaction-by-transaction analysis reveals rituals, games, and pastimes played. But relationships are more than a succession of transactions and pastimes. If we step back and look at the relationship as a whole we can see other aspects of it. We see, for instance, that some relationships are short-lived and some last long; that some are cooperative and some are loving; and that others are competitive and others hateful. We see that the people in the relationship are equals with equal rights and power or that they are unequal, some one-up and some one-down. We see that some profit all the persons involved; some profit some of the persons involved; and some profit none of the persons involved.

In *Transactional Analysis in Psychotherapy,* Berne discusses the analysis of relationships which he used "principally in the study of marital relationships and impending liaisons of various kinds." "In these situations," Berne says, relationship analysis "may yield some useful and convincing predictions and postdictions." Later, in *Sex and Human Loving,* he introduced an intricate classificatory scheme for relationships.

Relationship analysis is an extremely fruitful and helpful discovery, one which is intimately connected with the analysis of banal and tragic scripts.

Tragic and Banal Relationships

Tragic relationships, like tragic scripts, are the exception rather than the rule. Between man and woman, Romeo and Juliet is probably the most common of the tragic relationship scripts. Here two people in love are prevented by their families from being with each other for reasons of race, religion, or politics. Another tragic relationship script is Othello, who believes the lies of Iago about his beloved wife Desdemona and eventually kills her. Here a man violently rejects a woman he loves to appease others who hate her.

Ulysses and Penelope is really a non-relationship script on the part of Ulysses unless one assumes that he really would rather have been home than busy in his travels. But for Penelope, waiting for her husband was probably a devastating experience. The relationships between traveling salesmen, professional soldiers, politicians, doctors, and their wives often have a similar course.

The man who cheats and exploits a woman who continues to love him regardless or vice versa is again a one-sided tragedy, but not an uncommon one. In his book *Sex in Human Loving* Berne[1] classifies marriages into A H I O S V X and Y types. All eight of these seem to me banal-relationship scripts:

An A marriage starts off as a shotgun or makeshift one. The couple are far apart, but soon they find a single common bond, perhaps the new baby. This is represented by the crossbar of the A. As time goes on, they get closer and closer until they finally come together, and then they have a going concern. This is represented by the apex of the A.

An H marriage starts off the same way, but the couple never gets any closer, and the marriage is

[1]From *Sex in Human Loving,* by Eric Berne. Copyright © 1970 by City National Bank of Beverly Hills, California. Reprinted by permission of Simon and Schuster.

held together by a single bond. Otherwise they each go where they were originally headed.

An I marriage starts off and ends with the couple forged into a single unit.

An O marriage goes round and round in a circle, never getting anywhere, and repeating the same patterns until it is terminated by death or separation.

An S marriage wanders around seeking happiness, and eventually ends up slightly above and to the right of where it started, but it never gets any farther than that, leaving both parties disappointed and bewildered, and good candidates for psychotherapy, since there is enough there so that they don't want a divorce.

A V marriage starts off with a close couple, but they immediately begin to diverge, perhaps after the honeymoon is over or even after the first night.

An X marriage starts off like an A. At one point there is a single period of bliss. They wait for it to happen again, but it never does, and soon they drift apart again, never to reunite.

A Y marriage starts off well, but difficulties multiply and eventually each one finds his own separate interests and goes his own way.

Between man and man the relationship of two brothers who first love and eventually kill each other is a familiar one. This relationship can include a third person who is the reason for the tragic outcome. Similarly, two women can have a similar relationship involving a man as a third person. But far more common are the everyday failures in the relationships between parents and their children, men and women, women and women, men and men. I am best acquainted with the relationships between women and men and will speak mostly of them, though the others are all worthy of study and remain to be investigated.

The Three Enemies of Love

In my opinion, the three most destructive forces militating against the achievement of satisfactory loving relationships between men and women are Sexism, the Rescue Game, and Power Plays.

SEXISM

Sexism is prejudice based on gender which often (though not always) includes an assumption of male supremacy. Even when prejudices about the sexes don't give the man more power or privilege, they are harmful, as has been illustrated by Hogie Wyckoff in Chapter 13.

In any case, I wish to restate clearly what has been said earlier in this book. Men and women are given attributions and injunctions which force them into sex roles which are harmful and oppressive to both sexes though they are more oppressive to women than to men. The scripts that are generated by these sex roles prevent men and women from achieving their full potential and from being able to attain intimacy or to work with each other.

The myth of the differences between women and men finds a grain of justification in some of the actual differences between them such as their genitals, brute strength, body size, and possibly emotional make-up due to differing biochemical (hormonal) make-up. But these differences are in no way justification for the damaging expectations placed on males and females by our sexist society.

THE RESCUE GAME IN RELATIONSHIPS

As we begin to form relationships with other people, separate from our parents' arrangements, we find that we are almost irresistibly driven to assuming either a one-up or a one-down position. Every relationship seems destined to involve us either as one-down, more involved, more in need, more in love, insecure, and feeling generally needy, or else as one-up, less involved, less in need, less in love, secure, and not needy. Often people's lives consist of an endless chain of such relationships. Some people have the experience of being usually one-up and others have the experience of being usually one-down.

Being one-down in a relationship is often familiar to women, and being one-up is a more familiar experience for men. This is the result of the fact that most men are trained more thoroughly in the uses and abuses of power and are less likely to give themselves away to another person, whereas most women are trained to give of themselves and make themselves available, so that between a man and a woman there is usually a very unequal contest which too often ends with the woman in a one-down position. However, the tendency for one-up and one-down relationships operates between men and men and women and women, and the experience of equality between people is very seldom achieved and often not even sought.

In the relationships between grownup individuals, the roles of Rescuer, Persecutor, and Victim are commonplace. These roles manifest themselves not only in crude ways, in which one person is clearly acting powerless and helpless while another undertakes to take care of him or to persecute him, but in much more subtle ways as follows:

Any situation in which one person does something that she doesn't want to do in relation to another constitutes a Rescue. Often the Victims don't even know that they are being Rescued. For instance, it is a common occurrence between husband and wife that the wife, say, accompanies the husband to a football game or on a fishing trip which she doesn't have any interest in. She may do this because he has asked her, and would be hurt and perhaps even sulk if she didn't come along; but she may also be coming along even if he has not asked her to do so and when, it may turn out, he would prefer to go alone or with someone else. She may be afraid of being alone and prefers to Rescue than to be a Victim. In any case she

is Rescuing him since she is doing something she does
not want to do, and because she assumes he needs
her and is unable to be satisfied by and for himself.
People are constantly going places, doing things, participating in activities as Rescuers because they fear
that the people whom they would have to "reject"
would be hurt, upset, or in some way be unable to
take care of themselves.

Another way in which Rescues happen is when in
any joint activity one person puts in more effort or
more interest than the other. This is especially the
case when a person who presents himself as needy or
powerless (the Victim) ceases to put any effort into
his situation as soon as another person who is the
Rescuer begins to help. For instance, a woman may
be having a great deal of difficulty on some particular
afternoon taking care of her children, cooking dinner,
and doing different household chores. Another woman,
a neighbor, may come to the Rescue and as soon as she
does, the Victim, instead of pitching in and providing
at least one-half of the energy in the situation, falls
back and allows the Rescuer to take over. Or, in another situation, where a man and a woman are on a
camping vacation, the man, in the process of preparing
a meal, may run into some difficulty and ask for help.
As soon as his wife assumes the familiar role of the
cook (Rescuer) he falls back and ceases to put any
effort into the situation. Thus, any situation in which
one person asks another for help and then proceeds to
do less than 50% of the work constitutes a Rescue.

Another way in which people Rescue each other is
by not asking for what they want for themselves,
again because they're afraid of the other person's reaction. Husbands and wives are often locked into mutual
Rescues in which neither of them dares say what he
really wants for fear of the other's reaction. When
these Rescues are explored and people are encouraged
to talk straight and ask for everything they want 100%
of the time,[1] it is often found that large dissatisfactions

---

[1]Wyckoff, Hogie. "Between Women and Men." *Issues in Radical
Therapy* I, 2 (1973): 11:–15.

are present in both of the persons which are not expressed and often not known by the other person. In my work with couples in relationships I have found that when these mutual Rescues are made clear, it is often possible for cooperative agreements to be made in which both of the partners can ask for what they want and get it, therefore eliminating all Rescues in the relationships.

The main problem in achieving a No Rescue relationship is that people are so accustomed to compromising their own needs on behalf of others that they often need to relearn to recognize and express their real desires. In addition, asking for what one wants, even when one *knows* what one wants, is difficult too, and needs to be learned as well.

Power Plays will be explored in the next chapter.

17

Power Plays

Power

To date, the power aspects of relationships have been ignored in transactional analysis as being of insufficient importance to be systematically mentioned. As a consequence, in a routine transactional analysis of a relationship, the relative power of the individuals involved is not considered a relevant factor.

I should explain here what I mean by power. Power in physical terms means ability to exert force over a period of time. If I can drag you across the floor against your will, I have more physical power than you. This form of crude personal power, however, is not the only power to consider. I may be able to drag you physically across the floor, but you may have in your hire a bodyguard who will wipe me out if I as much as touch you. So you can intimidate me across the floor without even laying a hand on me. Or you may convince me to willingly walk across the floor, without any threat, based only on your attractiveness, personal magnetism, or convincing arguments, while I could not do the same to you.

Thus, power is the capacity to cause people to do things, and it is unevenly distributed among people so that some have more and others have less.

In drawing the script matrix, in which two parents and an offspring are portrayed, I unwittingly introduced the power factor into transactional analysis. Not only does the script matrix visually portray two

people who are higher, that is, one-up to the offspring, but there are also built into the assumptions of
the script matrix the assumption that parents are in a
position of being able to force the offspring into doing
things she or he would not otherwise do. With the
script matrix, power considerations were first introduced into the analysis of transactions.

The study of scripts extended into the study of
banal scripts that affect men and women, and the
understanding grew very quickly that men and wom-
en are scripted to perform along certain fixed role expectations, and that the role expectations include a
definite power relationship between them, namely,
with the man one-up to the woman.

The analysis of relationships between men and
women led to the conclusion that power arrangements
in relationships are crucial aspects of them, and that
a therapist who is unaware of them or does not relate
to them is simply not in touch with a most important
factor.

Psychotherapists are trained to ignore the relative
power of the persons that they work for. Generally
speaking, power or other political considerations are
considered to be irrelevant to the practice of psychiatry. This unawareness of power in psychotherapists
prevents them from becoming aware of the abuses of
power that occur between human beings and of the
unhappiness these abuses cause. Acknowledging
abuses of power would quickly lead most therapists
to the conclusion that as soul healers they must become advocates of those that are being oppressed
rather than neutral observers who take no sides. As a
consequence, because they would have to take sides
with the powerless against the powerful, therapists
are not too eager to become aware of such power
factors.

The understanding of power plays and the distribution of power has come to me through the study of the
relationships between men and women. This is the
case simply because as a therapist I do most of my
work with people who are in one way or another dissatisfied with their heterosexual relationships. It is be-

cause of this that the ensuing statements are focused primarily on the power plays between men and women. This is not to imply that power plays do not exist in other situations, or that they are in some way of a different caliber or nature; it is just that at this particular time I understand the power plays between men and women best.

As explained before, most human beings are scripted to be comfortable in relationships where they are either one-up or one-down to another human being. They are taught from birth that it is expected and appropriate to be one-up to certain people and to be one-down to others. All children are taught that one must obey certain persons of authority and relate to them from a one-down position. Children are also taught that human beings of the female sex are appropriately, naturally one-down to human beings of the male sex, that workers are one-down to bosses, blacks are one-down to whites, and so on. The effect of such intense scripting into acceptance of unequal distribution of power between human beings is that people continue to seek and expect inequality in their relationships. When relationships are such that a man and a woman are equal in power, it is unlikely that equality will remain, for that state of affairs is an unstable equilibrium which tends to be easily disrupted into the more stable equilibrium of a one-up/one-down situation.

Just as in other scripted situations, human beings tend to be comfortable when they are following the dictates of the script. By the same token, human beings have the tendency to feel good in situations in which they are either one-up or one-down to others, and not only to enjoy them but to seek them, as well as rejecting those in which power is equal.

It is easy to understand why people who are in a one-up position of power feel comfortable in it; the advantages of privilege are many. But why do people who are clearly one-down feel comfortable in their situation? When asked if they would trade places with their rich bosses, struggling workers often say that they would prefer not to: "They don't know how to live"; "They have too many headaches being in charge"; "They are half dead." People who are one-down and powerless often tend to see themselves as being better off than those who have more power than they. This tendency to disregard the inequalities in power between people and therefore not to seek equality is part of the banal scripting for Powerlessness which keeps one-down people one-down.

Only after a person has been one-down to another for a relatively extended time does the original gut enjoyment of the scripted one-down relationship give way to discontent and anger. At this point the person who is one-down will ordinarily begin to engage in guerrilla tactics designed to undermine the power of the person who is one-up. In the example given by Hogie Wyckoff (see Chapter 14), "Plastic Woman," after being one-down to her husband for many years, begins to undermine his power by attacking him where it counts most, in his pocketbook and in his genitals, by "beating him to death with a credit card" and refusing to enjoy sex. Both of these techniques are power plays from the one-down position designed to undermine and take away the power of the person who is one-up.

Marriages very often follow a typical sequence in which for the first seven years the man oppresses the woman, with her as a willing participant. After seven years she becomes rebellious and he may retaliate by terminating the marriage, or the marriage will go on for another seven years with her engaged in active guerrilla warfare to undermine his power. If the marriage lasts another seven years, it may arrive at an uneasy truce where both of the people live a separate and uncommunicative life in which they maintain their power separately and without interaction.

Power Plays

Power plays are techniques used to get people to do something they don't want to do.

When power playing, a person assumes that he can't

get what he wants by simply asking. Thus power playing assumes scarcity whether it exists or not. A good
relationship is based on the assumption that both of
the people in it are interested in doing things for each
other. When that is the case it would appear that one
person need simply ask for what she wants and it
would follow that the other person would do everything within his power to make it happen. This is the
case when the relationships operate smoothly and both
partners are getting what they want. However, when
this smooth cooperative process breaks down and scarcity sets in, it is likely that people will begin to use
power plays to satisfy themselves.

Typical relationships very often begin as a "turn on"
between the Childs of the two people involved. This
relationship, Child to Child, is often one which involves an awareness of the other's wishes and needs
and a strong wish to satisfy them. As long as the relationship maintains that Child to Child quality in which
feelings are openly expressed and responded to, it is
likely the people will get what they want from each
other. In time, however, the other vectors of the relationship are likely to emerge, and as these vectors
develop (i.e., the Adult to Adult vector, the Parent to
Child vector, and the Parent to Parent vector) difficulties may begin. Men and women are scripted so as
to have great difficulty in giving each other the two
things that they want most: strokes from a good mutual working situation, and strokes from intimacy.
Strokes from a working situation are scripted out of
relationships because women tend to be enjoined
against using their Adults. As a consequence, men and
women find it very difficult to work together. On the
other hand, intimacy, which is heavily based on the
capacity to be intuitive and nurturing simultaneously,
is strongly scripted out of men. This scripted, mutual
impossibility for achieving the two most rewarding
forms of strokes, work and intimacy, causes people to
start using power plays to get the strokes they want
from each other. Bernian games are power plays to
obtain strokes. Because strokes are in short supply and
much in demand, people play many games. But there

are other items for which people power play each
other (money, privileges, getting what they want how
they want it when they want it).

There are two major kinds of power play situations:
between unequals and between equals. In the first
kind, two people agree that they are unequal. This
situation can be called a master–slave relationship.
The acceptance of inequality can be total or less than
total. When people accept their inequality they may
cooperate and not power play each other. Examples
of total acceptance are rare; except in the most to-
talitarian situations (perhaps best exemplified by a
concentration camp or an insane asylum) power
struggles occur. In such situations, the master simply
expresses what he wants and the slave goes along with
it. However, most one-up/one-down relationships are
less than perfect and involve power plays to a greater
or lesser degree.

Both parties, the master and the slave, have to use
power plays to get what they want, and they are
different. Let us call them: *one-up power plays* (the
master's) such as "Hold the Line" or "Wipe Them
Out"; and *one-down power plays* (the slave's) such
as "Guerrilla Warfare."

Power plays between equals are a third kind and
they can be called "Pitched Battles."

ONE-UP POWER PLAYS

One-up power plays are used in successions of increasing power; they cascade. They start at a low intensity and if not successful they are followed up with
another power play of higher intensity; that is to say,
power plays are played in succession with the aim of
winning.

Let us briefly examine a situation in which Mr. and
Ms. White are deciding where to take their annual
two-week vacation. Mr. White would like to go to the
lake and Ms. White would like to go to the mountains.
The issue is met when, coming back from work, Mr.
White, knowing that Ms. White would probably prefer to go to the mountains, declares that he has ar-

ranged for his vacation time with his boss and that he has made reservations at the Lake Inn. This is the first one-up power play in a long series which, as described in this example, will get Mr. White what he wants.

Ms. White may give in on the first round. Making the decision without consulting her may be a sufficient display of power to cause her to abdicate. Let us, however, assume that Ms. White does not give up easily. Instead, she says: "But I want to go to the mountains."

In this example I will portray Ms. White as a "cool head" who does not get hooked into any power plays of her own. I do this to simplify the account which could become dizzying were I to portray a series of one-down power plays of her own simultaneous with his. Instead, Ms. White will be shown to simply ask for what she wants in a powerful, convincing way (power maneuver).

Mr. White will now try "If You Can't Prove It You Can't Do It." This power play is a demand for a logical reason justifying her choice. "Why do you want to go to the mountains rather than the lake?"

If Ms. White is hooked into this power play she will attempt to justify herself. She may say something like "Because the air is cleaner," or, "Because it will cost less money," or less rationally, "Because the kids might drown," or, "Because I'll be nicer."

At this point Mr. White will use his very strongly developed Adult reasoning capacities to his best advantage. He will logically defeat every one of the arguments, whether logical or illogical. For instance, he may argue as follows: "Who needs clean air? Clean air isn't that important; after all, we both smoke, anyway." Or he may say: "Yes, going to the mountains is cheaper, but look at all the money we save by not having to drive so far," or, "Don't be ridiculous, the children are excellent swimmers."

This power play may succeed; but if it doesn't and Ms. White still insists that she does not have to logically explain why she wants to go to the mountains, she just wants to go, Mr. White may attempt round three of the power play. This one is called "Man of the House," which is a revision of "It Says in the Bible."

"I'm the worker in this family, and it is me who needs a vacation. You are going to ruin my vacation by insisting that we go to the mountains. I wear the pants here and we are going to the lake."

Again, Ms. White may abdicate or she may go on and insist that she wants to go to the mountains. The fourth power play may be a heavy round of "Sulk (for Now)." Mr. White now says, "O.K., we'll go to the mountains." For the next month, whenever he comes home, he sinks into his chair, opens up a beer, sighs, and watches television a lot. He may get drunk too. He will make occasional comments about how his heart is in bad shape. He may point to a Sunday supplement article about how thin air is bad for a heart condition. He isn't really planning to go to the mountains, just biding his time until later, and seeing if he can change her mind meanwhile through guilt. While nothing is being said about it, it will be clear to Ms. White that Mr. White is very upset about not going to the lake, and she may be hooked into abdicating her position in the service of taking care of him. It is likely that in a series of power plays Mr. White will win over Ms. White since she has any number of tendencies which work against her, such as not having a strong Adult, and having a tendency to Rescue and Nurture him.

Let us suppose, however, that Ms. White continues to assume that they are going to go to the mountains. On the night before they leave Mr. White reopens the conversation. He may say, "Well, I have thought it over, and as far as I am concerned we are going to go to the lake and not to the mountains. There's no two ways about it. If you don't want to go to the lake with me I am not going on a vacation." This is a power play called "Ain't Budging."

It will be observed that as Mr. White does not get his way in this finely graded series of power plays, the power plays will become more and more crude, that is, more and more approaching the seizure of power through brute force. He is not at the point yet where he is using force offensively, but he is using it passively. At this point he is saying that he will not move physically until there is a change of plans. Again, Ms. White may give in. If she doesn't, Mr. White may begin to use physical power offensively, to make menacing, clenching gestures with his jaw and fist; and if Ms. White does not give in at this point he may actually settle the argument by hitting her or even giving her a beating. Situations that go to the point of the man beating the woman almost always result in the man getting his way. This last power play is called "Knock Some Sense into 'Em," a form of "Wipe 'Em Out."

ONE-DOWN POWER PLAYS

Unlike one-up power plays, one-down power plays do not tend to be played in sequence of increasing intensity. One-up power plays are played from an "I'm O.K., you're not O.K." position which includes an expectation of being right and winning in the end. One-down power plays are played from the one-down position of "I'm not O.K." and they are basically defensive. They are still trying to accomplish something that the other player doesn't want, but all they accomplish for the one-down player is to interfere with the one-up person's privileges. It is because of this that they are called Guerrilla Warfare power plays. Just as in guerrilla warfare, one-down power plays are engaged in by the weaker, oppressed of the two warring parties which has on its side the element of surprise and knowledge of the territory. The one-down power player will use his power selectively where it is most useful and then withdraw, succeeding only in interfering with the one-up person's drive for power, and without any immediate expectation of turning the tide or winning. Thus, one-down power plays do not cascade and do not necessarily follow each other in a graded series of increasing crude power.

As an example let us take again Mr. and Ms. White. This time Mr. White comes home and informs Ms.

White that he has set the vacation time with his boss and has purchased tickets for the Lake Inn. Instead of protesting, Ms. White goes along because she is accustomed to being one-down to Mr. White who usually makes all the decisions.

However, Ms. White is not necessarily happy and, while she has overtly gone along with the decision, she covertly intends to interfere with Mr. White's purpose. Periodically she will power play him from a one-down position, in order to diminish his control and well being.

One-down power plays come in three categories:

1. *Techniques to arouse guilt,* which is always present in the one-up person whose Little Professor knows the situation is unfair, and whose Pig usually tells her that she is selfish and mean. Crying, sulking, feigning illnesses such as headaches, insomnia, backaches, are this kind of power play.

Mr. White hears the muffled sobs of Ms. White beyond the locked bedroom door. He asks to be let in and when she finally does finds she has been looking at picture postcards of the Western Sierras. He asks (knowing full well what the answer is), "What *is* wrong?"; she answers, "Nothing." He is furious but can't do anything about the situation except feel guilty or become even more callous in his dominance. He exits, slamming the door; she smiles to herself.

2. *Techniques which are designed to hurt in retaliation.* These are most like Guerrilla Warfare.

Mr. and Ms. White are making love. He is very sexually aroused, she is angry. Because she is unresponsive he comes soon after they start intercourse. She turns her back to him and says, "I didn't come, you know!" He is deeply hurt and she is glad.

Or Ms. White notices that Mr. White has left his keys behind. When she goes out she makes sure that all the doors and windows are shut tight. When Mr.

White comes home, he has to wait in the car for an hour when he had planned to use the time to pack.

Or Ms. White buys herself an expensive summer wardrobe, thus adding a substantial amount to their already large debt, which he is holding down two jobs to pay.

3. *Techniques which waste the oppressor's time and energy,* causing tensions such as being late, making messes or costly mistakes, losing control, starting a fight, and so on.

Ms. White is supposed to go to the bank and get cash for the trip. He comes home and asks: "Did you get the money?"

"No, I couldn't because the car broke down."

"Good God! Why didn't you take a cab or borrow a car?"

"I thought we could do it tomorrow on our way out."

"Tomorrow is a bank holiday!"

"Oh, I *am* sorry. What *will* we do?"

"Well, I can call Fred, he usually keeps cash around." (Fred lives on the other side of town and, anyway, he left for his vacation two hours ago. Eventually, he cashes a check at the market but doesn't get enough money, so he spends the whole trip agonizing over his dwindling cash supply.)

Or she may get severely depressed and maybe even ill so that the vacation has to be canceled.

With every one of these power plays she interferes with his pleasure. At the same time she ineffectively hopes that he will catch on to the fact that she is unhappy and change his mind about the vacation. Needless to say, the only outcome of her power plays is that he gets angry, becomes even more oppressive and domineering, and that she gets even less of what she really wants.

She may, however, effectively interfere with his one-up stance and prevent him from getting what he wants, even though she does not get what she wants.

Pitched Battle

The other form of power play occurs between people who have approximately equal power and feel equal to each other. Both people want something which they are not capable of expressing. Instead of asking for what they want, they attempt to maneuver the other person into giving it to them. In a situation like this an agreement is never reached; every discussion escalates as each person scores a point in his favor and throws the "hot potato" to the other. A similar series of transactions, a game, has been identified by Berne under the name of a game called "Uproar." But Uproar is a series of power plays for strokes. In the case of Mr. and Ms. White a "Pitched Battle" might proceed as follows:

"Honey, I just found out when our vacation is going to be and made reservations at the Lake Inn."

"Well, you may be going to the lake, but I am going to the mountains."

"That's very interesting. How do you think you are going to go to the mountains? You certainly aren't going to take my car."

"So it's *your* car, is it? Go ahead, take the car! I'll just take along the credit card."

"If you spend one dollar on our credit card, I'm going to cut you off completely."

"O.K. You go ahead and try it. We'll see how you do. I think I'll take some money out of our savings account as well," etc.

As you can see, this type of power playing is quite different from the first example, since it is likely to escalate and become a raging battle and it is not very likely that either of the two people will win in the end. But each comment becomes a temporary victory, a partial strategic move which puts the other person down temporarily until forces are regrouped. "Pitched Battles" are like skirmishes, they erupt suddenly and unexpectedly whenever the opportunity for venting anger and resentment reaches a critical level.

These examples of how power occurs in a relationship can be contrasted with the way in which two people might ask for what they want from each other and get a satisfactory compromise without the use of power plays. In order for this to be possible, both people have to be able and willing to concisely express what they want and how they feel until they are satisfied.

A power play free discussion of that sort might proceed as follows:

"Honey, I just agreed with the boss that we are going on vacation from September 7 to September 21. I would like to go to the lake."

"I would like to go to the mountains."

"Would you feel very bad about going to the lake? I am looking forward to meeting a bunch of people and going to the lodge and having those good dinners."

"Well, I was thinking of going to the mountains because I'm really upset about the air pollution here, and I'm looking forward to some good air. You know how the lake is always full of gasoline fumes. Also, in my work I'm always surrounded by people, and I would really like to have some solitude. Then, too, I was hoping not to spend so much money so we can buy a car."

"I want to meet some people and have good meals, and you want some clean air and a new car. Why don't we go to the seaside then, and I'll have a chance to meet some people, and you can go to the beach alone if you don't want to always be around people. There is clean air there, and we can try to save money by taking a housekeeping apartment. That way we can go out and still have good meals and maybe save for a car. I will miss the lodge though . . ."

"Well, I like the idea, but I'm not so happy about keeping house while we are on the beach. I'd just as soon we kept the old car and stayed at the Seaside Hotel. How do you like that?"

The use of power plays in a relationship represents a situation in which two people who are after something from each other are willing to replace what they want from each other by the feeling of being one-up, however temporarily.

Power plays do not lead to satisfaction or equality. They always lead to increased or continuing one-up/one-down situations. The reward of winning through power is a sense of security achieved from having control over the situation. But control and power are not intrinsically satisfying; no quantities of power or control can ever fully satisfy the needs of any human being. Satisfaction comes from having enough of what we really need—food, shelter, space, strokes, love, and peace of mind. The way to those is not power plays but cooperation.

Analysis of Power Plays

Like games, power plays can be analyzed along a variety of lines. Let us take "You Can't Do It If You Can't Prove It." A detailed analysis follows:

Name: "Prove It"

Power (Is it played from one-up, one-down, or equal power?): One-up

Scarcity (What is being competed over? Is the scarcity real? If it is real, is it artificial or inevitable?):

The argument is over who is righteous in his demands. Mr. and Ms. White can't both be right. *The scarcity of righteousness is artificial,* since they are both right in what they want. When they agree that they are both right, they find a cooperative compromise.

Strategy: This one-up power play is based on the fact that most people feel they have to be "logical" in their behavior. The demand for a logical justification for the one-down person's claims is made. The one-down player gets hooked into accepting the demand and its challenge. Every justification is rejected. If the justification is illogical, this is pointed out. If it is logical, then it is skirted with fast talk and rhetorical tricks.

It usually takes the one-down person hours if not days to see the fallacies in the one-up arguments, but by then it is too late.

Moves:
Mr. W: I want A.
Ms. W: I want B.
Mr. W: You can't have B if you can't prove why you should.
Ms. W: Gives proof.
Mr. W: Refutes proof.
Ms. W: Capitulates.

Technique: Pseudo-logical arguments, fast talk.

Antithesis (How can the power play be stopped?):
Mr. W: "Prove It"
Ms. W: I don't want to prove it. I don't have to prove it. I want it because I want it and no one can judge whether what I want is right or not but me.

SECTION 4
Therapy

18

Myths of Therapy

Introduction

There are three main kinds of scripting and each kind of script can be found in banal and tragic dimensions. These three kinds of scripts—Lovelessness, Mindlessness, and Joylessness (depression, madness, and drug abuse)—cover the range of emotional disturbances that present themselves to psychiatrists. I am proposing that these three categories of scripts adequately substitute for all of the categories appearing in the American Psychiatric Association *Diagnostic Manual*[1] under the heading of functional disorders, namely disorders which do not involve visible damage to the central nervous system.

A person may be under the influence of any one or any combination of these three scripts. Lovelessness and its consequences, namely depression, are found either alone or in combination with Mindlessness (madness) or Joylessness (drug abuse). The Mindless and Joyless scripts tend to exclude each other so that people who have a great deal of Joyless scripting (often members of a powerful class, i.e., white men, well-to-do, etc.) tend not to have Mindless scripting, while people who have Mindless scripts (often members of an oppressed class, i.e., non-white, women, working-class etc.) tend not to have Joyless scripting. How-

[1] *Diagnostic and Statistical Manual, Mental Disorders,* second edition, American Psychiatric Association Mental Hospital Service, 1968.

ever, everyone has traces of each script since everyone is subjected to the basic training in all three areas which are ubiquitous in our society.

The three script categories suggest specific therapy approaches effective in dealing with the specific scripts. The only justification I find for the extensive analysis of scripts is in order to find or suggest ways to help people overcome them. The kind of script analysis, which has as its purpose primarily the identification and understanding of scripts, does not command a great deal of interest from me. Rather, it is my ultimate aim in writing this book to suggest methods whereby people can overcome their banal or tragic scripting and proceed to live their lives in a more autonomous fashion.

A few myths about emotional disturbance and psychotherapy need to be dispelled in order to clear the way for script analysis methods. These myths, which are widely accepted by people and their psychotherapists, are behind the failure of a great deal of the psychotherapy being done nowadays.

The Myth of the Value of One-to-One Individual Therapy

One-to-one individual psychotherapy is widely believed to be the therapy of choice, especially in the case of people who are severely emotionally disturbed. It is based on the physician–patient model of medicine and on the minister–faithful model of religious soul-healing. Both of these approaches are prestigious traditional approaches to human suffering, and it is easy to understand why people have come to believe that one-to-one psychotherapy is the only approach which has sufficient depth to lastingly affect severe disturbances. Group psychotherapy, when it is accepted as a therapy at all, is thought to be more superficial and only appropriate with people who have minor disturbances; or if used with severely disturbed people it is used not as therapy but as a cheap method of weekly review and maintenance without expectation of real help.

I believe this to be a myth. Competently conducted group psychotherapy is certainly as effective (I believe it to be *more* effective) as competent one-to-one psychotherapy. Except for the case of acute psychiatric emergencies when a person is temporarily so frightened or depressed that he is completely unable to relate to anyone, group psychotherapy does not only match the effectiveness of one-to-one psychotherapy, but in several aspects surpasses it.

First, individual one-to-one psychotherapy is not an effective method of exploring how people relate to each other. Instead, it tends to encourage the analysis of what goes on *within* a person and therefore tends to reinforce the view that the origin of people's troubles is to be found within them. To be sure, some individual therapists explore people's relationships and the external causes of their unhappiness. The point is that individual therapy is not conducive to that type of socio-analytic focus. Rather, it is conducive to the internal, psycho-analytic focus—the analysis of the person rather than her relationships and external circumstances.

Secondly, individual psychotherapy often becomes the most important relationship in the troubled person's life. When this happens, the relationship becomes a model of the ideal relationship which the "patient" then seeks to find in her relationships outside of therapy. It is not uncommon to meet people who speak of their therapist with the feeling and attachment which are usually accorded to an intimate friend, lover, or relation. I find that kind of a situation very saddening, the more so the higher the fees which the person is paying to maintain the "relationship" with the therapist. The one-to-one relationship is, in fact, artificial in the extreme and not an adequate model for the I–Thou loving relationships which people need and seek. One need only ask how long it will last after money or insurance coverage runs out to see what I mean. True friendship cannot be based on this model.

Lastly, individual therapy encourages the already strong tendencies in people to keep secret their difficulties or to entrust them only to special individuals, such as priests and doctors, in the privacy of their offices or confessionals. This colludes with the Pig Parent's purpose to keep us ashamed and guilty about ourselves (I'm not O.K.) and to keep us suspicious and separate (They're not O.K.) from others. It prevents us from seeing that we are not so wretchedly alone in our unhappiness, that others have similar problems to ours, and that there is no need to be ashamed because we can't find or give love, think, or enjoy ourselves.

Group psychotherapy, on the other hand, provides a situation where a person can experience and analyze his interactions with other people who are his equals. In effective group work the relationships that are highlighted are the relationships between the group members rather than the relationships between the group members and the leader; in transactional analysis, the leader is an adviser who tends to stay out of the interactions; he is not as needed or idolized as in a one-to-one situation.

Open discussion with a group of eight other people encourages openness about one's problems and discourages the sense of shame and guilt which people ordinarily have about their weaknesses and failures. Also, adequate therapy in a group is much cheaper than one-to-one psychotherapy, and is therefore more likely to be readily available to people who are not wealthy. In addition, the skills of a competent therapist are much more adequately used in a group where she can help many times as many people as she could help in individual psychotherapy in a given period of time.

All of the above is not to say that I believe one-to-one relationships or therapeutic contacts are undesirable; the above statement refers to extended (months and years) and intense (once or more weekly) individual therapy.

The Myth of the Uselessness of Common Sense

Another myth in psychotherapy is that somehow, for some reason, common sense is not only not useful, but in fact that the dictates of common sense are completely useless if not counter-productive in the emotional affairs of people. It is often implied that people cannot trust their senses and intelligence when it comes to matters of the mind. In fact, it is often even implied that to use one's common sense and intelligence will cause us to believe in the exact opposite of what's true and to do exactly the opposite of what is useful. If a therapist asks a person what he believes to be the cause of his difficulties, and he responds, "I hate my job and I need to find a new place to live," this common sense appraisal is apt to be subtly or bluntly discounted. Instead of considering the validity of his answer, it is not unlikely that the therapist will conclude instead that his troubles are caused by the fact that he has a passive-aggressive character disorder whose character defenses of displacement and projection prevent him from adequate reality testing.

Again, in opposition with what common sense would indicate, many psychotherapists believe that it is an error to suggest certain desirable courses of action to their "patients." This type of suggestion is labeled "manipulative." It will be shown later in this chapter that a crucial move in script analysis is Permission: a recommendation and often an insistence that the person take a certain course of action. This type of therapeutic strategy is viewed with suspicion by most traditional therapists, who would be reluctant to use it because it is "manipulative" and for fear of what is called the *paradoxical reaction*.

The paradoxical reaction refers to the reaction of a person who is asked to do something and does the opposite, as a result of being asked. Using alcoholism as an example, it is argued that it is not advisable to ask an alcoholic to stop drinking because it will provoke her into drinking even more. It is added that the alcoholic knows that he should stop drinking, and that it is unnecessary for the psychotherapist to ask him to do so.

Transactionally speaking, a paradoxical reaction is a very circumscribed phenomenon which may occur in the above example when the therapist's Parent either commands or begs the alcoholic's Child to stop drinking. Alcoholics who have entered into a contractual relationship with transactional analysts, when advised of the necessity to stop drinking, have either stopped or not responded; but never in my experience has an alcoholic proceeded to drink *more* because of this kind of request. This may be because the transactionally sophisticated therapist avoids the roles of Persecutor, Rescuer, or Victim, which are the source of paradoxical reactions; instead, he simply states the necessity that the person do certain things to effectively overcome her or his scripting.

Common sense indicates that therapists, being experts in human affairs, would have and give suggestions for their clients, and lay readers might be puzzled by this discussion. However, the myth of the desirability of non-directive, non-manipulative therapy persists among both laymen and professionals, and needs to be dispelled.

It has long been suspected, and it is now generally accepted, that no therapist can hope to avoid imposing her system of values upon the people she works for.[1] The issue of manipulation has now become simply a question of whether a therapist, consciously and overtly, is willing to expose people to his values or whether he prefers to do it without his own and his client's awareness. To the transactional analyst, the therapeutic contract makes it clear that the person wants the therapist to use whatever techniques he feels will help his condition, and it is the contract that gives the transactional analyst permission to apply

---

[1]Greenspoon, Joel. "Verbal Conditioning and Clinical Psychology." In *Experimental Foundations of Clinical Psychology*, edited by A. J. Bachrach. New York: Basic Books, 1962.

pressures based on her value system. On the other hand, people are justified in expecting the therapist to limit the application of his judgments to the confines established by the contract.

One final point regarding manipulation needs to be made. Once the therapist frankly admits that he expects to have an effect on the people he works for and as techniques of behavior change increase in potency, it becomes extremely important that the therapist obtain a previous, clear-cut agreement or contract (see Chapter 22) delineating what the person wishes to change in her behavior. Practicing therapy without such an agreement or contract leaves the choice of changes to the therapist who will then be clearly overstepping the boundaries of people's right of self-determination. No human being has the right, even if she is in the position of a therapist, to make decisions for another human being, and to do so is more aptly described as brainwashing than as therapy. A therapist must therefore take extreme care to limit his work to areas which are agreed to by contract.

Closely allied to the issues of common sense and manipulation is the issue of "self-discovery." For reasons never clearly specified, it is argued by some psychotherapists that whatever is discovered by the patient on his own is intrinsically more valuable than whatever he learns due to the therapist's teachings. This argument probably stems from observations of the futility of a strictly Parental or exhortative therapeutic approach, but it has been extended to encompass any behavior which willfully teaches or transmits information. Again the argument of "self-discovery," like the argument against "manipulation," defies common sense.

An analogy to the "self-discovery" approach is that of a man who pushes his stalled car to a gas station and is greeted by a mechanic who, believing in self-discovery, insists that his client deduce for himself the causes and remedy of his car's difficulty. Under the guidance of a good mechanic, the man will probably arrive at a correct diagnosis, and even be able to repair the car, but the value of self-discovery will

hardly compensate him for the expenditure in time
and fees that this approach implies.

Common sense expectations in therapy are that the
therapist teach, give her opinion, exert pressure, apply
her value system, and in fact actively participate in
doing anything and everything that will fulfill the
contract. I believe this common sense expectation to
be correct.

One more way in which common sense is denigrated
is in how people are expected to choose their therapists. Common sense indicates that length of training
and experience is of importance, but also that the
personality, warmth, and other attributes of the therapist are important. Common sense further indicates
that people should use their judgment in choosing a
therapist.

Yet it isn't considered sensible for a person to "interview" her prospective therapist. A person who
wants therapy for sexual problems isn't encouraged
to ask questions such as: "What is your experience (or
training) with sexual problems?" "Are you married?"
"Do you enjoy sex?" "Do you think sex is important?"
"Have you read Masters and Johnson's work on sex?"
and so on.

It makes perfect sense to me that people should ask
such questions, and evaluate the responses of their
prospective therapist, and that the time and opportunity for doing this be offered free of charge. It
further makes sense that therapists who won't agree
to be freely interviewed are suspect of being less than
open and candid. It makes no more sense that the
client should pay to interview the therapist, than that
the therapist should pay the client for interviewing
him.

The Myth of Mental Illness and the Relevance of Medicine to Therapy

The notion that emotional disturbances are in some
way similar to physical illnesses is another important

widely held myth in psychotherapy. This myth has been thoroughly and adequately exposed by Thomas Szasz.[1] Suffice it to say here that there is no justification whatsoever for thinking of the banal or extreme forms of tragic scripts, whether they be depression, madness, or drug abuse, as having any relationship to physical illness. As has been pointed out, the course of scripts parallels to some extent the course of illnesses in that they have an onset, a course, and an outcome. Yet none of the tragic scripts conform to the definition of an illness which requires that there be some "interruption or perversion of function of any of the organs, an acquired morbid change in any tissue of an organism, or throughout an organism, with characteristic symptoms caused by specific microorganismic alterations."[2] Because such micro-organismic alterations are not detectable in any of the so-called "mental illnesses," it is not proper to regard them as such, nor is it reasonable to expect that drugs could have a curative effect on them. At present no drug has proven effective to cure depression, madness, or drug abuse, and no drug is likely to ever have that effect, since these tragic scripts are not the result of chemical or micro-organismic changes in the body but the result of the scripted interactions between people.

Some readers might argue that people who are afflicted by the extreme forms of the tragic scripts are often sick and in need of medical attention, and this is indeed the case. However, it is important to distinguish malnutrition, liver damage, arthritis, ulcers, or any of the other illnesses which develop as a result of the neglect of the body and anxiety to which people in extreme scripts are subjected, from the actual script. Thus, alcoholism is not an illness, although the excessive consumption of alcohol over a long period of time can lead to liver damage and other medical

---

[1] Szasz, Thomas S. *The Myth of Mental Illness: Foundations of a Theory of Personal Conduct.* New York: Hoeber-Harper, 1961.

[2] Stedman, Thomas Lathorp. *Stedman's Medical Dictionary*, 20th ed. Baltimore: The Williams and Wilkins Co., 1962.

illnesses which require the assistance of a physician. The same is true of extreme depression and madness; they can over a period of time cause a physical illness, but they are not in themselves illnesses.

Since neither physical medicine nor drugs are directly relevant to emotional disturbance or unhappiness, it also follows that physicians are in no way uniquely qualified to be therapists and that when they attempt to exclude other capable therapists from helping people they are usurping for themselves a function which is not theirs. Competence as a therapist depends on training and experience in therapy, and medical training is of no particular relevance. People wishing to see a physician's documentation of this claim might read Allen Mariner, M.D., on the subject of the irrelevance of medical training to therapy.[1]

---

[1]Mariner, Allen S. "A Critical Look at Professional Education in the Mental Health Field." *American Psychologist* 22:4 (1967): 271–80.

19

How to Avoid
Rescue

Therapists who are paid for helping others (ministers, probation officers, social workers, psychologists, doctors, psychiatrists, therapists), as well as other people who are simply devoted to other human beings, often come to experience their "helping" activities in a basically negative way.

After the initial enthusiasm and pleasure of the first months or years of helping work they begin to experience frustration at having to work against difficult odds, a sense of bottomless responsibility, and heartbreak over failure.

The widespread occurrence of this unpleasant experience causes "helping" workers to accept it as being reasonable for them, and one that they teach their trainees to expect.

Working under such circumstances eventually fosters negative, persecutory attitudes about the people being helped; namely, that they are helpless and hopeless, or that they are lazy and unmotivated, or even that they are incurably ill.

Since persons in need of help come to be seen as helpless, hopeless, and unmotivated, helpers tend to assume the complete burden of caring and helping, responding to and dealing with every problem that presents itself, and expecting no effort in return from the people they help.

When a person enters into a helping situation with the attitude that the endless numbers of those being helped are helpless and yet that they all, somehow, must be helped, the burden becomes increasingly large until, soon, it is overwhelming and likely to crush the helper who will eventually feel powerless and victimized too. This is the plight of many mental health workers who work for public clinics where they are expected to take care of the emotional casualties of a whole city, county, or state.

The attitudes described above are the expression of the game of Rescue in the work of therapists.

The Rescue Triangle in Therapy

Once pointed out, the Rescue Triangle becomes quite apparent to therapists. For instance, in the psychotherapy of alcoholics, it is common for the alcoholic to present himself as a powerless Victim. The therapist accepts this presentation and proceeds to "do therapy" without insuring a commitment of any sort from the alcoholic. Without any assurances of interest and willingness to participate from the alcoholic, he begins to act in the role of a Rescuer in which he does more than half of the work because the alcoholic has not really manifested any interest in stopping drinking or doing anything at all other than, maybe, coming to therapy sessions. The alcoholic "makes progress" for a while, but eventually, just when everybody thinks he is really getting better, he goes back to drinking. Part of his reason is often a gesture of resentment and a retaliation to the therapist's one-up stance. This is an instance of the Victim turning Persecutor as the Rescuer turns Victim. After the alcoholic persecutes the therapist by his "failure," laced possibly with midnight calls and excessive demands for help, the therapist switches to the role of Persecutor and begins to act in vindictive ways. She may begin to think of him as a "schizophrenic," may discount him, be angry with him because he is no longer being a good little Victim but is being instead a bad little Victim. At this point the Rescuer has turned into Persecutor and the alcoholic is back in the Victim position.

Most therapists have worked enthusiastically in behalf of persons who eventually proved to have been not only disinterested in their help but actually disdainful of it. Most of us have had the experience of becoming more and more concerned and active with someone who subtly became more and more passive until it seemed that his welfare concerned us more than it did him. Most of us have, at one time or another, been lured into a false sense of accomplishment as therapists only to suddenly fall from our pedestals as our star "patient" got drunk, attempted suicide, or got arrested for shoplifting.

Most of us have, after "working hard" with a person, and having no success, gotten angry and subtly (or overtly) persecuted her.

These experiences are heartbreaking to therapists. I wish to present some ideas and approaches which will be helpful in avoiding the Game of Rescue in therapy.

Therapy is a situation in which the three triangle roles have a tendency to occur, especially Rescuer and Victim. Some therapy groups which use attack therapy methods, as pioneered by Synanon, encourage the Persecutor role as well.

For good therapy to take place, it is essential, however, that the persons seeking help be seen as complete human beings capable of taking power over their lives, and this is impossible as long as the therapist is willing to play the Rescuer role. The Persecuting role is completely without therapeutic merit as well, in my estimation. To be sure, when used, it does away with Rescuing tendencies in the group. But it adds nothing of value; and the kind of Persecution used in so-called "attack-therapy" is often terrifying and inhumane, frequently causing people to become hardened and insensitive rather than better, happier human beings.

In short, to avoid the Rescue Triangle the therapist needs to adopt an "I'm O.K., you're O.K." position with respect to the person seeking help. (See page 28 for elaboration on this point.)

How Not to Play the Rescue Game

It is fairly evident that some people, some relationships, and some organizations operate almost completely within the framework of the Rescue Triangle. In these situations a person is denied the freedom to act in any way other than that which fits one of the three roles. Relating to one of these persons, relationships or organizations almost requires that a person participate in the game. For instance, relating to a person who is an alcoholic and who almost constantly displays the role of Victim in search of a Rescuer may be impossible unless one is willing to play the role of Rescuer or Persecutor. That is to say, if one is not willing to Rescue or Persecute the alcoholic, the alcoholic will simply not be interested. The same is true of certain individuals who demand to be Rescued or who demand to be Rescuers in relationships.

There are some organizations in which, unless one is playing the role of Victim or the role of Rescuer, one cannot participate in the interactions. A psychiatric clinic is often this kind of organization in which there are only two slots for people: 1) the role of patient or Victim, in which one is treated as having no power and no choice; and 2) the role of therapist or Rescuer, in which one is required to treat people either as powerless good Victims, that is, people in need of help, or powerless bad Victims, that is, people in need of Persecution.

Relationships with such people and such organizations are personally stressful if one does not want to play the Rescue game. It may be impossible to do, in fact, because one might be Persecuted for *not* wanting to play, so that staying in the situation at all is a case of being willingly Victimized and not getting out.

In every case in which one person Rescues another, whether by going along with something she doesn't want to do, by doing more than 50% of the work, or by not asking for what is wanted, there is always the assumption in the Rescuer that the person is in some way powerless, unable to take care of himself, or in some other way one-down. In every case, the act of Rescuing another person reaffirms and maintains the power imbalance between the Rescuer and the Victim and prevents the possibility of people are O.K. and capable. Giving up one's one-up assumptions and giving up the belief that some people are just unable to take power over their lives is difficult to do, but it is the only path to cooperative, helping relationships.

Example: A young woman, disheveled and haggard-looking, appeared at the Radical Psychiatry Center Action Rap one afternoon (Figure 13). She slumped into a chair in the corner of the room looking desperate and ashen. Everyone noticed her and saw that she was in great need. Eventually, she looked up and got a greeting from a couple of the people in the room. As usual, after a round of self-introductions, the Action Rap Worker asked: "Who wants to work?"

Several people said they did, but Carol (that was the woman's name) said nothing. Everyone noticed; and somebody in the room, not the Worker, said: "How about you, Carol?"

Carol answered, "Oh, I don't know. . . ."

The Worker let a few moments pass, turned to someone else and said, "I guess you want to work, Fred. Let's go ahead and let Carol decide if she wants to work later." This was a very self-conscious effort not to Rescue. Carol looked disappointed but said nothing.

Fred worked for twenty minutes and when he ended by saying, "Thanks, I got what I wanted . . .," Mary jumped right in and reported on some work she had done during the week. Everyone in the room was aware of Carol's inaction and when Mary was done a silence followed.

The Worker turned to Carol and said, "You look like you need something. I would like you to ask for it so that we can see if we can help." Carol burst into tears. Jack, sitting next to her, put his arm around her but

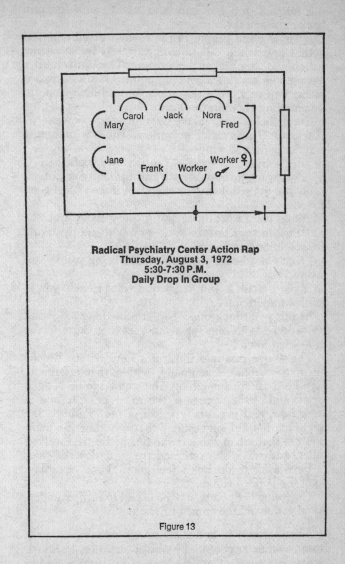

Radical Psychiatry Center Action Rap
Thursday, August 3, 1972
5:30-7:30 P.M.
Daily Drop In Group

Figure 13

she cringed and he, hurt and upset, took his arm back lightning fast.

By now some people in the room seemed annoyed with Carol while others seemed taken by her pain, which was very real at the moment. The Worker, after letting her cry for about a minute, said, "Carol, it seems you feel quite powerless and without hope to do anything about it. Am I right?"

Carol looked up, taken by the word "powerless." She said, "That's right, powerless. There is nothing I can do, I am such a mess."

The Worker answered, "The way we work here is that we want to do what we can to help you but we need you to use all of your energy or it won't feel good to us."

"I told you I can't do anything," answered Carol.

"You can start to take your power to act by asking for something. . . ."

"That's not being powerful, that's being weak!" answered Carol.

"I don't think so but, anyway, I want to help you to ask for something. . . ."

At this point Jack said, "I want something . . . ," and we worked with him for awhile, leaving Carol to decide what to do.

The above example illustrates how not to Rescue an active Victim. Eventually, within that afternoon, Carol did ask for something. She wanted to be hugged by several of the women in the room, cried in one of their laps, and eventually spoke of her troubles. She got some helpful suggestions that day, but the main point is that when she left she felt better, she walked taller, and when she returned the next day she said, "I have a lot to do but I feel good about yesterday. I got the point; I can do it!"

The following points may be useful to further understand and avoid the game of Rescue.

1. Every situation in which one person needs help from another is potentially also a situation in which one person can become a Rescuer and another person can become a Victim. The role of Rescuer is a role in

which one person, in a one-up position, denies to or
diminishes in another person, the Victim, the power
of helping himself by accepting a request for help
without making demands for equal participation or by
imposing help without a request for it. Therefore:

A. Don't help without a contract.

B. Don't ever believe that a person is helpless (unless he is unconscious).

C. Help people who are feeling helpless to find the
ways in which they can apply the power they
have.

D. Don't do more than 50% of the work in therapy;
demand that people do at least 50% of the work
at all times.

E. Don't do anything you don't really want to do.

2. The role of Rescuer is a role of power and superiority in relation to the Victim. The role of Victim is
the role of powerlessness and inferiority in relation
to the Rescuer. Behaving in either of these two roles
inevitably leads to accumulated feelings of resentment which will turn both of these roles into the
Persecutor role.

Persecution, the inevitable result of playing the role
of Rescuer or playing the role of Victim, will be
proportional in intensity to the intensity of the Rescue
or Victim role previously played. Therefore:

A. Avoid behavior which unnecessarily places you
in a one-up position.

—Don't use a special chair.

—Don't answer the phone during group sessions.

—Don't dress more expensively than the people
you work for.

—Don't take the center of the group's attention
unless you have to for therapeutic purposes.

—Don't interrupt people.

—Don't accept one-down statements or "Gee,
you're wonderful" strokes from group members.

—Maintain equality in all spheres except where
you are understood to be one-up, namely as an
expert in therapy. Strive to reduce this inequality

by teaching group members everything you know about therapy.

—Don't have an unlisted phone (unless you also have one listed).

B. If you feel anger toward a group member, assume that you have Rescued by either

(i) having done more than 50% of the work or by

(ii) having done something you didn't want to do and having failed to do something about it for fear of hurting the person. Examples of this are: listening to people when you are bored, doing therapy when it feels unproductive, having sessions when you don't want to, either because you don't like the person, or she bores you, or you are tired. The responsibility is half yours. The angrier you are at a group member or the angrier he is at you, the more you are likely to have Rescued or Persecuted him. Remember, there is no such thing as a group member playing a game with you without your being a full partner in it. If you get angry at members of your contractual therapy group often (more than once every six months), get yourself into a therapy group and work on *your* problem.

C. Don't allow feelings of resentment to accumulate in you or group members. Unload stamps or held resentments in the group and encourage people to give Adult, critical feedback to each other and you.

D. Don't allow yourself to invite Persecution or Rescue from your group members. Some therapists, in order not to be one-up, try to come on one-down. This can be done by dressing sloppily, being sick a lot, being late to meetings, being hungover, smoking incessantly, alluding to or talking about one's problems, or simply being an incompetent, fumbling therapist who cops out by saying once in a while, "Don't look at me, I'm just one of the group . . . ," and forgetting that if that were the case he would have to refund his fees to the group members.

Avoiding the Rescue game is a large measure of a therapist's effectiveness.

To summarize, we are rescuing another person when:

1. We do something for someone else which we don't really want to do.

2. We put in more than 50% of the effort in helping another person.

Arriving at contracts with every group member is an important step in setting up a Rescue-free group.

20

Contracts

Drawing up a contract is the indispensable first step of transactional script analysis. Transactional analysis is a contractual form of group therapy which needs to be distinguished from any number of activities which may be undertaken in groups and which may be of therapeutic value. When practiced in a group, observing a boxing match or football game, finger painting, dancing, screaming or "expressing feeling," can be therapeutic, but they can also be harmful. A basic difference between transactional analysis groups and other group activities is the existence of a contract. This section defines the therapeutic contract and presents a practical approach to obtaining one.

Therapeutic contracts should be regarded with as much respect as are legal contracts in courts of law, and the legal aspects of contracts are fully applicable to therapeutic contracts.[1] Legal contracts must contain four basic requirements to be legally valid. Inasmuch as these requirements have been historically evolved from innumerable litigations over hundreds of years, they may be accepted not only as legally necessary but also otherwise desirable when establishing a therapeutic contract.

[1]Thanks are due to Mr. William Cassidy who first suggested to me the similarity that should exist between legal and therapeutic contracts.

Mutual Consent

Mutual consent implies an offer by the therapist followed by the client's acceptance. The offer must be explicitly communicated and certain in its terms. The offer made by the therapist is an attempt to remedy a certain unhappy state of affairs or disturbance. In order to make an intelligent offer, the therapist should know the nature of the problem and it is his duty to elicit this information during the beginning stages of therapy. Thus, the person seeking help should state what he wants in specific, observable, behavioral terms. For instance, in the case of the alcoholic or other drug abuser this involves gaining control over drinking or drug use, and this specific, observable change is a good basis for a therapeutic contract. Other contracts can be experiencing pleasure and getting rid of headaches and other chronic pains and tensions without drugs. Enjoying strokes, the outdoors, learning to laugh, dance and cry. Having good sex, stopping eating or spending too much as a means to experience pleasure are all good contracts.

In the case of a depressed person, being happy most of the time, establishing good, enduring, cooperative friendships and love relationships, learning how to get strokes, being able to go to sleep or wake up, eat or not eat, as desired, and abandoning thoughts of suicide are all good contracts.

For people with madness scripts, being able to think, to figure out problems, to stop attacks of madness, feeling in control most of the time, learning accounting, asking for what one wants, or not being scared most of the time are good contracts.

On the other hand, the attainment of happiness (rather than being happy most of the time), better relationships (rather than good relationships), emotional maturity, responsibility, self-understanding, and other vague achievements, sometimes expressed as the desired effect, cannot be used in a therapeutic contract because these terms are unclear and non-specific.

It is not possible to enter into a therapeutic contract on the basis of such desired but vague goals and, generally speaking, words of more than two syllables are largely unusable in contracts because of their vagueness. In order for a contract to satisfy the requirement of mutual consent, it is necessary that both parties be able to specify what they are consenting to. Since a person often has little knowledge of what the therapist's offer is, he may grasp at any offer no matter how unclear. The therapeutic offer should contain a clear description of proposed services, and the conditions which will be considered to constitute the fulfilment of the contract.

When the person has no clear understanding of the offer, it may be advisable to arrange a short-term contract of some four to six weeks' duration during which the therapist can explore the person's situation, and the person can acquaint himself with the therapist and her methods. After the short-term contract elapses, the final offer and acceptance, which implies mutual consent, can be attempted again.

This issue of mutual consent is very important. Many people come into therapy due to pressures applied by family or through the courts, and a therapist may make the mistaken assumption that there is mutual consent in the ensuing relationship. The basic transactions of mutual consent are 1) request for therapy; 2) offer of therapy; and 3) acceptance of therapy. It is not unusual for a therapeutic relationship to develop which is lacking in one or more of these transactions. Consider, for instance, the following conversation taking place in the first interview with an alcoholic patient:

THERAPIST: *What brings you here, Mr. Jones?*
MR. JONES: *I'm here to get treatment for my alcoholism.*
THERAPIST: *Fine. I will be able to see you weekly on Monday at 10:00 A.M.*
MR. JONES: *O.K. I'll see you next Monday.*

This conversation may seem a satisfactory achievement of mutual consent. If examined closely, however, it may turn out that the patient's "request" was as follows (if one reads between the lines):

THERAPIST: *What brings you here, Mr. Jones?*
MR. JONES: *[My wife is threatening to leave me and I have a drunk-driving charge against me, and my wife and my mother and the judge say I need treatment, so] I am here to get treatment for my alcoholism.*

This is not a request for therapy, and it probably constitutes a beginning move in a game of Rescue. There is only one response the therapist can make which would not further the game, and that is to make explicit the fact that the person is not really requesting therapy. On the other hand, consider the following conversation:

THERAPIST: *What brings you here, Mr. Jones?*
MR. JONES: *I'm drinking too much, I have made myself physically sick, I'm losing my wife, and I am in trouble with the law. I want to stop drinking so I am here for treatment.*
THERAPIST: *Fine, I will be able to see you weekly on Monday at 10:00 A.M.*
MR. JONES: *O.K., I'll see you next Monday.*

This constitutes a request for therapy but not an offer, in that the therapist has in no way stated what he intends to do or what he hopes to accomplish. Therefore Mr. Jones is free to assume whatever he pleases about what the therapist's role will be, and he will probably assume that it will be one of the roles of the Alcoholic game.[1]

This could also easily be the first move in a Rescue game in which the therapist will eventually wind up as a Rescuer. Any further interaction between the person and the therapist without clarification of the contract would further the game.

The therapeutic offer by the therapist implies that

---

[1]Steiner, Claude M. *Games Alcoholics Play.* New York: Grove Press, 1971.

he is willing to work on the problem and that he feels that he is competent to do so with success. Occasionally a person will request therapy for a condition which the therapist is not competent to work with, at which time it is the therapist's duty to decline making a therapeutic offer. People on occasion apply for therapy of a minor problem but do not want a major problem such as drug addiction or alcoholism to be included in the contract. Making an offer to work on a relatively minor disturbance such as marital disharmony without dealing with the much larger problem of addiction can be compared with doing plastic surgery on a terminal patient and should be declined on the grounds that addiction is such a destructive form of behavior that it will disrupt and defeat any efforts to deal with minor disturbances.

The above view should not be confused with the view held by some therapists, i.e., that it is improper to make an offer to treat a symptom such as drinking, sexual impotence or frigidity, or a phobia, because these disturbances are caused by "deep" dynamic disturbances—and treating the symptom will not only be of no value to the person but, in some mysterious way, may be harmful instead. The argument may run approximately as follows: "This young lady requests treatment to overcome her sexual frigidity. But her incapacity to enjoy sex is related to a deeply buried hostility against men which will overwhelm her if she in fact enjoyed sex, causing her to become psychotic. Therefore we cannot offer to treat her frigidity but must treat her hostility instead." This strange but not unusual thinking process is not communicated to the person and has a certain similarity to the situation in which a person goes to a store to buy a whiskbroom and emerges with a five-year contract for home maintenance, a vacuum cleaner, and a one-year supply of soap.

If the woman in question asks for therapy with the aim of learning to fully enjoy sex, then the therapist must pursue that goal or refuse to do therapy. He doesn't have the option to secretly work on his own aims no matter how convinced he is of the validity of his theory.

Finally, returning to Mr. Jones, consider the following conversation:

THERAPIST: *What brings you here, Mr. Jones?*
MR. JONES: *I'm drinking too much, I have made myself physically sick, I am losing my wife, and I am in trouble with the law. I want to stop drinking so I am here for treatment.* (Request)
THERAPIST: *O.K., Mr. Jones, I think we can work together on your problem. While you are in therapy you'll attend group therapy once a week, and perhaps an occasional individual session. I'll expect you to stop drinking entirely as soon as possible and to continue to abstain for at least one year, since it is my experience that individuals who do not abstain for at least a year tend not to recover from alcoholism. If you remain abstinent for a year while in therapy, you will probably gain control over your drinking to the point that drinking will no longer be of concern to you. This contract implies that you will be actively pursuing not only sobriety but any number of other things which might be helpful to you. I, as the therapist, will be guiding and working with you as long as you want to work on your problem. I will be able to see you on Monday at 10:00 A.M.* (Offer)
MR. JONES: *O.K., I'll see you next Monday.* (Acceptance)

This highly condensed example contains a request for therapy, an offer, and an acceptance, and satisfies the requirements of mutual consent in a therapeutic contract.

Mutual Consent Implies Mutual Effort: In every situation in which one person helps another and therefore one person is for that moment one-up to the other, it is also true that the person who is one-down or being helped has a certain amount of power available to him. In order for the situation to be effective, the power that is available to the person being helped has to be used in its entirety. That is to say, the person being helped has to contribute to the situation everything that he has to contribute. Mr. Jones, above, should be expected to come to meetings on time, be involved, do homework (see p. 281), and in general put out a visible effort toward the fulfillment of his contract. If he ceases to do so, the effort is no longer mutual and the situation becomes a Rescue. This is true of any situation in which a person is being helped, even those in which it seems that the person being helped is totally without power. Take, for instance, a person who has been run over by a car and badly hurt. As long as she is unconscious, she has no power to contribute to the process of help delivered by ambulance drivers, doctors, nurses, etc. But as soon as she regains consciousness she is able to apply her energy, her power toward the healing process, and if she doesn't, whoever is helping her is engaging in a unilateral effort which is a Rescue.

Consideration

A helper is giving of herself. To avoid a Rescue the person helped needs to give something in return. This is called in legal parlance the *consideration*.

Every contract must be based upon a valid consideration. Valid consideration refers to benefits conferred by the therapist and the person being helped, which may be bargained for and eventually agreed upon. The benefit conferred by the therapist should always be a competent attempt to remedy the disturbance. Given that a person and a therapist specify an undesirable state of affairs in observable, behavioral terms, when the person, the therapist, and the majority of the members in the group agree that the problem as described is no longer present, the therapist has delivered her consideration in the contract. Clearly, it is impossible to state that a person was helped unless the condition from which she was to be helped was precisely described at the beginning of therapy. The consideration delivered by the client can vary.

Take as an example the following *teaching* (rather than therapy) contract:

Mr. Smith is an accomplished pianist. Charlie comes to Mr. Smith asking to be taught how to play the piano. Mr. Smith may decide to teach Charlie to play the piano for a $3.00-an-hour fee, or he may teach Charlie the piano in exchange for Charlie's taking care of his garden. Mr. Smith was taught to play the piano by someone who detected that he was very talented and who taught him for free, making it clear to him that she expected her teachings to be passed on to other talented people. Therefore, Mr. Smith might teach Charlie, whom he sees as a very talented young man, in repayment for the teaching he received from his own teacher. Or, Mr. Smith may teach Charlie for free in exchange for the benefits that he receives from the community in which he and Charlie live. Finally, it is possible that Mr. Smith would have such pleasure in teaching Charlie, either because Charlie is very talented or because of some other personal quality of Charlie's, that Mr. Smith is willing to invest the effort to teach Charlie in exchange for being in Charlie's company. Charlie may also be able to teach Mr. Smith something.

All of these alternatives are valid arrangements for consideration as long as they are understood and agreed upon by both parties. When consideration does not exist or ceases to exist, then the situation becomes a Rescue.

In therapy the benefit or consideration conferred by the client is usually money. But any of the above described kinds of consideration are possible (though not often plausible) in therapeutic contracts.

Competency

Contractual ability is limited in certain cases:

1) *Minors.* Legally, minors cannot enter into a valid contract. The likelihood of establishing a contract with such a person is very slim, unless the parents enter

into the contract as well. This necessity arises with minors as it often occurs that the legal guardians will, for one reason or another, decide to discontinue his therapy—particularly if the child begins to exhibit some changes after a period of therapy. Frequently, this decision is based on their notion that their child is getting worse, instead of better. This phenomenon is easily understandable in terms of the script, since it is assumed that children who need therapy are performing according to the wishes of their parents. When they cease to behave according to parental injunctions the parents will interpret this change as a negative effect of the therapy.

Thus, with minors, it is important that at the beginning of therapy a contract be made not only with the minor but with her parents as well. In practice I have found that this difficulty is adequately dealt with by an agreement with the parents that the child will not discontinue treatment unless both the guardians and she consent to it.

2) *Incompetence.* Those whose mental faculties are so impaired that they are incapable of understanding the consequence of their agreement cannot enter into a contract and are therefore not appropriate for contractual therapy. Persons who cannot cathect an Adult ego state, such as acutely (temporarily) psychotic individuals or profoundly retarded individuals, are included in this group.

3) *Intoxicated persons.* Intoxicated persons are a subgroup of incompetents and represent persons under the influence of mind-altering drugs to the extent that Adult ego functioning is impaired so as to prevent mutual consent. Contracts entered into while a person is intoxicated are invalid; and therefore people who are heavily dosed on any drug, be it alcohol, tranquilizers, or stimulants, cannot make a contract until they "sober up." It should be pointed out here that persons who are excluded from entering into a valid contract for reasons of competency are not necessarily unable to profit from other therapeutic measures available to helpers. The above statements apply only to

contractual treatment, which is only one of the avenues available to people who want to alleviate their condition.

Lawful Object

The contract must not be in violation of the law or against public policy or morals, nor should the consideration be of such nature. This stipulation seldom applies but must be considered with care in the treatment of users of illegal drugs or persons with criminal involvement.

Transactional analysis of scripts cannot be effectively pursued without a contract because unilateral therapy is intrinsically contradictory to the principles of transactional analysis outlined in the Introduction to this book. The absence or presence of a contract most clearly distinguishes transactional analysis from other forms of therapy, especially psychoanalysis where contracts are referred to but in a completely different manner than outlined above;[1] one which binds the client but not the analyst.

---

[1]Menninger, Karl. *Theory of Psychoanalytic Technique.* New York: Basic Books, Inc., 1958.

21

Strategies of
Script Analysis

Any experienced therapist probably has an intuitive grasp of the need to avoid the Persecutor, Rescuer, and Victim roles in therapy, though he may not know how these roles interrelate. Avoidance of these roles is the reason why many therapists hide behind a mask of noncommittal passivity in their work.

Unfortunately, by retaining a strictly noncommittal Adult-to-Adult relationship, psychotherapists have rejected the kind of behavior which is essential to effective therapy, especially therapy of scripts. Games and scripts are played from the Parent or Child ego state and their therapy requires what may be called "tissue" or "gut" responses from the therapist. By rejecting all tissue responses and using only their heads, their Adult, therapists have thrown out the baby with the bath water, so to speak, since without tissue responses, that is, transactions from the Parent and Child, effective script analysis is not possible.

By making it possible to dissect and evaluate the possible transactions in therapy, transactional analysis makes available to the therapist a number of strategies in addition to Adult-to-Adult Work which are needed to help people with scripts. These therapeutic strategies (namely, Antithesis, Fun, Permission, and Protection, outlined in the following discussion) involve the therapist's Parent and Child ego states. They will be distinguished from harmful tissue responses which they resemble but which are roles in the Rescue Triangle.

Work

The Work transaction (Figure 14A) is most common among "rational" and "insight" therapists. It represents Adult-to-Adult communication in which 1) data is gathered—the person's life history, patterns of unhappiness, childhood or recent events in her life, her dreams; 2) conclusions are drawn—interpretation of dreams, diagnosis of ego states, games and scripts, interpretation of resistances; and 3) recommendations are made which are Adult statements of logical consequences or predictions, such as "Well, given what you've told me, it would seem that you are no longer able to control your drinking," or, "It seems that your love affair with Jack is very harmful for you; you probably won't feel good until you stop seeing him."

Work transactions represent the largest percentage of transactions occurring in a group and take a certain predictable course. Work tends to be carried out with one group member as the focus. Either by his own choosing or by being singled out by someone else, one group member will become the center of attention. This does not necessarily mean that he will be placed on the "hot seat" where he becomes the focus of *all* interaction but simply that he tends to be at the center of it. The first phase of this process is one of *clarification.* The person presents a problem or someone else suggests that a problem exists, and some exploration is needed to ascertain whether there is, in reality, something to work on. The problem suggested may be a "red herring" or "bone" thrown at the group instead of a more serious problem which is difficult or scary to bring up. Or the problem, suggested by another group member, may represent a projection or misperception. In any case, the process of clarification continues until the feeling develops that the group is working on a real problem in which some change can or should occur.

Now the process shifts from clarification to *challenge*

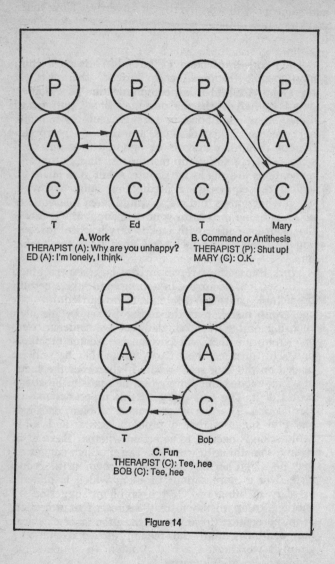

A. Work
THERAPIST (A): Why are you unhappy?
ED (A): I'm lonely, I think.

B. Command or Antithesis
THERAPIST (P): Shut up!
MARY (C): O.K.

C. Fun
THERAPIST (C): Tee, hee
BOB (C): Tee, hee

Figure 14

and someone will ask, overtly or covertly, "Now that you know the problem, what are you going to do about it?" The person ordinarily is at a loss for solutions or unwilling to use those which are suggested. A cherished old pattern of behavior is being reexamined, a parental injunction is being challenged, and the person's Adapted Child is expected to balk. This is the *impasse* beyond which the person will not go unless pressure is applied, pressure which can only come from another person's Child or Parent.[1]

At this point, a purely Work-oriented therapist has to rely on one of the group members to supply the tissue transactions needed. The transactional analyst, however, has at his disposal the Permission transaction and will use it when appropriate. Now the process shifts from challenge to *climax* if the person accepts the Permission, or to *anticlimax* if he deflects it. If Permission is accepted, the group members will ordinarily have an experience of well-being and closure, and a silence will follow after which the process starts anew with another person as the focus of attention. If Permission occurs within the group itself, such as getting angry, crying, being honest, asking for strokes, or exposing the Pig Parent, the person may be quite shaken and Nurturing and Protection may be indicated.

Sometimes, the person will be frightened enough to be unable to continue in her Adult ego state during the clarification or challenge. She might feel defensive, not O.K., guilty, ashamed, or angry. When this happens it is important to stop the Work process and Nurture and provide Protection. Some therapists prefer to use *attack*, a technique borrowed from Synanon, to "break through the defenses" of the person.

I will comment on the uses of attack therapy later. Suffice it to say here I believe that when a person becomes defensive, Protection rather than continued Work or attack is the appropriate response.

---

[1]Perls, Fritz S. *Gestalt Therapy Verbatim*. Lafayette, California: Real People Press, 1969.

At times the impasse is not resolved by a climax or anticlimax but becomes a game of "Why Don't You— Yes, But." Here the therapist is faced with a question of strategy. Should she continue to press or should the group go on to someone else? In a hard-working group the therapist is always under time pressure and has the dual responsibility of not allowing time to be wasted and of pursuing matters to their completion. Skillful decisions along these lines distinguish the experienced therapist from the novice who will either pursue matters endlessly to no avail or drop them just as the impasse is ready to be broken. In any case, if the matter is dropped, the feeling in the group is anticlimactic and again a silence follows, after which a new person becomes the focus of attention. It should be noted here that in a cooperative group all the group members, and not just the therapist, are responsible for deciding whether to stay with something or go on to something else. In my groups, people sign up on the blackboard if they want to work and everyone is expected to make sure that time is used to the fullest and allocated fairly.

GAME PLAYING

It takes a skillful leader to maintain the work orientation of a group. When a group loses its work orientation it will fall into game playing. Game playing can take several forms. The group can play Rescue in a situation where one of the persons presents himself as a Victim and the rest of the group scramble madly in an attempt to Rescue. A group of this sort will be taken up by games such as "Why Don't You— Yes, But," "Do Me Something," "If It Weren't For Them (or Him) (or Her)." The general outcome of such groups is that the Victim and Rescuers all end up in a state of heightened frustration and anger. Very often when a group has played a Rescue game the Rescuers will switch to Persecutors and attack the Victim. Now the games will be "Uproar," "Kick Me," "Now I've Got You, You Son of a Bitch," "Stupid," and so on. Or the Victim becomes Persecutor and

plays "Nobody Loves Me," or, "See What You Made
Me Do." The roles of Victim, Rescuer, and Persecutor
will switch around in the group with different people
taking different roles so that everyone eventually plays
every role in an endless merry-go-round.

The role of Rescuer is the natural game role that
group leaders tend to fall into. For every long minute
that a leader plays Rescuer, he will eventually have
to play an equally long minute as Persecutor. A group
leader must be aware of the possibility that a group
member may no longer be holding to the original
contract, and when this is the case should stop the
process until a new contract is arrived at. The
tendency for group leaders to engage in Rescuing
usually comes out of a sense of guilt or exaggerated
responsibility for the group member. When a group
leader maintains a position of "I'll help you as long as
you are willing to work on your problem as hard as
I do," she will avoid the dangers of the Rescue role.
Needless to say, Persecuting any one person in a
group is even less desirable than playing Rescue. I
have concluded that therapy can be done without
any necessity of yelling, screaming, attacking, goad-
ing, and other "therapeutic" maneuvers which are really sadistic versions of "I'm Only Trying to Help You"
and are found to be unnecessary when a leader learns
how to confront people in a human and loving way.

Antithesis or Command

This is an emergency transaction from Parent to
Child which is used to arrest or interfere with certain
transactional sequences which the therapist feels are
dangerous. (Figure 14B).

For instance, if a teenage girl who has a history of
unhappy sexual relationships and an older married
man get into a flirtation in group, the therapist may
wish to arbitrarily say, from his Parent to their Child,
"Don't get together by yourselves outside of group."
Or if one person verbally attacks or "pigs" another,
the therapist, again Parent to Child, may want to

demand that he stop. If an intoxicated patient in the group continually interrupts the proceedings, the therapist might need to say, "Shut up!" This transaction has to be available to a therapist dealing with people who have self-destructive scripts, since they are often on a dangerous or disruptive brink and require direct commands to stop. I have seen dramatic evidence of the effectiveness of the Antithesis transaction with self-destructive individuals. It has become routine to use a script Antithesis such as "Don't kill yourself," or "Don't beat your children," with suicidal or violent people who later reported hearing the therapist's voice and injunction whenever tempted to kill themselves or beat their children. These people often express their appreciation for the positive effect of the therapist's injunction without which, they feel, they might have committed a suicidal or violent act.

ATTACK

The antithesis or command is to be distinguished from the attack transaction in which the therapist also uses her Parent in a critical and authoritarian way.

There is a vast difference between command and attack. My opinion about the attack approach is that it is cruel, that it serves the oppressive purposes of the Pig Parent, and, above all, that it does not work.

My feelings on this subject are strong. I have seen many casualties from groups where attack techniques were used. Some become frightened of groups and are enormously relieved when I tell them that I personally do not use or allow attack in my groups. Others have learned to "deal" with attack and have become hardened, defensive, uptight, and insensitive to feedback. I have heard of the misuse of attack therapy combined with transactional analysis in prison groups where attack becomes a nightmarish experience akin to a third-degree police interrogation. Attack therapy is especially noxious when the group members are captive, that is, not free to leave at any time.

I know that some will argue that they know people who have been helped by attack therapy and that it can be used lovingly as a technique. Perhaps; but nevertheless I believe that attack has as little place in a therapy situation as a cattle prod, even if it is used (mostly) as a pointer, and I object to its use in connection with transactional analysis.

Fun

Fun is a transaction in which the Childs of the group's members are able to experience joy together (Figure 14C). This transaction is hard to distinguish from its destructive counterpart, the *gallows transaction*, and is therefore avoided by some experienced therapists because they fear its possible dangers. Yet Child-to-Child fun seems to be a basic requirement of efficient therapy, and while a therapist may be able to help without having any fun, the work is likely to be more speedy if they are having fun together. Fun also has the advantage of making the therapist's task more enjoyable, something which is of benefit since a zestful, happy therapist is likely to have fewer days out of work from sickness, and less interference by depression than a therapist who is not having fun in his work.

Fun is most readily expressed through laughter. Because of this, a group member or a therapist who doesn't laugh heartily at least once per meeting should consider seriously whether he is not being unnecessarily glum, and whether he is Rescuing the group.

THE GALLOWS TRANSACTION

The *gallows transaction*, as opposed to Fun, takes place when a person, in one way or another, cons the group members (and sometimes the therapist) into smiling at his script behavior. In hamartic individuals, self-destructive behavior is always associated with a smile. The person who explains the smile by saying, "I'm smiling because it's funny," "I'm smiling in order not to cry," or, "I'm smiling because I am embarrassed," is falling prey to sophistry. A smile is associated with pleasure or more precisely, just as it is in the infant, with well-being. The pleasure in this case is the result of the approval and smile of the Pig Parent rewarding the Child for his self-destructive behavior. The smile of the therapist of group members parallels and reinforces the smile of the Pig Parent who is pleased when the person obeys the injunction. For instance, White, a self-destructive alcoholic, may come to the group and say, "I had a terrible car accident last night, ha, ha." The verbal content is Adult-to-Adult and the "ha, ha's" are from Child-to-Child or from Child-to-Parent and from Parent-to-Child. The person's smile is primarily addressed to the Pig Parent. The Child learns by conditioning and is stimulus-bound, so that the smile of the respondent serves to reinforce the Child's self-destructive behavior. A therapist dealing with self-destructive individuals must determine which behavior is self-destructive or script-bound, and must never smile in response to it. When the gallows transaction is explained in a group and is thus prevented from occurring, the effect is startling, and often the person's Child reacts as if the therapist is a party-crasher who made away with the goodies. Curtailing the gallows transaction does not mean that therapy should not be fun, but simply that self-destruction is no fun. Avoiding the gallows transaction allows the group to laugh at whatever is joyful rather than tragic in the person and discourages the self-destructive aspects of her behavior by denying the strokes she expects, and usually gets for it.

Permission

The first of the three P's of transactional analysis (Permission, Protection, Potency)—Permission—is a transaction which is intimately tied to the theory of scripts (Figure 15A).

The concept of Permission in script analysis was elaborated in my work with alcoholics.[1] In puzzling

---

[1] Steiner, Claude M. *Games Alcoholics Play*. New York: Grove Press, 1971.

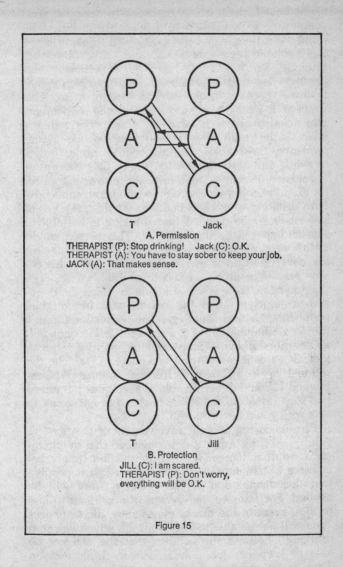

T   Jack

A. Permission

THERAPIST (P): Stop drinking!   Jack (C): O.K.
THERAPIST (A): You have to stay sober to keep your job.
JACK (A): That makes sense.

T   Jill

B. Protection

JILL (C): I am scared.
THERAPIST (P): Don't worry,
everything will be O.K.

Figure 15

about how to help, some therapists propose that alcoholics need permission to drink without guilt. The implication here is that the guilt about drinking keeps the alcoholic feeling not O.K. and provokes further drinking. Script analysis takes the superficially surprising view that an alcoholic needs permission *not* to drink, because he is under duress to do so. This concept is really not surprising if one remembers that an alcoholic is involved in a script, and that a script is the result of parental injunctions. As a consequence, theoretically the alcoholic is under orders to drink, and needs permission not to. The concept of Permission becomes clear in practice when applied, for example, to a young alcoholic who is surrounded by hard-drinking co-workers and who would feel a loss of self-esteem if he decided that drinking is harmful to him and should be discontinued. This person would clearly need permission to stop drinking and go against the covert and often even overt challenges of his co-workers and co-drinkers to continue drinking.

Permission, then, is a transaction in which the therapist attempts to align the person with her original script-free, Natural Child ego. The permission transaction is a combination of a Parent-to-Child command, as described above—"Stop drinking"—and a rational, logical explanation, Adult-to-Adult, in which the rational or logical reason for the command is explained ("You will not be able to keep your job unless you stop drinking," or "Your husband is not going to stay with you unless you stop.")

Permission requires the involvement of the person's Adult, and if his Adult is not convinced that the therapist's Adult statement is valid, Permission simply becomes a Command that may be resisted. It is possible that decontamination of the person's Adult will be needed. For instance, the person who is about to lose her job because she drinks may ignore the statement "You will not be able to keep your job unless you stop drinking," because she believes that she will not be able to keep her job unless she can drink *socially*. Thus, if the Adult-to-Adult message is not received and accepted, Permission will not work. The therapeutic task at this point would·be to recognize the contamination involved, namely, that the person believes that she has to drink in order to keep her job.

Every script injunction requires a separate Permission. As major injunctions are defeated, others become salient and need to be dealt with. For instance, an alcoholic who had very visibly improved her situation by remaining sober for a whole year never initiated social relationships herself, but rather relied for her social contacts on whatever activities her few friends initiated. When this was noticed it became evident that she needed Permission to ask for strokes from people. She was told, as part of her homework, to call someone and ask them to a movie. This proved to be a very difficult task for her, and she was not able to perform it for a few weeks. This difficulty became the focus of the therapy, the person's impasse beyond which she had to move in order to proceed toward permanent improvement. The therapist's insistence and interest in this specific action eventually had the desired effect and she finally overthrew the strong injunction against asking what she wanted from people, an achievement which later proved to be crucial to her well-being.

It must be remembered that the parent giving Permission should be the grownup Parent (P_2), and not the Parent in the Child (P_1 in C_2) (see Figure 2). The difference between the first-order Parent and the Parent in the Child has been elaborated in Chapter 13, but it should be further noted that the Parent in the Child plays the part of impotent Rescuer or Persecutor. The potency required to countermand parental injunctions is not available to the Parent in the Child but only to the first-order Parent. Every therapist should be aware of the difference between these two ego states in himself, since any transactions coming from the Parent in the Child (the Pig Parent acting as Rescuer or Persecutor) of the therapist are an indication of difficulty.

Protection

The concept of therapeutic protection was first postulated by Patricia Crossman and has become an indispensable part of script analysis.[1] When a person under the influence of the therapist's Permission takes a step which involves rejection of the parental injunction, he may find himself alone and terrified, having declined parental protection. The existential vacuum and fear that follow cannot be ignored by the therapist. If the therapist does not replace the Protection the person has lost from his parents, the person will probably return to his prior mode of behavior within which he feels safe, and allow the bad witch to "return." This constitutes a re-embracement of the script and, psychologically speaking, it represents the person's belief that the therapist is not as powerful as the bad witch and that he cannot be trusted when the chips are down.

Because the person has to rely on the therapist's Protection, the timing of Permissions is important. They should be given only when both the therapist and patient feel that Protection is possible. Thus, major Permissions should not be given before going on vacation, or when schedules are likely to be overcrowded. The need for Protection may arise at almost any time; therapists who prefer to isolate themselves may fail to be available for Protection when needed. Protection is often provided over the telephone, since the panic that follows Permission does not always coincide with therapeutic appointments. My experience has shown that a therapist working with about forty people will need to provide Protection about twice a week outside of the regularly scheduled appointments. I have made my home telephone available to all the people I work with and have encountered very little

[1]Crossman, Patricia. "Permission and Protection." *Transactional Analysis Bulletin* 5,19 (1966): 152–53.

difficulty because of it. By remembering that any "distress" phone call may be either an invitation to play Rescuer over the phone or a genuine call for Protection, it is relatively simple to separate the "game" phone calls from the calls for Protection. In general, a genuine call for Protection takes less than fifteen minutes and is a highly satisfying experience for both the therapist and the caller. An invitation to play Rescuer has a totally different feel to it since whatever reassurance the therapist gives is received with "Yes, but," which is simply a further invitation for another move within the Rescue role. When a person calls and is clearly attempting to hook the therapist into a Rescue role, the therapist should quickly decline any further conversation and remind the person of his responsibility for his own actions. Consider the following conversation:

JANE: *Hello.*
THERAPIST: *Hello.*
JANE *(crying)*: *I'm scared.*
THERAPIST: *What's the matter?*
JANE: *I don't know, I'm scared and I feel like killing myself.*
THERAPIST: *I understand. It's pretty scary to try to do things differently from what your script calls for. I suggest that you call up a friend and go to a movie tonight.*
JANE: *That sounds like a good idea. I think I'll do it.*
THERAPIST: *That's good, hang on tight, and feel free to call me any time you get scared again.*
JANE: *I feel better now. Thank you.*
THERAPIST: *Goodbye.*
JANE: *Goodbye.*

The above conversation is a typical Protection transaction. Notice that Jane is willing to accept responsibility for her emotional state, and is willing to accept the therapist's recommendations to change it. Jane is genuinely scared and responds in a favorable manner in a relatively short period of time. Consider in contrast the following conversation:

JUNE: *Hello.*

THERAPIST: *Hello.*

JUNE *(crying): I'm scared.*

THERAPIST: *What's the matter?*

JUNE: *I haven't been able to sleep for ten nights and I feel like killing myself.*

THERAPIST: *I understand how you feel. It's pretty scary to try to do things differently from what your script calls for. I suggest that you call up a friend and go to a movie tonight.*

JUNE: *I don't feel like doing that. I don't have any friends. Can't you do better than that? If you can't do better than that, I'm going to take all my sleeping pills.*

THERAPIST: *What would you like me to do?*

JUNE: *I want you to talk to me, or give me some different medication, or something.*

THERAPIST: *I want to help but what are you going to do about the situation?*

JUNE: *I don't know, I think I'll end it all.*

THERAPIST: *Well, I hope you won't, but I don't exactly understand what you want me to do. I suggest that you get out of the house and go to a movie.*

JUNE: *Yes, but . . . , etc.*

The above conversation is an attempt on the part of June to draw the therapist into a Rescue role. If the therapist is willing, this conversation can go on for hours and have essentially no results. If the therapist is unwilling to play, June may decide to abandon the attempt. If she does, she is much less likely to think of the therapist as a possible Rescuer and will probably not repeat the attempt in the future, but instead ask for and accept Protection.

The therapeutic effectiveness of Protection needs to be distinguished from what is called "transference cure" in psychoanalysis, in which improvement is predicated on a continuing involvement with the therapist. Ordinarily, a person does not require Protection for more than three months following abandonment of a script injunction. If the panic and need for the person's therapist do not subside by that time, the therapist is probably playing a Rescue game.

Protection is the function of the Nurturing Parent. If it were possible to rank the importance of the ego states, I would put the two Adults (A_1 and A_2) first and the Nurturing Parent a close second with the Child running an important third. The Pig, or Critical Parent, however, has no usefulness in therapy.

Thus a good Adult, rational as well as intuitive, a loving, caring Nurturing Parent, and a happy Child are important attributes of a script analyst. His Pig Parent should be left outside the door and if it manages to intrude in the proceeding, it is the therapist's responsibility to get some help from his own therapist.

Potency

These four tissue transactions (Command, Permission, Protection, and Fun), in addition to the Adult-to-Adult Work transaction, constitute the transactional analyst's basic tools. Adding Antithesis, Fun, Permission, and Protection to the Work transaction gives the transactional analyst flexibility and latitude and provides him with increased therapeutic effectiveness or Potency. Therapeutic Potency refers to the therapist's capacity to bring about speedy improvement. The Potency of the therapist has to be commensurate with the potency of the injunction laid down by the parents of the person, and it is an attribute which transactional analysts seek in their work. Eric Berne[1] said, "A timid therapist is as out of place trying to tame an angry Parent as a timid cowboy is trying to ride a bucking bronco. And if the therapist gets thrown he lands right on the patient's Child." Potency implies that the therapist is willing to attempt to truly remedy the problem, to permit himself to do so, and to estimate the time and expense involved. It means that

[1]Berne, Eric. *What Do You Say After You Say Hello?* New York: Grove Press, 1972.

she is willing to confront the patient at the *impasse* and to exert pressure, and it means that the therapist is willing to provide Protection when it is needed. Potency, when striven for by therapists, is often interpreted as implying a wish for omnipotence. However, the difference between Potency and omnipotence is quite clear; and transactional analysts, aware of their limitations as well as those of the concept of therapeutic Potency, are seldom plagued by what psychoanalysts call "fantasies of omnipotence" or, in transactional terms, by being hooked into the Rescuer role.

The desirability of therapeutic Potency makes transactional analysts willing to consider for use any technique which demonstrably accelerates therapy. Some techniques which contribute to therapy are Permission classes, Marathons, and Homework.

1) *Permission Classes.* Group sessions have their limitations as therapeutic tools. They are arranged primarily for the purpose of verbal interaction among ten or fewer individuals and they tend to take place in a room of limited size. In addition, time is limited and many therapists feel that they are bound by their ethical code to limit their physical contact with their patients.

Transactional analysts have amplified the potency of group therapy by adding to it Permission classes led by a Permission teacher (see Steiner and Steiner,[1] and Wyckoff.[2] These classes are recommended to selected group members whose parental injunctions inhibit them not only in their thinking and talking (which can be dealt with in group), but also in more physical ways, such as in touching and being able to be touched; moving in an expansive, graceful, or assertive way; laughing or crying; dancing or cutting up; moving sexually or aggressively; relaxing; and so on.

[1]Steiner, Claude M., and Steiner, Ursula. "Permission Classes." *Transactional Analysis Bulletin* 7,28 (1968): 89.

[2]Wyckoff, Hogie. "Permission." *The Radical Therapist* 2,3 (1971): 8–10. Reprinted in *Readings in Radical Psychiatry*, Claude Steiner, ed. New York: Grove Press, 1974.

Permission classes preferably meet at a dance studio with mirrors on the wall and soft mats available for the floor. Each patient is referred to the Permission class with a specific contract such as "Permission to dance," "Permission to touch others," "Permission to be sexy," "Permission to act assertively," or, "Permission to lead instead of follow," to mention a few.

2) *Marathons.* Marathons, or protracted therapy meetings lasting between eight and thirty-six hours, are another technique which amplified therapeutic Potency. I have found Marathons extremely useful for people who, after several months of therapy, have arrived at an impasse beyond which they seem unable to move. People who are on an improvement plateau in therapy and who have not made any recent progress are encouraged to participate in Marathons.

Marathons can have different aims. Permission marathons are simply enlarged Permission classes. Wyckoff describes Amazon Power Marathons designed to put women in touch with their physical power.[1] A Stroke Marathon or Stroke City is a situation exclusively devoted to breaking down the stroke economy. Body Marathons focus on getting people back into touch with their bodies. Off the Pig Marathons are devoted to exercises to get rid of the Pig Parent.[2] Typically, the session begins with a discussion of the goals each person hopes to achieve during the Marathon. These goals are written on a large sheet of paper or on the wall to be clearly visible to all the members participating,[3] and work toward achieving these goals continues throughout the period of the

---

[1]Wyckoff, Hogie. "Amazon Power Workshop." *Issues in Radical Therapy* I,4 (1973): 14–15.

[2]Wyckoff, Hogie. "Permission." *The Radical Therapist* 2,3 (1971): 8–10. Reprinted in *Readings in Radical Psychiatry,* Claude Steiner, ed. New York: Grove Press, 1974.

[3]Dr. Franklin Ernst was the first to utilize wall markings or graffiti as a technique which improves therapeutic effectiveness. (Lecture delivered at the summer conference of the Golden Gate Group Psychotherapy Association, San Francisco, 1968.)

Marathon. At the end every person evaluates his own
work and writes his accomplishments next to his contract on the wall.

The success of these sessions is unquestionable; people are usually quite elated and feel a great sense of
accomplishment and satisfaction at the end of a Marathon, a sense of euphoria which usually lasts from one
to two weeks. Work in group is usually invigorated
and pushed forward by a good Marathon experience.

3) *Homework.* Homework is assigned work that
group members do between therapy meetings toward
the fulfillment of the contract. Often people will do
homework without any urging from the therapist or
the group. It is not unlikely that it is those people who
profit from "insight" therapies in which much emphasis
is placed on what transpires during the therapeutic
hour. A person who generates his own homework is
likely to assume responsibility for his situation and assume that he must do something about it. I pointed
out earlier that all the diagnostic labels or categories
heretofore applied to people seem to make very little,
if any, sense. Based on the concept of homework,
however, one valuable distinction seems to emerge:
workers versus nonworkers. The latter category is not
to be confused with the familiar term, "unmotivated."
Many people who would be called motivated, because
they attend regularly, pay fees, participate in the
group, are nonworkers. The concept of motivation is
hypothetical: a worker, on the other hand, is a person
who uses suggestions given her by the therapist or
group members and tries them out, discarding those
that do not work and keeping those that do. Whether
a person is a worker or not is the best predictor of success known to me. Workers who seemed to other
therapists to be hopelessly psychotic have achieved
their goals within a year of group therapy, while nonworkers with minor neurotic symptoms have made
little change in one or two years.

I don't mean to imply that there is, after all, a category of people who are not O.K., namely nonworkers.
I am really only saying that some people's scripts have

built into them permission to work toward getting better. This means that they apply their Adult to their situation, listen to feedback, experiment with suggestions, and so on. These people have a much easier time giving up their scripts than others who don't have Permission to do the above. Giving nonworkers Permission to work is the first and most difficult task of therapists. Having a good contract and not playing Rescue are essential in the task.

The kinds of homework assigned are as varied as the problems they are intended to counteract. Some homework assignments are devised to overcome social anxiety by systematic desensitization, an approach borrowed from behavior therapy. A shy person, for example, is given increasingly difficult social tasks starting with one he finds simple to perform. Beginning with such things as asking the time of day on a busy street, the homework includes a number of items, each one to be performed repeatedly. Each homework assignment is more difficult than the last one: asking the time of day, then asking for elaborate directions; smiling at people in the street, then complimenting someone on his appearance; making small talk, and so on. The purpose is to teach how to obtain strokes. Another type of homework is assertion with significant persons. A person's homework may be to ask her boss for a raise, to tell her husband that from now on she will take a night out, to tell her mother-in-law to move out, or to call a man she likes and ask him for a date. The conversations involved are often rehearsed in group, and this procedure—as well as the whole activity of devising and assigning homework—is often the source of much fun.

A person who suffers from a contamination of the Adult such as "I am no good," "Everyone who says that they like me is lying to make me feel better," "The people in this group are communist agents," may be asked to write an essay defending the opposite point of view: "I am a good man," "People love me and like me," "The people in this group are just people like myself." One woman who called herself a monster was asked to draw a picture of it because she had

no words to describe it. Having done this, she was
able to realize what a distorted and unreasonable view
she had of herself.

Other forms of homework such as following a tight
schedule of activities, having fun, and looking up old
friends are assigned to teach people how to structure
time to replace an abandoned game. Homework can
be as varied as people's problems and has included
writing love poems, masturbating, spending a thousand dollars, fasting, staying awake for a whole night,
etc.

When homework is assigned, it is important to expect a report on it the following week. If the group
member did not do his homework it is reassigned,
and if this reoccurs his sincerity is challenged. Often
the assignment is too difficult and the homework has
to be redesigned to fit the capacities of the person.

These auxiliary techniques of group treatment am-
plify the therapeutic potency of the transactional
analyst. Clearly, as therapists experiment with new
techniques and creative practitioners explore the vast
array of possibilities which may increase their effectiveness, other approaches will be added to the tired
and tested approaches available today.

Unloading Negative Feelings

Another approach that amplifies the potency of a
group therapist is the use of two techniques designed
to clear up two common obstacles to effective group
interaction. These obstacles are stamps or held resentments, and the harboring of paranoid fantasies between group members. These two procedures can be
ritualized and performed at the beginning of every
meeting or they can be done more spontaneously
throughout meetings.

Held Resentments. I learned this technique at Ask-
leipieion, a therapeutic community within the Federal
Penitentiary at Marion, Illinois. It consists of making

it possible for people to release the accumulated feelings of anger, which people in the group may be holding from previous transactions. These feelings, called stamps in transactional analysis, are generated by game playing (see page 50) and when accumulated hinder frank communication and work between people. The process works most smoothly when it is done contractually, that is, the offer and acceptance of the stamps is prearranged. Once the stamp is delivered, the recipient of it is asked not to respond. If the person doesn't understand the nature of the stamp, he can ask for clarification. Example:

JACK: *I have a stamp for you, Fred. Do you want it?*
FRED: *O.K., I'll take it.*
JACK: *I resent the way you cut me off in the middle of a sentence during the last meeting.*
FRED: *I don't recall. Do you mean when you were talking to Mary?*
JACK: *No, when I was talking to John and you started talking about your own thing.*
FRED: *I understand.*

Notice that Fred needs only to understand the stamp, not necessarily to agree with it. It is also important that stamp exchanges alternate from person to person so that Jack will not follow up with another stamp for Fred nor will Fred respond with a stamp for Jack before someone else gives someone else (preferably neither Jack nor Fred) a stamp.

Paranoid Fantasies. A paranoid fantasy is a suspicion, a feeling of distrust, or a belief that another person does not mean well, which usually has a reason for existing. When people harbor such paranoias, it is very difficult for them to openly and freely work on their intimate problems. As a consequence, it is important that these be cleared by being openly expressed. The proper response to paranoid fantasy is an attempt to account for it by providing the grain of truth for its existence. Obviously a total discount of it will only heighten it and make it worse. Example:

FRED: *I have a paranoid fantasy for you.*
JACK: *O.K., I'll take it.*

FRED: *I think that you are jealous of me and actually really hate me. I think that you are especially
angry at the fact that I get along with Mary.*
JACK *(thinks carefully)*: *I don't hate you, but I am
annoyed at you and a little bit jealous. Part of my
jealousy is because of the way Mary listens to you but
won't listen to me.*
FRED: *Thank you. That makes sense.*

Unloading of held resentments and accounting for
paranoid fantasies is not just useful in group therapy.
Indeed, it is extremely useful when it precedes any
kind of meeting in which people wish to work fully
and cooperatively with each other.

Being able to express resentments and hearing justification for our paranoias makes the difficult work of
therapy easier and clears the way for Work.

22

The Therapy of the Three Basic Scripts: The Therapy of Depression

Scarcity of essential life support causes depression. People need food, shelter, space, safety, drinkable water, breathable air, and human contact (or strokes). Hungry, crowded, scared, and alienated people are sad and unhappy (the folk word for depressed) no matter what else is going on.

Scarcity can be caused by natural accidents or can be artificially created. Competition creates scarcity for many while providing for the few. I say this in spite of the fact that competition is touted to do the opposite, namely bring plentitude. Actually, the way it works in western society, competition between people brings about increased productivity, the major benefit of which is reaped by a privileged few with enough given back to people to keep them competing.

Because the audience of this book is Middle America—the average citizen who has a reasonable supply of food, shelter, space (maybe), safety, water, and breathable air (just barely)—I speak of the therapy of depression being aimed at the artificial scarcity of strokes which in this group is usually the cause of depression.

Depression is the single most common complaint of people who seek therapy. Whether in its mild, banal form or its severe, acute, tragic form, depression, as has been pointed out before, is the result of stroke deficit. Therapists who bother to ask their clients why they are depressed will find that most people (except

323

for the few who are couch-broken by previous therapists and have come to disbelieve their own common
sense) will say that they are depressed because they
have no friends or loving relationships or that their
loving relationships are not satisfactory. When depression becomes severe and begins to manifest itself in
the form of physical symptoms such as apathy, sleepi-
ness or sleeplessness, overeating or loss of appetite, a
constant tendency to cry, or suicidal thoughts, people will often lose sight of what it is that they are
missing. But in most cases of depression it will be
found that the person readily sees how her or his depression would be lifted if she or he could get a certain specific kind of stroke from a certain, specific
kind of person or persons. Thus the appropriate strategy for depression is teaching people the procurement
of the strokes that they want.

Breaking Down the Stroke Economy

The process of defeating the rules which maintain
the artificial scarcity of strokes is called *breaking down
the stroke economy*. In order to break down the
stroke economy and free up available strokes people
need to overthrow the injunctions that interfere with
stroke procurement—asking for strokes, accepting
strokes, offering strokes, rejecting strokes that are not
wanted, and giving oneself strokes are all permissions which will generate strokes and ultimately get
rid of depression.

People need to know what kind of strokes they
want. Strokes can be roughly divided into physical
and verbal. Physical strokes can be hugs, kisses, back-
rubs, being held, squeezed, touched, caressed. Physical strokes can be strong or light; they can be sexy,
sensual, or just friendly. They can be nurturing or
slightly teasing. Verbal strokes can be about a person's
physique—her face, her body, his posture and movements; or about a person's personality—her intelligence, his lovingness, sensitivity, courage, and so on.

People have specific needs for specific strokes, and these needs are often kept secret because people are ashamed of needing something and not being able to get it. In the same way in which people who are hungry blame themselves for being poor and not being able to afford food, so do people who are in need of strokes feel ashamed and embarrassed about their need. As a consequence, they keep the nature of the strokes that they want secret, the more so the more they crave them. A person who gets a lot of physical strokes, hugs, kisses, in some form, will have little difficulty asking for them (again, a case of the rich getting richer). However, a person who for some reason or another gets very few physical strokes and is in dire need of them, is very likely to be ashamed of his need and keep it secret. Samuels[1] points out that people *give* the kind of strokes that they want as a way of indicating their need. It can be seen that this method of getting strokes is very ineffective and in fact it creates even more scarcity. Typically, for instance, a man might want sexual strokes from his wife while she wants verbal strokes about being loved. As a consequence he gives her sexual strokes which she doesn't really want, and she gives him verbal strokes which he doesn't really want. The more she gives what he doesn't want, the less satisfied he is, the less he gives her verbal strokes, the more resentful she is —because she's not getting what she wants in return, and because she is giving away what she wants herself (creating an even greater feeling of need). The same is happening with him. This example is given to demonstrate that it is important that people learn to ask for (and give) what they want (and are asked for) in the way of strokes. In group work, Permission is given to disobey the injunctions about strokes in a number of different ways. In breaking down the stroke economy it may be useful to remember the following points:

[1]Samuels, Solon D. "Stroke Strategy: I. The Basis of Therapy." *Transactional Analysis Journal* I,3 (1971): 23–24.

Faith in human nature. Therapists are often afraid that certain individuals simply will not get strokes even if they ask for them. As a consequence, they are afraid of proposing stroke exercises for fear that certain people will not get the strokes they want. This fear is evidence of the fact that the therapist, like everyone else, believes that strokes are in fact a commodity and that they are in actual rather than artificial scarcity. The fact of the matter is that in a group of eight people, it is highly unlikely, if at all possible, that any person who asks for strokes will not be stroked to satisfaction. True, if a person asks for very specific kinds of strokes from a specific person, she may be disappointed. But if the strokes that are asked for are not specific and if the whole group is asked for them, it is a certainty that there will be enough strokes to satisfy the request. It is the nature of human beings to be loving, and therapists need to develop the kind of trust in human nature which will make it possible for them to fight against Stroke Economy without hesitation or apprehension.

Stroke starvation. Persons who are completely stroke-satisfied are rare. Because of this it is hard to describe the behavior of stroke-satisfied people. Certainly, it would be an extraordinary, novel and satisfying state to achieve. It would probably free the person for activities other than stroke procurement and it would be accompanied by a feeling of calm in the "I'm O.K., you're O.K." position. It is also likely that a stroke satisfied person would have no interest in consumer items which are strictly related to stroke hunger, such as new cars, new clothes, cosmetics, etc.

Because negative strokes have a certain value for the satisfaction of stroke hunger, people, when they get hungry enough, will be willing to take negative strokes just to keep going. Thus, depending on their stroke Survival Quotient,[1] some people will be able and some will be unable to reject negative strokes.

---

[1]Capers, Hedges, and Holland, Glen. "Stroke Survival Quotient." *Transactional Analysis Journal* I,3 (1971): 40.

One can't expect a stroke-starved person to reject "Plastic Fuzzies" any more than one can expect a starved person to reject rotten food.

Some people get stroke-starved because they reject good, available strokes. For instance, some men's tastes (see "Playboy," Chapter 15) have been perverted by the media so that they come to crave very special kinds of strokes[1] and will only accept them from *Playboy* centerfold models or their earthly look-alikes. Thus, they reject strokes from real, loving women around them and eventually wind up in a stroke deficit, "starving in the midst of plenty." This situation is similar to that of a city-dweller starving in a forest surrounded by roots and berries which he doesn't recognize as nutritious.

Acceptance and Rejection of Strokes. Taking in or accepting a stroke is a biological process, like eating, which requires a certain amount of time to be completed. Strokes have to be allowed to "soak in." Just as when one waters a plant in very dry soil where the water takes a certain amount of time to penetrate the soil, so do certain strokes and certain people have different "soaking times." In any case, when a stroke is given, it may take anywhere from five to fifteen seconds (or more) for it to be completely accepted.

A stroke can be rejected at a number of different levels. Some strokes are received with an obvious discount such as a shrug, a grimace, or an overt denial. For instance, a group member says to another: "I think you're a very intelligent person." The person might respond: "I don't think so; I don't believe that you really mean it. You probably are just trying to make me feel better. Anyway, I know I'm not intelligent, you must be putting me on." This kind of a discount is easily detected. However, strokes can be discounted in more subtle ways. It is because of this that it is important to carefully observe how a person receives the stroke and whether the stroke is "soaking

---

[1]Samuels, Solon D. "Stroke Strategy: I. The Basis of Therapy." *Transactional Analysis Journal* I,3 (1971): 23–24.

in" or being rejected. Stroke rejection is revealed by certain gestures, pauses, looks, sighs, reciprocation of the stroke, or a speedy "thank you." Very often when people receive strokes they immediately hear a statement from their Pig Parent to discount it. That statement is usually detectable in the face and body of the person in the form of a minute muscular change. It is important to demystify stroke discounts and to pinpoint the Pig Parent message which causes them.

The clearest indication that a stroke has been accepted fully is when a person receives it, smiles broadly and comfortably, and says nothing.

When a person receives a stroke that she does not want, it is important that she reject it outwardly and overtly. Sometimes it is hard to know whether a stroke that we receive is genuine or not, especially when our Pig Parent tells us that it isn't. As a consequence, it's important to air the fact that the stroke is, for the moment at least, not acceptable. Further investigation might result in the conclusion that the stroke was genuine and the rejection was caused by the influence of the Pig Parent or, and this is quite possible as well, that the stroke was not really a wanted stroke or, indeed, that it was actually not genuine. Which is which is best determined in a group context where the observers are usually objective and capable of helping to discriminate between the above alternatives.

Nurturing. Strictly speaking, strokes go from one human being to another (though it is possible to get strokes from other animals). However, people can accumulate strokes like food and water and stroke themselves with them. We are able to accumulate things we need to different degrees. Our bodies can only accumulate oxygen for about three minutes' worth of life, but we can store food and water for weeks. Strokes are stored, too. Kupfer[1] speaks of the Stroke Bank. I believe the ego state where strokes

---

[1] English, Fanita. "Strokes in the Credit Bank for David Kupfer." *Transactional Analysis Journal* I,3 (1971): 27–28.

are accumulated is the Parent. Positive strokes are accumulated in the Nurturing Parent and negative strokes are accumulated in the Pig Parent.

People with scripts have strong Pig Parents always willing to defeat the Child and weak Nurturing Parents that have no reserves of strokes to help them through rough times.

Thus, having a big, well-stocked Nurturing Parent for self-stroking is very important to maintain an O.K. feeling, though no matter how strong the Nurturing Parent, it is not possible to keep an O.K. feeling without a steady supply of strokes from others. Ultimately, feeling O.K. depends completely on the strokes we get. No one can maintain the "I'm O.K." position very long with no stroke input, and even less long when the only input is negative strokes.

Sometimes the Nurturing Parent accumulates strokes but can't use them because they are reserved exclusively for others. "Mother Hubbard" (see Chapter 14) is an example of such a person. Self-nurturing of self-stroking has to be learned by most people, and I will describe exercises to do this later.

Plastic vs. Warm Fuzzies. Strokes vary in their genuineness. Some strokes are thinly disguised critical statements, as, for instance, "You are very beautiful for someone's who's fat," or, "You are trying real hard." Other strokes are comparative in nature and arouse competitive feelings in people. For example, "You are the most beautiful person in this group," or, "I love you more than anybody," instead of "You are very beautiful," or, "I love you." It is important that people learn to give strokes which are genuine and not contaminated with competitiveness or critical Parent content. Contaminated strokes are called colloquially "Plastic Fuzzies," and people should learn to not give them and reject them when given.

One major situation in which people give phony or "plastic" strokes is when they feel they should give strokes and actually have none to give. Either because they are directly asked, but usually because a person is coming on Victim and hooking her, a person

may feel that she should "come across" with strokes.
Under such circumstances, it is often the case that
people will manufacture strokes that they do not actually feel. Needless to say, in a free stroke economy this is to be avoided, since it throws it completely
out of kilter by undermining its basic assumptions.
People need to believe that it is O.K. not to give
strokes to a person when they are not felt, since, in a
free stroke economy, someone else who feels them
will.

Touching. Touching is a therapeutic maneuver of
great potency which has fallen into disrepute, probably because of the problems associated with it. As
in the example of laughter where Fun is therapeutic
and the gallows transaction is harmful, the use of
touch needs to be thoroughly explored and its thera-
peutical potential isolated from its harmful possibilities. Touch is the most basic tissue transaction, and I
believe that it is an essential ingredient when working with the tragic extreme of scripts. In my opinion,
physical strokes are also a specific and powerful antidote to depression, except in the rare cases where it
is clearly related to organic causes.

It seems prudent at this time, though, due to a lack
of clear understanding about the negative effects of
touching, to handle this potent therapeutic tool with
care.

In groups, I avoid touching the people I work for
and encourage a maximum of touching between them.
I also discourage social contact between myself and
group members as well as intimate contact between
them outside of group sessions. I encourage social contact between group members and hope that they will
be available to each other for support and Protection.

Organizing a Stroking Community

The problem-solving group is an artificial situation
in which the rules of the stroke economy do not apply.

In time, people in the group will operate within this free stroke economy. However, clearly this is not a sufficient solution for a person who suffers depression and is unable to get strokes. That person needs to be able to obtain strokes in the world as well as in the group. Part of the task of the therapy in depression is to teach the person how to obtain strokes in the outside world where the rules of the stroke economy are usually in force. This requires that the person choose her friends and partners carefully and that she make agreements with them with respect to the free exchange of strokes. It is important for people who are depressed to relate to people who are willing to abandon the rules and to exchange strokes freely. Without being able to develop relationships with such people, it is not possible for a person who has a Lovelessness script to "close down the show" and put a new one on the road. As a consequence, working on a Lovelessness script requires that a person organize a circle of friends and loved ones outside the therapy group in which strokes are readily available. Only when a person has learned to ask for strokes, to give strokes, reject strokes, and to give himself strokes freely, and when he has learned to relate to people in such a way that strokes from other people are forthcoming, will it be possible to give up the Lovelessness script.

The following exercises have been useful in breaking down the stroke economy.

Exercises

1) *Giving Strokes.* The person needing to learn how to give strokes ("It") goes around the group and gives a stroke to every person in the group. Or "It" chooses one particular person in the group and gives her a series of strokes, as many as he can think of. Or each person in group asks for a specific kind of stroke and "It" gives it (only if he genuinely can do so, of course). This latter exercise is difficult and requires careful Protection.

2) *Asking for Strokes.* "It" stands up in the center of the room, and people give her strokes. She works on accepting them as they are given. Or, "It" asks a certain person to give her a certain specific kind of stroke that he has trouble taking, and she works on accepting it. In all of these exercises the whole group watches for "plastic fuzzies," how strokes "soak in," and gives Permission and Protection.

3) *Self-Stroking and Nurturing Parent.* "It" stands in the middle of the room and makes a series of positive statements about himself with the help of the group members who suggest ideas, object when the self-strokes are "plastic" or become self-criticism, and applaud when the strokes feel good. This exercise is called *bragging*. Bragging can be combined with asking for strokes and learning how to reject strokes that are not wanted.

Wyckoff[1] describes her exercise to develop the Nurturing Parent. In it, two or more people start by writing with crayons with their left hand (if right-handed)[2] on a large piece of paper what their ideal Nurturing Parent would be like—adjectives like "warm," "big," "smooth," "giving," "loving," etc. Next, on the other side of the paper, people write what they would like to hear from their ideal Nurturing Parent; sentences like "I love you," "You are beautiful," "Enjoy yourself," etc. Following this, each person reads, with appropriate feelings, what she has written.

Other group members help decontaminate the strokes, taking out veiled criticism, hidden conditions and expectations, and other Pig Parent content.

Now people exchange their lists and read them to each other in groups of two or three while they hold and stroke each other accordingly.

People can also read the list to themselves while looking in a mirror.

---

[1] Wyckoff, Hogie. "Permission." *The Radical Therapist* 2,3 (1971): 8–10. Reprinted in *Readings in Radical Psychiatry*. New York: Grove Press, 1974.

[2] It is believed that the dexterous hand is dominated by the Adult; therefore we use the other hand to elicit the feelings of the Child.

This exercise is especially good for people, particularly men, who have a Joyless script which is associated with the inability to use their Nurturing Parent on themselves and others.

4) *Massage*. Occasionally a group member is so stroke-starved that she can't take any verbal strokes offered. In those cases it is useful to suggest a group massage. Anonymous, clearly non-sexual strokes in large quantities along the head, the neck, the back, legs and feet. This "emergency stroke ration" is occasionally the best stroking for a person to get and paves the way for his being able to accept more specific strokes from specific people. Often it is the only way for a person to be able to cathect her Adult so as to work.

All of the above described exercises are for use in a group therapy situation. However, asking for, giving, accepting, and rejecting strokes, as well as self-stroking, can be practiced and rehearsed in the world at large. As has been mentioned before, it is necessary for people to take their experiences and learning from group into their everyday lives. Every one of these exercises can be practiced at home, at work, on the bus, while shopping, and so on. To be sure, the situation isn't as safe and protected as the group therapy situation, but if some care is exercised it is possible to successfully break down the stroke economy outside of the group, too.

It may be necessary to revise one's vocabulary and use words like *compliments* and *hugs* instead of strokes, and it is always important to be ready for a rejecting reaction from people. But while it is true that to attempt to break down the stroke economy in the "cruel world" could be met with an occasional rejection or discount, the facts are that most people are interested in strokes and warm fuzzies, willing to react generously, and able to enjoy attempts at freeing strokes.

In people's intimate lives outside of group, it is important that cooperative agreements about the desirability of freeing up the stroke economy be made. For instance, Mary, a group member, early in the therapy discussed with her husband Jack the ideas of strokes, warm fuzzies, and the injunctions against their free exchange. He agreed that these notions made sense and that he was willing to work cooperatively with her. His problem was a difficulty in giving nurturing verbal strokes, and hers was in giving sexual non-verbal strokes. Mary and Jack agreed to work cooperatively in these two areas of difficulty and succeeded in giving each other the strokes that they wanted, even though Jack was not himself in a therapy group.

Occasionally it happens that a person who, like Jack, is not involved in this type of therapy rejects and actually is unwilling to cooperate with strokes. When that is the case, and Mary has made every possible effort to no avail, it may be that Mary will not be able to continue in a relationship with Jack if she wants to give up her Loveless script, since the main source of strokes in her life is inadequate and likely to keep her in a stroke-starved state.

23

The Therapy of
Madness

As has been explained before, madness is the result
of systematic discounting, over a long period of time.
Discounting is a transaction. Like any other interpersonal situation the discount involves both the *discounter* and the *discountee* equally. The discounter
refuses to react to the discountee's statement. The discountee, on the other hand, is willing to go along with
the discounter's lack of reaction and does not pursue
the matter, letting the discount be. This is why certain
people are discounted more than others; because they
are willing to accept and compromise on being discounted. This is not to disregard an important additional fact, however, namely that discounters use power
plays to back up their discounts so that the discountee
is often one-down and unable to deal with the power
used against her. Thus, people who are frequently discounted, and come to experience the disorientation
and perhaps the eventual madness that is the result
of discounts, need to learn the antithesis to the discount which I called Accounting, and to deal with
power plays.

Accounting

Accounting is a process whereby a discount is neu-
tralized and the feelings that need to be accounted

for are responded to. Let us reconsider one example given previously:

JILL: *You think I'm stupid.*
JACK: *I don't think you're stupid.*

This time Jill is not willing to accept the discount and the ensuing confusion in her mind. She can now attempt to give an accounting of her feelings and demand that they be accounted for.

JILL: *Well, if you don't think I'm stupid, then why do I feel that you think I'm stupid? I would like to tell you. Do you want to know?*
JACK: *Yes.*
JILL: *The reason why I think so is that you continually interrupt me in the middle of sentences and that you often disagree with my point of view. When I try to explain something to you you often get a vacant look in your eyes and you stare through me. Finally, you repeatedly call me, albeit in jest, "dummy," "stupid," "dingbat," and refer to me that way to your friends. Because of this I have come to think that you think I'm stupid. So, I would like to know. Do you think I am stupid?*

You will notice that Jill's reaction to Jack's discount is no longer a series of confused and confusing internal or external statements. It is, instead, a systematic accounting of the reasons for her feelings and a demand that Jack respond to this accounting.

Jack now has to respond and either admit that he thinks Jill is stupid or, if he doesn't, he has to explain why he acts as if he does. In any case, he can hardly discount her feelings, and as a consequence Jill avoids the confusion that comes from being discounted.

One of the most frequent discounts happening in relationships is when one person asks another for strokes. Take as an example the following:

JILL: *Do you love me?*
JACK: *What is love?*

Jill may now try again.

JILL: *Actually, I don't think you love me.*

JACK: *For God's sake, how many times do I have to tell you that I love you?*

The above is a power play designed to stop Jill from asking that question. It is also a discount.

Let's assume that Jill is not stopped by Jack's power play and proceeds.

JILL: *I don't think you love me, and I'll tell you why. You haven't told me that you love me in the last five years unless I asked you and then you did so in a most grudging tone. You have not given me a single special present except on my birthdays. You have acted as if I was married to you, but not as if you are married to me. You seem to resent everything you do for me. And as a consequence I feel that perhaps you don't love me any more. I'd like to know, one way or another.*

Accounting is best taught in the group situation through role playing. The person learning Accounting acts out the situation with a discounter who does everything he can to evade the Accounting. Very often, when role playing, the discountee is dumbfounded at every renewed discount and has no idea how to proceed. At this point the rest of the group members can fill in suggestions on the best strategy to deal with the particular discount.

Discount Power Plays

Learning to account for one's feelings usually includes with it learning how to deal with power plays since discounters will often use cascading power plays (see Chapter 17) to back up their discounts. Thus, it isn't only necessary to know how to present one's feelings so that they are accounted, but it is also important to be able to use *power maneuvers* to stop the discounter's power plays.

Very often the discounter will refuse to continue a conversation when an accounting is demanded. She may stomp out of the room in a huff; she may refuse to discuss the matter any further; or she may change the subject. In every one of these cases, the discount is being backed up with a power play. Thus, it is important that the discountee learn how to deal with power plays.

The essential approach to discounts that are backed up with power plays is to stay in the Adult and to refuse to engage in any further cooperative aspects of the relationship until the discount is taken care of. For example, let us say Jill asks for an accounting of her feelings, having been hurt when Jack criticized the food she cooked, and he discounts her by storming out of the dining room. This is a unilateral decision by Jack to end the discussion, a frequent one-up power play called "The Meeting Is Adjourned." Later, when Jack wants to go to bed and have sex, Jill needs to bring up the discount and asks for an Accounting again and refuses to proceed with "business as usual" until an accounting of her feelings is forthcoming. The reader will perceive that this can become a highly emotionally charged procedure, and a person who is working on accounting for her feelings needs a great deal of support and backup (Permission and Protection) from her group.

Accounting is most likely to go smoothly and to be a rewarding experience between people who are in a cooperative relationship (see Chapter 25). It is quite possible, if the discounter is not committed to cooperate, that an accounting may never be forthcoming, as every attempt is stopped with a one-up power play. When that is the case, the person who is being discounted has no other choice but to terminate the relationship since as long as Accounting does not occur the relationship is one which necessarily feeds the madness script. Of course, some people would rather be driven mad than be alone; this can only be decided by the person himself. Yet, just as depression cannot be defeated without breaking down the rules of the stroke economy, so madness cannot

be defeated without obtaining an Accounting for
every discount that is absorbed.

Accounting for Paranoia

It is not possible for a therapist who herself discounts the people she works with to do effective work
with the Mindless script. Therapists discount the people they work with in a number of different ways. For
instance, it is not unusual in the first stages of therapy
for a therapist to form a notion of what is wrong with
the person and what the reasons are for his unhappiness, quite apart from and even in disagreement with
the person's own ideas of what is wrong. For example,
the person might feel that his difficulty is the result
of having a bad boss and living in the wrong part of
town. The therapist may conclude that the "real" reasons are quite different.

In this instance, the therapist might decide that the
person's problem at work is the result of a homosexual
attraction toward his boss, and that what the person
needs to do is to come to terms with his attraction.
As far as changing residences, the therapist might decide that it is an evasion of what is "really" wrong (latent homosexuality) so that the person should not
even think about changing residence.

Or the therapist, a transactional analyst, might decide that the problem is that the person isn't getting
enough strokes. If the therapist comes to and holds
his opinions irrespective of the person's differing
opinions about what's wrong, this is a discount. If the
therapist takes the discount to the point of not even
communicating these opinions to the person, then this
constitutes a lie in addition to the discount. The discount and the lie together will be perceived by the
person's Little Professor and will only add to his feeling of confusion, suspicion, and despair. As a consequence, it is absolutely necessary that therapists do
not discount the people they work for in any of the
ways exemplified above and that they be accountable
to them.

The therapist must see the relevance of the person's ideas and feelings in a situation. If the therapist can't, then it is necessary for the therapist to demystify this fact. For instance, in the case described above of the person who comes to group and speaks of his discomfort only in terms of how mean and ugly his boss is, the therapist may have a different opinion and express it as follows:

JACK: *I'm still really upset. My boss is getting worse. Yesterday he chewed me out for a mistake that somebody else made. I can't stand the guy. The other day he actually . . .*
THERAPIST (*interrupting*): *Jack, what I want to know is if you are getting any strokes this week.*
JACK: *Strokes? Are you kidding? I can't stand people! What I need is to get away from people. I have to move somewhere else. . . .*
THERAPIST: *Well, I think that the real problem is that you're not getting strokes. Until you get strokes you are not really going to get better.*

This is a transactional analysis discount of Jack's feelings. It may be in fact true that Jack needs to get strokes. But the therapist will not succeed in making this point because a much more important fact is being ignored, namely Jack's actual perceptions and feelings regarding the situation. These feelings are important; they have at least a grain of objective validity, and they must be taken seriously and accounted for. Consider the following alternative.

JACK: *I'm still really upset. My boss is getting worse. Yesterday he chewed me out for a mistake that somebody else made. I can't stand the guy. The other day he actually . . .*
THERAPIST: *Jack, I want to interrupt. I know that you're having problems with your boss and that it's hard for you to live where you are living. I am having some difficulty thinking that your boss and your living situation are the real reasons for your unhappiness. I believe that things would be a lot better for you if you were getting some strokes, and*

*I don't see you getting any. Instead, I see you being
so upset about your boss and your neighbors that
you're getting fewer and fewer strokes.*

JACK: *Well, I want to get strokes, but I just can't
stand the situation. And you should see my
neighborhood. It's nothing like where you live. I'll
tell you. . . .*

THERAPIST: *Well, perhaps we need to figure out
some way in which you can handle your boss and
your neighbors and eventually move out of your
neighborhood. I'm willing to help you work on that,
but I would like to know that you are willing to work
on your stroke situation as well, because I don't
think things are going to get better permanently
unless you do that. Is that a deal?*

JACK: *O.K., but I've got to take care of my boss first.*

THERAPIST: *O.K. Let's work on it.*

A therapist must account for people's feelings and
must realize (unless the person is simply lying, which
occasionally happens in public mental health agencies
where people are compelled to see therapists and
therefore lie about what's going on) that whatever the
person says he feels and perceives as the reason for
his difficulties is important information that needs to
be used and accounted for.

The most extreme case of Accounting that therapists
will need to do is the accounting that is necessary with
cases of paranoia. The usual reactions of therapists to
paranoid delusions and fantasies in their clients is to
decide that they are psychotic symptoms, completely
unfounded in reality. Thus they either ignore them,
try to work around them, or try to systematically dis-
prove them. None of these approaches is likely to have
any success whatsoever. I have found in my work
that the only approach that works with paranoia is to
account for whatever grain or large measure of truth
exists in the paranoid fantasies.

If a woman comes to therapy in the grips of paranoid jealousy about her husband in which she accuses
him of having sexual intercourse with every woman
in the apartment house and of trying to poison her, it

is important that the therapist, no matter how bla-
tantly paranoid the woman is, concentrate and focus
not on the obvious untruth of her views about her
husband, but on the possible truth about them. The
therapist should investigate closely why she thinks that
her husband is having intercourse with all of the
neighbors or why the husband is trying to poison her.
I have found, time after time, that in the case of such
paranoia, there is always a grain of truth which is
being discounted. The husband may not be actually
having intercouse with all the neighbors, but he
flirts with a number of them and is very attracted to
one of them! When his wife confronts him with this
fact he denies it repeatedly and admits to no attraction or interest at all. The husband may not be trying
to kill her, but he may be entertaining fantasies of
divorce or having her committed to a mental hospital,
to which she is attuned and, once again, he may completely deny these thoughts. Both of these actions by
the husband backed up by discounts are sufficient
to lay the foundation for acute paranoia in the woman,
and if demystified and accounted for will bring her
paranoia to an end.

Therapists need to have a healthy respect for the
mental lives of the people they work with. All of their
"bizarre" fantasies, "inappropriate affects," "thought
disorders," are part of the legitimate mental life of
people whose minds have been battered by discounts
and lies. Any person exposed to similar discounts and
lies will eventually react similarly. A therapist who
regards these reactions from the detached, one-up
position of seeing them as symptoms of some underly-
ing mental illness is simply going to make the situation worse and is certainly not going to be able to help.

I have found the above approach to madness, or
what is called in psychiatric circles "schizophrenia,"
to be speedily effective in the cases of people coming
to me for help, when they are relatively untouched by
the destructive machine of psychiatric hospitalization,
drugging, and shock therapy. An excessive dose of
this kind of oppressive, damaging treatment can, in
my estimation, make success in therapy a more diffi-

cult task. The torture of psychiatric commitment
leaves a deep mark upon the souls of people, one that
may take much love, nurturing, and devotion to
neutralize and replace with feelings of trust and well-
being. People who have Madness scripts should avoid
involvement with psychiatric commitment, especially
if it isn't *completely voluntary*. By completely voluntary, I mean that there are no locked doors and the
person can call out or leave with all of his belongings
at will, at any time, and that no "therapeutic" procedures (individual or group therapy, medication, shock
therapy, etc.) will be administered against the person's will or be a requirement of his stay in the hospital. If entering a hospital is necessary, it is a good idea
to have the name and phone number of a lawyer
sympathetic to the person's rights as a "mental patient," who can intercede speedily in her behalf if the
treatment "suddenly" becomes involuntary. Even so,
it will be difficult for a person in a mental hospital to
resist the subtle pressure applied for voluntary "informed consent" to oppressive psychiatric procedures.

24

The Therapy of
Joylessness

Establishing contact with one's bodily responses of joy and pain is the process of Centering indispensable in work with drug abuse.

Centering body work as applied to script analysis is in its pioneering stages. However, enough is known to be able to make some preliminary statements which readers may find useful.

Centering body work is based on the systematic re-establishment of contact with one's bodily functions. This process can be effectively approached through the breathing function. Breathing is an effective approach because it is both involuntary and under voluntary control. Most of the time we breath involuntarily; it happens "by itself" just like our heartbeat, the movement of our bowels through out intestines, the filtering of the blood in our kidneys, and so on. However, unlike the other functions mentioned, breathing is also under voluntary control. As a consequence, control of breathing is a very good beginning in the process of regaining touch with the rest of our body's functions.

Our breathing is usually shallow and insufficient. If we force air in and out of our lungs, by breathing first into our bellies, then into our chests, and up into the shoulder areas, and then exhale completely, we drive an unusual amount of oxygen into our lungs, into our blood stream, and eventually into the cellular tissue of our whole body. The result of this hyperventilation is that areas of our body which are split off and operate at very low levels of feeling energy become ener-

gized. When these areas of our body which are split
off from our Center and are basically dead to us—
hypertense or inactive and flabby—are oxygenated
and energized, we become aware of them; they actually *feel* dead, paralyzed or highly wound up. The
person now experiences the part of the body which is
split off as it really is: paralyzed, inactive, clumsy,
tight, twisted, detached, and so on.

For instance, a woman, Ann, who had beautiful,
long legs was usually not aware of them except when
people stared at them or as she put garments on them
to show them off or hide them. (She did not think
them beautiful but silly and ugly-looking.) Her legs
did not *feel* like anything except occasionally when
they hurt from walking too much. Generally, they
just "moved around down there" getting her from one
place to another. Her gait was slightly awkward as
she walked with her weight placed on her toes rather
than on her whole feet. She felt about her legs as one
feels about a bicycle: they were locomotion devices
and not part of her—unlike her face, head, shoulders,
and breasts which she felt very connected with and
where she felt her Center to be. Deep breathing, energizing her legs with excess oxygen, caused her to suddenly *feel* her legs. The split between her legs and her
"self" was temporarily gapped. She now was aware of
how her legs always felt, without her head, her Center, knowing it. The feeling in her legs was, she
realized for the first time, that they were dead, and as
if wrapped in a tight bandage like a mummy's legs
are. She also realized that they (her legs) longed to
take great strides; that they wanted to be bare and
exposed to the wind and sun; that they hated to be
certain of leering looks which usually came from men.

Later, the vividness of her "leg feelings" subsided,
but she retained a tenuous yet very real sense of them.
She was especially aware of her legs longing to walk,
climb, run in the air and sun. She became aware of
the body injunctions about her legs, mostly sex role-
based, which said "Don't spread your legs (it's sexy),"
"Don't bare them (they are provocative)," "Don't run
(it's not ladylike)," and attributions like "You have

beautiful legs (sit still and let the gentlemen look at them)." She decided to buy short hiking pants and let herself walk wherever she wanted to. If people looked at her legs, she hid them if she disliked their looks and let them be if she enjoyed them. Her legs changed physically; they became firmer, more grace-ful; but, more importantly, they became part of her Center, gave her much pleasure, and received much welcome attention from herself and others. She prob-ably will get around on them gracefully and vigorously for as long as she lives, unlike her mother who at age sixty-five can only shuffle from place to place and has lost all sense that her legs could be able to transport her swiftly and competently.

This single, dramatic example of Centering through breathing is just one of the ways that Centering body work can help in defeating banal and tragic life scripts.

I am aware of the fact that the above account is incomplete, especially with regard to the techniques of deep breathing that bring about such changes in con-sciousness. This is not unintentional; as I said before, my understanding of this approach is incomplete. Bio-energetics as developed by Wilhelm Reich is being practiced by people who have a great deal more experience in it than I. Interested readers can learn or seek therapy from one of them. Needless to say, I recommend that the choice be made carefully, just as I suggested in the section on Common Sense in Chap-ter 18. There are some techniques for Centering which I have used effectively in groups and which I shall describe now.

Breathing

As explained above, deep breathing brings us in touch with our body and our emotions; it can tell us what parts of our body are dead, what parts of our body are alive, and so on. Ideally, breathing should be slow and deep, with the lungs going from complete in-flation to complete deflation at every breath. This

would keep the body fully oxygenated in the most
efficient way. Instead, people take short, frequent
breaths at the top or at the bottom of the breathing
range and often hold their breath completely when
scared or anxious. With some people it is as if a large
invisible hand were wrapped around their chests, making it impossible to inhale fully and forcing them to
breathe into their bellies. With others the squeezing
hand is wrapped around the belly preventing full exhalation.

Incomplete inhalation or exhalation causes shorter,
more frequent breaths; oxygenation is chronically incomplete. Inhalers never clear their lungs completely.
When they do, through deep exhalation or coughing,
the air is stale and old. With lungs fully inflated, it is
easy to shout and scream but hard to plead, cry, or
whisper. Exhalers never fill their lungs completely.
With lungs deflated, it is easy to whisper or cry but
hard to speak with conviction and volume. Thus,
when I feel that people need to express tender feelings, I ask them to exhale repeatedly. Conversely, I
ask people who need to be strong, angry, or convincing to breathe repeatedly at the top of their breathing
range.

People in group therapy often launch into long,
emotionless accounts which leave the observers without the slightest idea of what's going on. Their statements seem to emanate from their mouths automatically, while their body, racked in fear or pain, huddles
tightly into itself. By the simple device of deep
breathing it is possible to facilitate the establishment
of the connection with the body so that an actual,
clear account of the situation emerges. When the person is asked to do three or four minutes of deep breathing and then to repeat the story, having now established some contact with the feelings associated with
the situation, her story now becomes comprehensible.
It has a point; it feels real; people can empathize
with it and comprehend it; it can be dealt with. The
above two techniques are, so far, the only ones I can
recommend with confidence to transactional group
therapists for routine use.

Centering

Centering is barely hinted at in this chapter. It needs to be understood and explored and translated for use in group therapy. At this time I am personally involved in investigating this form of script analysis. I don't have additional techniques to offer here. I can only suggest what benefits this work could bring for people who might pursue it.

Free of bodily injunctions and attributions, I believe that people could learn to use, train, and control their own bodies in the same elaborate and intricate way in which they have learned to use, train, and control their minds. People would be able to regulate their heartbeat and blood pressure; they would be able to slow down or hurry up their digestion and metabolism. Women would be able to bring on their menstrual periods. Men would be able to control ejaculation. As people learn to have power over their bodies they might be able to kill malignant tumors by controlling their blood supplies. They would be able to fight infections and eliminate toxic substances far more effectively than most people can now. They would be able to do things with their bodies which are considered "miraculous" by medicine today.

On the other hand, people would be more sensitive to pain and noxious stimuli and would be unable to smoke or drink coffee excessively or tolerate, much less enjoy, oppression and persecution without constant painful awareness of it and a resulting constant tendency to throw it over. They would become sensitive to the side-effects of drugs and unable to overlook them. They would not need drugs to regain touch with their bodies.

Such persons would deeply enjoy their body functions. Moving, breathing, standing, running, sleeping, straining, relaxing, crying, defecating, sex, and orgasm would all be unitary, organic functions involving the whole person pleasurably.

Having been spared script attributions such a person would not overuse and eventually overdevelop any part of the body, such as his head, to neglect the rest of it. He would not have an inflated chest within which the heart works itself to early exhaustion. She would not have an overdeveloped belly, full of feelings which have no place to go because she can't have them accounted for.

People whose minds are in good touch with the rest of their bodies can be said to be Centered as opposed to being split-off. When Centered, all of the physical functions work in harmony and unison; the person is physically focused. Centering has been taught and mastered in the martial arts for centuries. When a martial arts black belt is under attack and she means to defend herself, the whole of her faculties and functions is focused on that task. Her breathing, heartbeat, circulation, vision, hearing, and all her senses and masculature are Centered around self-defense. She hears no voices in her ear saying "You're going to die" or "Better run." Her legs don't tremble. She has no contradictory impulses to flee or plead or surrender. When she receives, deflects, and retaliates a blow it is done with as nearly all of her concentration as humanly possible: a fearsomely powerful, completely focused, thoroughly honest act in which every fiber of her being is involved.

In the same manner as described above, people can think, play, love, intuit, speak, listen, or be completely quiet. People who are Centered emanate energy and are seen by some to show a special aura, sometimes called charisma, which never fails to inspire others (mostly favorably but at times with antagonism). The kind of personal power that comes with Centering, when complemented with the full use of one's loving capacities and one's capacities to think rationally and intuitively, is a firm basis for autonomy. Cooperative relationships between autonomous human beings are, in my mind, the foundation for the Good Life to be explored in the next section. So far as Centering goes, I hope to learn a great deal about the subject in the next years and encourage my readers to do the same.

SECTION 5
The Good Life

25

Cooperation

About three thousand years ago, Moses descended from Mt. Sinai with the Ten Commandments. One of these Commandments was "Thou Shalt Not Kill." At that time it was a novel thought that one was not free to kill one's fellow human beings. In order to conform to it people had to believe that it was a command from God Himself. Today we may be coming to a point in history where sanctioned killing will not only not be permissible but it may actually come to a virtual end. When killing and torture are no longer allowed in the affairs of people, the next step may be to get rid of lying and deception. And eventually, perhaps, the misuse of psychological power—power plays—will be given up by people as well. Perhaps people will come to believe that everyone is born equal, and equality will not only be talked about, but will be reflected in the feelings and actions of most people. Cooperation between autonomous, independent, powerful human beings could then be the rule rather than the exception.

Cooperation on a large, international scale is a far distant dream. However, cooperative relationships are possible between people under special circumstances; and, as far as I can see, large scale cooperation can only come about after many people in many small groups learn to cooperate with each other.

Cooperation Rules

How then are we, who live in a society in which there is plenty, to take advantage of this plenitude? The answer is: cooperation. Cooperation is a mode of interpersonal relations which, based on the assumption that there is no scarcity of basic needs (food, shelter, space), provides an opportunity for everyone to have everything they need.

One very good context in which to learn and struggle against individualism and competitiveness and toward achieving cooperation is the couple. The situation in which two people are in an intimate, long-term relationship is a situation in which the seeds of individualism and competitiveness cause great trouble and can be successfully defeated. Individualism and competitiveness are best pursued as a person standing alone. If one has no close ties to anyone, one hardly notices how individualism and competitiveness are destructive forces. It first becomes clearly destructive in a couple or family situation. The couple is the most available and protected laboratory for personal relationships, and a situation for which people have a great deal of energy to struggle. Thus, cooperation is most easily worked on in a couple. Also, cooperation is easier between two rather than three or more people. Therefore, this section devotes most of its attention to cooperation between two people, but applies to all sizes of human groups.

Two people who decide that they want to enter into a cooperative relationship need to agree on several things:

1. *No scarcity*. There is between them a satisfying quantity of what they need from each other. This agreement is not necessarily always obtainable since in some cases people do not have what they need for each other. Some people cannot provide the freedom, security, willingness to share, support, and knowledge that others need. For instance, with respect to sexual

needs, one person may want to have sexual inter-course twice a day, and the other person may not want to have any sex at all. When the discrepancy between what people want is so large that there can be no compromise, there is in fact a situation of scarcity which cannot be remedied. In the above situation it's not very likely that a cooperative compromise can be achieved. However, in most situations the discrepan-cies are not so large, and a cooperative compromise can be arrived at. A more common situation might be the one in which one person wants to have daily sexual intercourse while another person would prefer to have sex only every third day. Here, based on the assumption that there need not be scarcity, compro-mises can be arrived at so that both people can feel satisfied. For instance, one couple in such a situation agreed that the person with larger sexual needs would be willing to masturbate while the other person held and gave her loving strokes. This took the pressure off both and eventually equalized their sexual wants.

We have found that cooperation of this sort tends to bring about a plenitude of what might at first have been scarce. The above exemplifies how artificial scarcity comes about. This couple had a "sexual" prob-lem which could easily have become complicated into a case of "impotence" for the man as he became more and more anxious due to her sexual demands, ending in complete scarcity of sexual strokes for both. The "problem," however, was based on their strict ad-herence to stroke economy rules which do not allow sexual self-stroking, especially in the presence of an-other person. But, as he asked for what he wanted and she compromised, they broke down the stroke economy and created sufficient and satisfying sexual strokes for both of them.

2. *Equal rights.* Given that there is enough of what is needed "to go around," the next agreement is that both of the persons have equal rights to satisfaction and equal responsibility in the process of cooperation.

A person may be aware that there is enough to go around and still not be willing to share and struggle to bring about the equalization of what there is. For instance, sex-role scripting causes relationships between men and women to have built-in inequities which, on the whole, favor the man. For example, it is expected that women will do a larger proportion of the housekeeping even if both are employed, and most certainly if she is not. She may work at home as long and hard as he does at his job, but it is assumed that he is entitled to more leisure time than she. If she asks for equal leisure time he might agree that he gets more but be unwilling to equalize it based on his male privilege.

On a more subtle level, men are encouraged to expect to get more nurturing strokes than they give. Typically, when confronted with this inequity, they acknowledge it, but may not work to change it—once again, holding on to their privilege.

The inequities are not always in favor of the man, however. For instance, women expect men to do most of the work in their sexual life. Men are supposed to initiate, direct, and successfully complete sexual relations. When this inequity is pointed out women often balk at giving up their privilege, and refuse to work to change it.

One couple's work toward cooperation developed as follows:

She wanted nurturing and caring strokes when she got sick or when she was afraid. He knew this, and even though he knew what she needed he did not comply with her needs. He didn't work on the problem on his own accord. He would give her the strokes when she asked, if she asked "nicely," but never initiated nurturing. He didn't show any interest or put any energy in sharing the strokes he had for her.

For a while, she tried to deal with the problem by withdrawing her strokes for him, but this only created further scarcity and did not solve the problem even though it equalized the flow of strokes.

Eventually, they worked the problem out by a mutual giving up of privilege. They agreed to the following: He would work on his difficulty with giving strokes to her if she worked on her jealousy about his giving strokes to other people, including other women. He became willing to give up his unequal share of her strokes, and she became willing to give up her unequal share of his.

3. *No power plays.* The effective establishment of a cooperative relationship is also based on the agreement that power plays are not an option under any circumstances. Power plays are based on the assumption of scarcity and competitiveness and are the antithesis of cooperative behavior and must be given up as a method of getting what one wants in a cooperative relationship.

This point seems simple at first, but it turns out to be one of the most difficult cooperative agreements to honor. We are deeply immersed in fears of scarcity and thoroughly trained to use power of one sort or another to get what we want. Threats, sulking, yelling, banging doors, discounting, and so on are more accessible to us as approaches to what we want than discussion and negotiation. Both partners need to be on the lookout for power plays and willing to call, and be called, on them and stop as soon as they happen.

4. *No secrets.* If cooperation is to exist, there must be no secrets kept, especially about what one wants. Thus, everyone in the situation must ask for everything they want 100% of the time.[1] The tendency to use power plays to get what one wants is coupled with the inability to know or ask for what one wants clearly and openly. The reason for this is that in a competitive situation to reveal what one's needs are is to warn one's competitor of where the demand is going to be so that fears of scarcity for the supply will be aroused. As a consequence, people in a competitive, individualist situation are thoroughly trained and indoctrinated into not saying what their wants are, and for good reason, since to express one's needs will immediately decrease the supply of what is needed and create further scarcity of it. However, in a cooperative situation,

---

[1] Wyckoff, Hogie. "Between Women and Men." *Issues in Radical Therapy* I,2 (1973): 11–15.

to ask for what one needs is a basic requirement for
satisfaction. Given a context of willingness to struggle
against competitiveness, to say what one wants is the
first step to getting it. It will immediately enlist the
interest and energy of the others to provide satisfaction of those wants. In the work to achieve cooperation
one of the biggest problems is that people either will
not say what they want or are not actually in touch
with it and eventually become resentful because they
don't get it.

Paradoxical as it may seem, to ask for everything
that one wants 100% of the time seems an individualist and competitive move, yet it is an essential aspect
of the struggle against competitiveness and individualism. One only needs to understand that to ask for
what one wants 100% of the time is *not* the same as to
grab, to outfox, to cajole people out of what they
want; it is simply stating one's position, a position with
which everyone who has stated theirs can cooperate
and negotiate.

I do not mean to imply that in a cooperative situation everyone will get what she or he wants immediately. However, the process by which what one wants
is modified by what others want in a cooperative
situation is amazing, an almost magical event, so that,
often, when it doesn't seem possible that there will be
enough for everyone it turns out that there is. It
appears that people's drive toward cooperation is as
strong as their drive for food, for shelter, for strokes; so
that one's need for food, for shelter, or strokes can be
very strongly modified by one's need to cooperate.
The pleasure in supplying for others what they need,
which is a function of the Nurturing Parent, the
source of the cooperative instinct, in many cases over-
rides the needs for sex, food, and other material goods.
Felt needs for items which are in short supply actually
decrease in the presence of others with whom one
can cooperate by sharing, while the artificial consumer
needs created by merchandising and advertising are
dramatically diminished.

The effect of cooperation on consumer needs becomes most visible in larger groups. This country is

made up essentially of pairs of people and their children living under separate roofs with one refrigerator, one stove, one washer, one or two cars, etc. Eight people and their children could live equally well, provided they were able to cooperate, with the same refrigerator, stove, washer, and perhaps three cars. Further, the decrease in competitiveness would diminish their need to "keep up with the Joneses." Finally, strokes would be in less scarcity, so that consumer needs which are based on stroke hunger (cosmetics, drugs, new clothing, automobiles, and so on) would be sharply diminished.

In the event that in the cooperative process a person does not get what she wants, it is part of the agreement that she continue to ask for what is needed as often as possible and that she make clear that she is satisfied. Her dissatisfaction, if not expressed, will be accumulated in the form of resentment which can build into the tendency to become angry and resentful and, once again, individualist, competitive and grasping. Generally, a person who does not get what he wants, a person who is in need of something, is scripted in a competitive society to blame himself for his unfulfilled needs. As an example, poor people blame themselves for their poverty, with ample help from the rich. They attribute it to lack of drive, lack of will power, etc. People who are hungry often feel ashamed of the fact. People who are sexually in need find it hard to admit to it. It is extremely important that the self-blame, the taking onto oneself the cause of one's oppression, be fought by not going along with the feelings of shame and worthlessness and asking for what one wants. A cooperative society is based on the assumption that everyone is O.K., everyone wants to contribute, and everyone deserves enough of everything she or he needs.

5. *No Rescues.* A fifth requirement for an effective cooperative situation is that there be No Rescues. While people are supposed to ask for 100% of what they want, it is also important that if they do not ask others to provide for their needs, others do not act out of

shame or guilt or misguided nurturing without having a clear sign that the need exists. In this particular situation, a Rescue would be to do things or go along with situations which one does not want because one suspects that the other person, now seen as Victim, powerless to fend for himself, wants them. This is a Rescue which violates the contract to ask for what one wants, for both the Rescuer and the Victim. It also re-creates the situation in which power plays to arouse guilt and shame can be used to get what one wants instead of asking for it.

On the other hand, it is also important that in a cooperative situation people do not persecute each other through anti-Rescue, which is an exaggerated disregard of what one guesses other people want. Anti-Rescue, which is a kind of hardening of one's perceptions of other people's needs for the purpose of not Rescuing, is Persecutory. For example, in one couple, the woman decided to stop Rescuing her husband's needs for nurturing, which she had routinely satisfied without his requests or thanks. She stopped guessing what he needed and took a hard anti-Rescue stance which frightened and angered him. This was an incomplete solution; in group, she worked out a non-Persecutory, non-Rescuing stance in which she would still be aware of his needs and make this awareness clear to him, but refused to nurture him unless he asked for and actively appreciated her nurturing. She also made a trade agreement for nurturing from him, when she needed it. This was not a Rescue because she did not do anything he didn't ask for, but it also defeated the tendency to Persecute because it offered a vehicle for the satisfaction of his needs.

No matter how smoothly a cooperative struggle goes, it often happens that one person is reluctant or unwilling to cooperate at one time or another. The proper response in this temporary non-cooperation is to be quite explicit about one's feelings of disappointment. The withdrawal of sharing, as a response to a clearly uncooperative move on someone else's part, is a legitimate maneuver in a cooperative struggle. This is especially clear in situations with children, who often either overtly refuse to cooperate or give up completely in their cooperative efforts. In this case it's legitimate to act in a manner which withdraws one's own willingness to cooperate and share. This is not a power play because it is an honest, above-board, and overt maneuver based on one's feelings. One simply loses interest in cooperating in the presence of unco-operative people. Therefore, once again, based on the rule that one should say what one wants all the time, it is a legitimate approach.

For example, in a cooperative household involving children, the expectation is that they contribute their efforts. Chores, being helpful, anticipating people's needs, not disrupting, entertaining, and taking care of themselves, all are ways in which children can co-operate. Children who contribute their energy to the household are appreciated and liked. One wants to do things for them, spend time with them.

When children refuse to cooperate, the opposite re-action occurs. One dislikes them, one does not want to do anything for them. In one household the parents stopped being helpful in many small ways to a ten-year-old who was not cooperative. They stopped making special treats, taking her to her friends, invit-ing her to movies, cooking minor meals like breakfast or snacks. This was done without vindictiveness or anger, but simply because it no longer felt right in light of the girl's behavior. Cooperation was the child's renewed choice soon after she saw the loss incurred due to her lack of cooperation.

Two, Three, or More

The struggle for cooperative behavior, which as I said before is most easily engaged in within a couple, can be expanded to a couple and children, or to three, four, five, or more people. In every case it requires that the above agreements be respected; and while the struggle between people who are not cou-ples is often not as committed and has less cohesive-ness to carry it through difficult spots, it is also quite possible and desirable. Clearly, the difficulties multiply the more people there are involved, and the two-person situation seems an almost indispensable first step. It appears to me that in a gradual process where one moves from competitiveness to cooperation, from acting alone to acting in groups, the first step is cooperation between two people in which the struggle is most easily pursued and moving from there to larger groups of people.

26

Child-Rearing for Autonomy

Looking at the script matrix, one can put oneself in the position of the offspring or the parents. Transactional script analysis deals mostly with the difficulties that people experience as offspring, but an inescapable question in relation to scripts is, "As a parent, how can I bring up my children in the best possible way, given these ideas?"

How much should children be taught? How much should they be disciplined? How much should they be left alone? How much should they be told or not told? Injunctions are made to sound harmful, but isn't it necessary to enjoin children from certain behavior harmful or to their disadvantage? How do we make certain that our feelings about our children aren't unwitting programs for them to follow against their own better judgment? How do we raise children to have a maximum amount of autonomy without taking the risk that they will be neglected, without self-discipline, goals, values, or ideals? How do we raise libertarians without raising libertines?

Once again, the solution is based on faith in human nature; the firm belief that people, including children, are O.K. and, if given a chance, will do O.K. As a consequence, if one follows this point logically, bringing up children is a matter of allowing them to discover what it is they want and not interfering with their spontaneity, their awareness, and their intimacy.

Children *will* do what is right for them, given the freedom to choose and circumstances in which the

362

choices can be made without stress or pressure. Power plays are not necessary to cause or help children to do what is good for them; they will do it on their own accord.

Take, for instance, the example of an eight-year-old who on a weekday wants to stay up late to watch television. Parents know that a child needs about ten hours of sleep to be able to function adequately, and most parents would be inclined to set a bedtime and insist that it be kept. Suppose now that Mary, who has to get up at seven o'clock in the morning, wants to stay up beyond nine o'clock in the evening. What are her parents' choices in this matter? Should they enforce a nine o'clock bedtime by insisting on it and using power tactics such as withdrawing strokes, commands, yelling, turning off the television, spanking, or maybe even forcibly undressing the child and putting her to bed if necessary? To be sure, most children wouldn't rebel against a nine o'clock bedtime to the point where they'd have to be forced into bed. However, some sort of resistance, we assume, will be encountered from Mary who wants to stay up beyond nine o'clock. The parents in this situation are up against their own faith in human nature. If we assume that Mary is an intelligent human being capable of making valid decisions in the affairs that concern her, I as a parent would like her to exercise this capacity and trust her to choose well. As far as I'm concerned, Mary has the right to stay up as late as she wants, to get as little sleep as she will, and to be cranky all the next day if she so chooses.

You may ask, "What if she oversleeps and misses her bus and therefore has to either be driven to school or put in a cab or even stay at home the next day?" Mary's selfishness of the night before might result in her missing school or creating a large inconvenience for her parents the morning after.

This is a good question; and the answer is that autonomy does not include the freedom to cause inconvenience or pain to others. So long as a certain action affects the person alone, cooperative child-rearing for autonomy demands that the person be given the choice and be allowed to make it. If the choices made result in some harm or inconvenience to other people, then the people inconvenienced have a right to demand that that kind of a choice not be made again. If Mary stays up and oversleeps, misses the school bus, and has to be driven to school, then—but only then—can the parents begin to make certain demands with respect to her bedtime.

Suppose that Mary stayed up and overslept. Now she wants to stay up late once again. The parents notice this and ask her to go to bed.

"Mary, I would like you to go to bed. It's past nine o'clock."

"But I want to watch this program, and it ends at eleven o'clock."

"I don't think that's a good idea, Mary, because last time you stayed up you overslept, and I had to drive you to school."

"I won't oversleep this time. I'll set the alarm."

Mother could now power play Mary and force her to go to bed, or she could once again give Mary a choice; but this time with some reasonable, cooperatively arrived at conditions.

"O.K., Mary. I don't think it's a good idea. I think you're going to have trouble getting up. But I think you should do what you think is best for you. However, I'm not going to get up to wake you tomorrow morning or drive you to school; and if you oversleep I would like you to pay for the cab out of your allowance, or walk to school, no matter how late. Do you agree?"

"O.K., Mom. Can I pay for the cab by doing dishes?"

"Fine. Enjoy your program."

Chances are that Mary will wake up and go to school in time. If she doesn't and has to walk to school, she will probably choose not to watch television next time rather than take a chance on being too sleepy in the morning.

The above example shows how it is possible to allow Mary to choose what she wants to do, to allow her to experience the consequences of her choice, without, at the same time, allowing her to interfere with other people's well-being. When Mary is given this kind of freedom in a host of situations beginning as soon as she is able to make such choices, she will grow accustomed to making decisions which are based on her own judgment. Her judgment will include her responsibilities toward others. Children who are obedient and follow orders become accustomed to doing things as they are told without understanding why and without autonomy. Children raised under this kind of program are mysteriously expected, once they are emancipated, to suddenly be able to make decisions and choices on their own. The fact is that most children's upbringing gives them no opportunity to choose, gives them no opportunity to experience the consequences of their choices, and gives them no opportunity to make cooperative choices which respect the rights of other human beings.

But suppose now that the reason why Mary stays up late at night has something to do with the fact that she really doesn't want to go to school and that she would rather watch television than ready herself for school the next morning. She may even secretly hope that if she stays up late she will oversleep and not have to go to school. What are parents to do— since at this point Mary would not only welcome oversleeping but would also welcome missing the bus and perhaps even not being driven to school? This is a more complicated situation. What are parents to do about the fact that some children don't like to go to school and that they'll do anything to avoid it? I want to answer this question with another question. What interests *you* more: freedom, or school attendance? Do you want to bring up children to do things they don't enjoy, and which are not likely to be good for them? If a child does not enjoy school, chances are that the school is not a good place for the child. Once again, faith in human nature demands that we assume that children will be interested in learning when learning is interesting, that children want to go to school when school is a good place for them. It stands to reason that if school is a nasty, uptight, competitive place filled with social and racial strife, authoritarianism, and injunctions against spontaneity, awareness, and intimacy, children might want to stay away from it. But the law says children have to go to school. So what are parents to do?

Clearly, the problem now proliferates. Parents who want to raise children who are free and not bound by oppressive and defeating scripts may have a great deal more to do than to follow certain simple cooperative formulas at home. It is not conducive to autonomy to force a child to go to a bad school no matter how cooperative the home situation. As a consequence, parents may have to choose between not sending children to the school (which means sending them to a better school which they may not be able to afford, or keeping them out of school altogether), or putting demands on the school, organizing, and becoming social activists in behalf or their children so that school becomes a better place and the child may want to go to it.

Personal freedom, autonomy, scriptlessness cannot be achieved in the midst of oppressive circumstances. We are not able to raise our children without scripts unless we deliver them into a social situation in which they can make free choices.

When parents have to work excessively hard or do not have the means to provide reasonable environments for their children, when families live in isolated, competitive units, each fending for its own, each desperately struggling to eat, sleep, and stay alive from day to day, there is very little room for awareness, spontaneity or intimacy.

But let us imagine now a home situation which has a certain measure of ease. The parents are not overworked and underpaid. The schools are reasonable. There is enough room, food, and leisure, so that cooperation and child-rearing for autonomy can be given a try.

In such a situation the parents can work cooperatively with the children. Children can be raised reasonably free of injunctions and attributions. That is to say, they will not be prevented from doing things they want to do, nor will they be induced into doing things they don't want to do. They will regulate their behavior according to what they want and their desire to cooperate with what others want. Thus, if they want to do something and it is not wanted by someone else they love, they may choose not to do it of their own free will. Children will, to a large extent, conform to the wishes of their parents. They will do this out of a wish to cooperate with them because they love them rather than out of a wish to avoid punishment or to obtain reinforcement. They will not always conform to their parents' wishes and, at times, they will choose to do or not do what they, rather than their parents, want; but this will be accepted and understood by the parents as a reasonable price to pay for the fact that these children will be autonomous and self-sufficient rather than dependent, passive, and powerless.

One thing is very clear, however. In a situation of this sort, children will definitely not do things that they experience as painful, obnoxious, or holding no benefit for them. Under such circumstances, children will refuse to go to bad schools, they will refuse to follow oppressive rules, they will demand to be heard when they speak, they will ask for everything that they want 100% of the time and demand that their wishes be considered on an equal footing with the grownups in the household. Difficult as this may sound, the parents of such children have a number of rewards. First of all, they will be living not with Victims that need to be Rescued at every turn, but with fully participating human beings. They will see the results of this in the way in which children will use their capacities to the fullest extent as they express their innate wish to cooperate. When these children grow up they will be truly self-sufficient and autonomous and much more likely to fend for themselves and to do a good job of it; they will not tolerate injustice, oppression, lies, and exploitation. Finally, parents who choose this child-rearing approach will know that their children are shaping their own destinies and following their O.K. constructive nature, provided as they are with the freedom to choose and the tools to choose wisely. Children raised in this manner, because they are not subjected to long years of Rescues and Persecutions as powerless Victims, are very likely to grow up to be loving children, respectful of their parents and appreciative of what they've done for them rather than turning on them after years of sacrifice only to accuse them of in some way having harmed them. I say this with a conviction which is strengthened by my experience with my own two children, Mimi and Eric, now twelve and ten years old.

Raising children for autonomy is a project that cannot be done in isolation of a larger community which is supportive and understanding of the process. When everything in the community is decided on the basis of competitiveness, individualism, discounts, Rescues, and Persecution, it is very difficult for a specific household in that community to operate on a totally different basis. It is therefore important that people congregate in larger numbers, teach each other the principle of cooperation, start alternative schools for their children if necessary, and support each other in their struggles to achieve the good life. No one can enjoy the benefits of the above lessons while everyone else is oppressed and defeated. One person can only rise a few inches above the rest; and in order for one person to be liberated completely everyone else around him has to be traveling the same path and achieving the same benefits.

Raising Children for Autonomy: Ten Rules

1. *Do not have a child to whom you can't extend an eighteen-year guarantee of Nurturing and Protection.* Once you have the child, endeavor to shorten the years during which it needs you by allowing it to achieve autonomy as soon as it can.

2. *The principal aim of child-rearing for autonomy is to provide the child with freedom to fully exercise the*

faculties of intimacy, awareness, and spontaneity. No other goal (discipline, good manners, self-control, etc.) is put *above* autonomy, although it may be desired and pursued by the parents, but never if it contradicts the main goal: autonomy.

3. *Intimacy is defeated through the Stroke Economy.* Do not prevent children from fully and honestly expressing their love or lack of it. Do encourage them to give, ask, accept and reject strokes, and to brag.

4. *Awareness is defeated through Discounts.* Do not Discount your children's rationality, feelings, or intuition. Do teach children how to Account and do respond to their demands for accounting when addressed at you.

5. *Do not lie to your children ever*, either by omission or by commission. If you choose to hide the truth from them, say so and say why, truthfully.

6. *Spontaneity is defeated by arbitrary rules applying to the use of the body.* Do not regulate the moving, seeing, hearing, touching, smelling, tasting of children except when it clearly interferes with your own well-being or puts them in clear and present danger—and then only in a cooperative manner. Do remember that the wisdom of your child's body about itself is surpassed by yours in almost every case. Don't take the advice of "experts" (educators, physicians) too seriously either; they have been wrong before and will be again. *Never* physically assault, attack, or trespass the sanctity of your child's body. If you do, apologize, fully, immediately; but do not compound the error by proceeding to Rescue out of guilt. Take responsibility for your actions and do not repeat those that you disapprove of.

7. *Do not Rescue and then Persecute your child.* Do not do what you would prefer not to do for your children. If you do, don't compound the error by Persecuting them later. Give your child a chance to fend for itself before you "help."

8. *Do not teach children competition.* They'll learn enough of it from watching TV and reading the newspapers. Do teach them, by example, how to cooperate.

9. *Do not allow your children to oppress you.* You have the right to time, space, and a love life of your own separate from them. Demand that your needs be taken into consideration; they will do so out of love for you.

10. *Trust human nature and believe in your children.* They will reward this trust by growing up to love you for it.

27

Men's and Women's Liberation

The oppressive exaggeration of differences between men and women into banal sex role scripts described by Wyckoff in Chapter 13 has been under attack on a different front by the Women's Liberation Movement. American women are afraid of "Women's Lib" as it is called by the media. In the early phases of the Movement the press managed to make it the laughingstock of the nation by its portrayal, out of context, of the actions of some of its most radical members.

But the Women's Liberation Movement (as opposed to the media's Women's Lib) has a steadily growing following of American women, half of whom now support "organized efforts to improve women's status."[1] My experience is that when the aims of women's liberation are explained in their everyday, bread-and-butter, birds-and-bees, sex-role scripting aspects, only a minority of women disagree with it.

I am personally a committed feminist and in working for the liberation of women (mostly by not interfering with women and their work), I have come to see how men are privileged with respect to women and how they use this privilege to their advantage and to women's disadvantage. But, looking further, I also see how most men are being damaged as human beings by taking advantage of their privilege. Men need women for companionship, friendship, strokes,

[1] Staines, Graham; Jayaratne, Toby Epstein; Tavris, Carol. "The Queen Bee Syndrome." *Psychology Today* 7,8 (1974): 55–60.

love, and work partnerships; and these needs cannot be enduringly met by one-down, passive, slavish, or angry women. Being the master in a master/slave relationship takes its toll in the hardening of feelings, lovelessness, and guilt which accompany it. The Women's Liberation Movement speaks loudly and well for itself; in this chapter I wish to speak for the Liberation of Men, my brothers who stand to gain in happiness what they may lose in privilege if they join women in their struggle for freedom.

Men's interest in working against sexism has very murky and unclear motivations. Unlike the Women's Liberation Movement, which is obviously a thrust out from under and which has clearcut logic both for the mind and the gut, the men's struggle against sexism does not understand itself nearly as well.

If we participate in the movement to help women find freedom or, worse, to give it to them, then we are patronizing them and are rightly told to mind our own business. If we become a sort of one-down men's auxiliary to the women's movement, we take on a role reversal which is humiliating and unproductive. We have trouble knowing what is in it for us, though we can head-trip for hours on the subject, and we have real trouble feeling any *need* for it. We know we like women to be free, mostly because when they are free they don't hang on us and are more sexually responsible. But we don't like it so well when, once free, women look at us and say, "Buzz off brother, come back when you grow up!" or when we find that women prefer each other to us and leave us out in the cold.

So why should we struggle against sexism? Why should we give up our power to take what we want and need from women? Why should we yield our one-up to women who are often hostile to us and no longer appreciate our manhood?

I think it is useful to divide men into several types. There are male chauvinist pigs and there are male chauvinists. Male chauvinist *pigs* can be crude or subtle. Crude male chauvinist pigs know that they are male supremacists and are proud of it; they are honest bigots and Norman Mailer is their king and Bobby Riggs their court buffoon.

Subtle male chauvinist pigs usually give lip-service to the women's liberation movement with respect, say, to wages, especially if they are not employers. But they also make a point of calling women "girls" once in a while, always with a grin on their face, and of drawing women into debates in which they will rib them about "women's lib." Because they mystify their chauvinism they are even more oppressive than their crude brothers. Either way, whether crude or subtle, male chauvinist pigs hang on to their privilege as men and get the best of it while the getting is good. A man who wants to shed his pig status can do it by being concerned with and admitting to the facts of his and other men's oppression of women and deciding to earnestly struggle against it.

All of us have undergone thorough training in male supremacy from the day we were born, and it is not very likely that any of us, our most militant sisters included, have escaped or undone the indoctrination completely. The problem with most (51% or more) men is not that they are chauvinist *pigs* since they are willing, as sincerely as they know how, to struggle against their chauvinism and give up their male privilege. Rather, most men are unaware of their chauvinism and where it has its impact, and also unaware of how they would benefit by ridding themselves of it.

I feel that we men have difficulty seeing this struggle as a struggle for our own freedom. We don't feel oppressed, even if we know we are; we are not only being robbed of our freedom, but robbed of our awareness of the robbery and being given the illusion that we benefit from it. Our mystification is buttressed by the petty (wearing the pants, sitting at the head of the table) privileges that accompany our oppressed lives. While we have no awareness of what we would gain in the way of well-being when we overthrow our chauvinism, we very clearly see what we would have to give up in the way of privileges: the privilege of first and last choice, our one-up to women.

So what is in it for us? How does one explain a brotherly glance to the blind? How does one translate the sounds of love-making to the deaf? One hopes that words will suffice; that they will evoke from the forgotten memories of childhood and occasional accidents of freedom the understanding, however misty, of what liberation can mean to a man, of what the reclaiming of our full human potential signifies for us.

Does freedom to love fully without fear of being trapped strike a cord? Does ease and comfort without backbreaking, life-shortening work, ring a bell? Does full awareness of love, hate, fear, joy without shame sound good to you? Does relating to a woman as an equal partner in a cooperative relationship in which you get as much as you give turn you on? Would you like *not* having to take care of every problem that comes up? Can you dig giggling, tears streaming down your cheeks, trembling loins? Would you enjoy the weight on your shoulders being lifted? Would you like to rage without fear of hurting or killing, or the freedom to feel all your power without oppressing anyone with it? Can you dig it, brother?

I assume that I am not speaking to anyone so crude in his chauvinism that he still has beliefs such as that women are *by their nature* unable to think as logically as men; or are inherently more emotional and therefore more unstable than men, or more likely to be satisfied doing domestic chores than men; happy only when being dependent and submissive while raising children and "making a home." If you fit into this category we live in different worlds; we must part company in this chapter.

Our real problem lies in subtle chauvinism. Subtle chauvinism is usually held by a man or a woman who believes in the equality of the sexes but who, nevertheless, in many subtle ways, acts in a manner which systematically oppresses the woman.

Men who are subtle chauvinists usually believe in the liberation of women. Often a woman who is in a relationship with such a man is puzzled by the fact that, even though he protests that he is in favor of her liberation and gives effusive lip-service to it, he ultimately and irrevocably winds up in a one-up rather than equal position with respect to her. How and why does this happen?

Sex Role Oppression

None of us are given the choice to develop fully, and there are a number of human capacities which are badly diminished in men due specifically to sex role training or scripting. A lesser number of different capacities are equally taken away from women.

When human beings are born they are divided into two groups. One group is told: "When you grow up you will be a girl. A good woman should be a very nurturing, supportive person; so much so that every time someone in her family needs something, she can provide it. In order to be truly good at it, it is useful for her to be very intuitive and capable of reading people's minds so that if a person around her needs something, it would be ideal, especially if it's a man, if she could figure it out before he even said anything. Since your major task will be to be nurturing, you won't need to be very rational; you don't need rationality in order to be supportive and nurturing; in fact, rationality might interfere with nurturing. It is best not to try to understand certain things."

By contrast, children of the male sex are told: "When you grow up you will be a man. A good man should be able to work hard at making things. He must be able to think clearly and logically and understand the laws of nature since his main task is to solve problems, especially problems related to power and its accumulation. On the other hand, the function of being tuned-in and sensitive to yourself or other human beings is one that you should not make use of, because it is difficult to think logically when you are aware of how you or other people feel. The accumulation of power will be interfered with if you become aware of the emotions of the people with whom you are dealing, nor will it be valuable or advisable for you to be nurturing since, once again, the world of men and power does not allow for the considerations of needs and emotions. Leave emotionality and sensitivity to women; they are better at it than you."

These banal script injunctions and attributions insure that women will apply their energies to nurture men while men will apply their energies to external reality and the accumulation of power. Men and women are alienated from their full human potential by the oppression of these various functions and the justification of this oppression under the guise of "proper" masculinity and femininity.

As has been pointed out by Wyckoff (see Chapter 13), men's scripted incapacity for being loving prevents the equitable exchange of strokes, thus creating a stroke deficit for women in the long run.

On the other hand, men's training in the uses of power makes it easier for them to get what they want in the world than it is for women. And it makes it easier for men to get what they want from women than for women to get what they want from men.

The above two inequities express themselves in the relationships between men and women in subtle but powerfully erosive ways which ultimately defeat *at least* every other serious effort at heterosexual relationships.

Thus, to rectify the distorting effect of sexist scripting, men need to work on two areas:

1. Men need to learn to be loving. This is done by developing intuition and nurturing.
2. Men need to learn to use their power without abusing it. This is done by learning to be cooperative and by giving up competitiveness and individualism.

The reclaiming of the human potentialities that men are oppressed away from is an arduous process which requires energy and struggle. The process is similar to teaching Johnny how to read. Children, if left alone in a literate world, will learn to read, quite easily and without difficulty. The same process applies to men relearning their human potentialities.

The capacity to love is dependent on possessing the two interrelated faculties of nurturance and intuition.

Intuition is essentially the capacity of human beings to know others, especially to be able to read their emotional states. Only a person who is sufficiently tuned in to other people's emotional states and can sense them without there being a need for elaborate explanations can be in a position of applying the nurturing which is appropriate. The capacity to be nurturing is dependent on the capacity of knowing what others feel. Reclaiming one cannot happen without the reclamation of the other.

Men's Trust Circle

Eight men stand in a circle. Jack steps into the center, closes his eyes, and moves toward the periphery. He is stiff, smiles bravely until he bumps into one of the men in the periphery, then flinches. He turns around and starts another tentative walk through the circle. When he reaches the center, Fred says:

"You look scared. . . . Are you?" Jack answers quickly, "No!"

Silence follows. Jack asks, "Am I scared? I feel something strange."

"You look scared," says John.

"I guess I am."

"What of?"

"I am afraid someone is going to trip me. I know it's silly."

Ed says: "Nobody would trip you here. I promise you. Don't worry."

Jack keeps walking, bumps into Ed. Ed gives him a hug. "Don't worry, brother. . . ."

The Trust Circle is a good exercise for men. Jack learns to recognize his fear, shame, distrust, and to express it. Ed, John, Fred learn to read Jack's mind; they learn to intuit how he feels and to be supportive and nurturing. Nurturing helps Jack trust the others with his feelings and safety.

The process whereby we teach intuition is called *feelback* and is quite similar to the process of bio-feedback in which a person is capable of getting in touch with and controlling involuntary, unconscious bodily states through a feedback mechanism which monitors these states. In this case, instead of having a device which provides the feedback, one has the other person who either confirms or disconfirms whatever intuition happens to be. Obviously, this process requires that everyone in the context be open and willing to expose her or his feeling states to others so as to make feelback possible. Jack has to be willing to be honest; the others have to instill enough trust in him to make it safe to be honest.

Men's Great Curses: Responsibility and Guilt

Not only are men unskilled in reading people, but they also respond with guilt when in the presence of other people's emotional states, especially women's. This guilt is based on a very strongly scripted tendency to feel responsibility for other people, to Rescue them rather than let them take care of themselves.

Example: A man and a woman meet at the park. Their innermost wishes are quite similar to each other's. They both want to hold hands, run in the grass, stroke each other's hair, touch each other's skin, and talk about themselves to each other. Were they acting freely, they would proceed to do so and continue until one or the other decided to stop, and then their relationship would either change or end. However, the usual course of events is quite different. From the man's vantage point, the simple response of reaching for her hand while looking into her eyes and stroking her hair is immediately censored and replaced with a guilty response. The average male will feel guilt with respect to having such a carnal, animal desire. He tells himself he should want to know the woman better before he touches her; he should take her to the movies and out for dinner and give her something before she gives him access to the physical strokes that he wants. Or, his reaction to the spontaneous wish to touch and relate physically to the woman is that it is sexist and objectionable; that it turns the woman into a sexual object that he can only relate to physically. He therefore squelches his initial free *sensual* response and replaces it with a "more acceptable" response which allays his guilt. If she really likes him and expresses love, tenderness, expectation, or disappointment he often panics. Suddenly he is in a position of responsibility. He *has* to love her back or satisfy her in all her needs. If he doesn't he feels guilty. Most probably he will adapt and wind up Guilty and Trapped.[1]

Men's reaction to guilt is a retreat from those feelings and emotions that cause the guilt into a passive intellectual pursuit which makes use of their most developed capacity, the capacity of Rationality. A man who has squelched his true feelings because of guilt is prone to engage in a head-trip about what he is supposed to want. He may feel that he is supposed to want to appreciate the woman's mind instead of her body. Or perhaps he is supposed to want to marry her. Or he is supposed to be sensitive; he is supposed to "struggle" with his chauvinism. He proceeds to do so in his head by thinking about it, talking about it, and doing things which he sees as discharging his obligations so that he can escape guilt.

The outcome of this process is usually disastrous. The natural, sensual reaction of both persons is denied even though it might have led to the very thing that they both want. The woman's wishes are, usually, a deepening and enriching of the relationship in which not only her most superficially attractive aspects are appreciated, but also all of the succeeding layers of her personality which a continuing relationship will uncover. The man's wishes are a relationship in which he can act freely without having to fear being trapped. Instead, the man does things which he is *supposed* to do, but which he doesn't want to do, which create resentment and often generate a series of lies which escalate the guilt even further. As a consequence,

---

[1]DeGolia, Rick. "Thoughts on Men's Oppression." *Issues in Radical Therapy* I,3 (1973): 14.

the development of their relationship is interfered with and destroyed, and its future potential nipped in the bud. Resentment builds because the man is not doing what he wants to do, but doing what he doesn't want to do, and feeling a responsibility to continue doing it, while the woman becomes disappointed and increasingly mystified. He continues to adapt; he continues to be out of touch with what he really wants, and feels more and more guilt about his true feelings. The end result is that after a certain period of time he suddenly breaks away from the relationship, fleeing what has become an unfulfilling and intolerable situation.

These developments do not occur in a vacuum, however. Women have a complementary set of responses which encourage and maintain the male guilty response. In many cases women agree with men that their initial physical interest in them is one that is inappropriate and deserving of guilt. They often feel the need for guarantees that "he wants more than sex," that "he will marry me," or "take care of me." Yet a growing number of women who have no such expectations find with exasperation that even though they would be willing and eager to hold hands and tumble through the grass and will even say so, men cling to their guilty responses and "don't come across."

Guilt is a response taught human beings by their parents in the service of oppression. Guilt prevents children from striving for the things that they want but which their parents do not want them to have.

When boys grow up into men they are expected to get married and create a family. Ours is a society that thrives on working men, exploited labor. It is important that men be neatly trapped into a relationship with a woman and their children in an isolated house or apartment. In that setting they can best work hard for their employers for eight full hours daily. After work it takes eight further hours to wind down so that they can sleep eight hours and then go on to work again. In order for a man to be optimally exploited in his labor he must live with a woman who, on his eight hours of off-work time, re-supplies him with energy. He spends all day making cars, and when he comes home, his wife plugs in, fills him up with strokes and nurturing, then they both sleep (preferably without using up any sexual energy), and he is a much more effective source of labor than a man who is single and alone. So men are instilled with the sense of an obligation to allow themselves to be trapped in a relationship with a woman in order to be exploited by their employers. Guilt is intensely felt by men who attempt to break out of this pattern by refusing to get married or have children.

The liberation of men from sexism usually follows a certain pattern. Guilt is the first overt manifestation in men of their resolve to fight their chauvinism. Guilt is usually followed by passivity, a sucking in of energy and power in an attempt to become less of an oppressive force. This passivity which men tend to assume as a stance when they begin to feel guilt over their chauvinism is an improvement over the active oppression of a *"macho"* man, but it is only the beginning of the process. Men in this passive phase completely neutralize their energy, turning it inward, and not knowing what to do with it. They become scared, defensive, cagey, unspontaneous; but do not necessarily give up their one-up position which now is bolstered by subtle (rather than crude) power plays to maintain the status quo. A man in this passive phase, which is often laced with a little boys' game of "All or Nothing at All," can become lusterless and ineffectual while he holds to a heavily intellectualized, head-trippy illusion that he has effectively coped with his chauvinism—when he has, in fact, only begun the long road to his liberation.

Potency is often, but mistakenly, mixed up with *machismo*. This has caused many men to confuse their strength, energy and potency with *machismo*. *Machismo* is the use of physical energy in a manner that is oppressive to women and other human beings. But energy or power does not need to be oppressive, and when properly used it is a good human quality. Women want to have energy and power, too. Struggling men's response to the attacks of women should not be withdrawal into passivity but learning to use their power without oppressing people with it.

The phase in which men pull in their power, necessary as it is, needs to be followed by a rebirth of power free of power plays, crude or subtle, and free of stereotyped masculine roles: human power based on the full exercise of *all* of the human faculties—Nurturing, Rationality, Intuition, and Spontaneity. Cooperation is the antithesis of the abusive use of power; and in learning how to cooperate rather than compete men are able to once again enjoy the full expression of their energy and assertiveness, only this time without the burden of guilt.

Liberated Relationships and Life Styles

Men and women can live their lives separately and with each other as autonomous, cooperative, equal individuals. Women can pursue careers without becoming "Queen Bees" who shut out female competition, or they can be mothers of a crew living in a large house with many rooms and a big kitchen full of cupboards without turning into overweight "Mother Hubbards."

Men can be bachelors relating to several women in a warm, affectionate, ongoing, caring way without being "Playboys," or they can be married and have many children whom they support without being a one-up tyrannical "Big Daddy." Men can live to be ninety-nine years old and women can be beautiful as long as they live. Women can be athletes and surgeons and men can be nurses and homemakers. Men can find their life's love with other men and women with other women without having to hide in dark closets for fear of being discovered. People can live alone, with another loved one (see Wyckoff's "Rules for Liberated Relationships"[1]), or with many in a cooperative commune; people can be homosexual, bisexual,

---

[1] Wyckoff, Hogie. "Between Women and Men." *Issues in Radical Therapy* I,2 (1973): 11–15.

or heterosexual. Human needs can be fulfilled in many ways that avoid the banal alternatives which we are handed to choose from. Fulfillment may mean struggle—but the Good Life is worth fighting for.

In this book I have promoted a number of human ideals which I consider valid alternatives to banal oppressive life styles, and I would now like to list them all at once:

Equality (I'm O.K., you're O.K.)

Autonomy (choices rather than scripts)

Truthfulness (rather than lies, secrets, and games)

Cooperation (rather than competition and power plays)

Love (a plenitude of strokes, rather than a controlled stroke economy)

28

After Scripts, What?

Over the ages, every newborn cave-age child has smiled expectantly at its "civilized" parents. From generation to generation, humanity has a brand-new chance for self-fulfillment. Fulfillment may take some time, but our day *will* come. The newborn is enormously adaptable and is capable of surviving the chambers of horrors of its most sadistic fellow humans.

Human potential is as infinite as human adaptability. Each generation of parents has the option to oppress its offspring with age-old curses, or to protect its children's spontaneity, encourage their awareness, and respond to their intimate needs that they may reach their full potential. Pushing through to the surface, people's basic nature is like a perennial virgin spring, ever ready to feed life with its sweet waters.

Intimacy, awareness, and spontaneity are innately human and, even if crushed, will re-emerge again and again within each succeeding generation.

Graciously, Mother Nature in this way guarantees ever renewed hope for humanity; without hope for the whole human race there can be no hope for individual members of it.

Bibliography

Aldebaron, Mayer. "Fat Liberation." *Issues in Radical Therapy* I,3 (1973):3–6.

Allen, Brian. "Liberating the Manchild." *Transactional Analysis Journal* II,2 (1972): 68–71.

American Psychiatric Association. *Diagnostic and Statistical Manual, Mental Disorders,* 2d ed. American Psychiatric Association Mental Hospital Service, 1968.

Aristotle. *Poetics.* New York: The Modern Library, 1954.

Berne, Eric. "Away from the Impact of Interpersonal Interaction or Non-Verbal Participation." *Transactional Analysis Journal* I,1 (1971):6–13.

——. *Games People Play.* New York: Grove Press, 1964.

——. "Intuition v. the Ego Image." *Psychiatric Quarterly* 31 (1957):611–27.

——. *Sex in Human Loving.* New York: Simon and Schuster, 1971.

——. "Staff-Patient Staff Conferences." *American Journal of Psychiatry* 125 (1968): 286–93.

——. *Transactional Analysis in Psychotherapy.* New York: Grove Press, 1961.

——. *What Do You Say After You Say Hello?* New York: Grove Press, 1972.

Bernstein, E. Lennard (Berne, Eric). "Who Was Condom?" *Human Fertility* 5,6 (1940): 72–76.

Cameron, Norman. "Paranoid Conditions and Paranoia." In *American Handbook of Psychiatry,* edited by Silvano Arieti. New York: Basic Books, 1959.

Capers, Hedges, and Holland, Glen. "Stroke Survival Quotient." *Transactional Analysis Journal* I,3 (1971):40.

Comfort, Alex, ed. *The Joy of Sex.* New York: Crown Publishers, 1972.

Crossman, Patricia. "Permission and Protection." *Transactional Analysis Bulletin* 5,19 (1966):152–53.

DeGolia, Rick. "Thoughts on Men's Oppression." *Issues in Radical Therapy* I,3 (1973):14.

Dusay, John M. "Ego Games and the Constancy Hypothesis." *Transactional Analysis Journal* II,3 (1972):37–41.

——. "Eric Berne's Studies in Intuition." *Transactional Analysis Journal* I, 1 (1971):34–45.

Ellis, Albert. *Reason and Emotion in Psychotherapy.* New York: Lyle Stuart, 1962.

English, Fanita. "Episcript and the 'Hot Potato' Game." *Transactional Analysis Bulletin* 8 (1969):77-82.

——. "Sleepy, Spunky and Spooky." *Transactional Analysis Journal* II,2 (1972):64–67.

——. "Strokes in the Credit Bank for David Kupfer." *Transactional Analysis Journal* I,3 (1971):27–29.

Erikson, Erik H. *Identity: Youth and Crisis.* New York: W. W. Norton, 1968.

Frank, Jerome D. "The Role of Hope in Psychotherapy." *International Journal of Psychiatry* 5 (1968):383–95.

Freud, Sigmund. *The Interpretation of Dreams.* In *The Basic Writings.* New York: The Modern Library, 1938.

——. *New Introductory Lectures on Psychoanalysis.* New York: W. W. Norton, 1933.

Frumker, Sanford C. "Hamartia: Aristotle's Meaning of the Word & Its Relation to Tragic Scripts." *Transactional Analysis Journal* III,1 (1973):29–30.

Goldstein, Arnold P. *Therapist-Patient Expectations in Psychotherapy.* New York: Pergamon Press, 1962.

Greenspoon, Joel. "Verbal Conditioning and Clinical Psychology." In *Experimental Foundations of Clinical Psychology,* edited by A. J. Bachrach. New York: Basic Books, 1962.

Harris, Thomas A. *I'm OK—You're OK.* New York: Harper & Row, 1969.

Hartmann, Heinz. "Ego Psychology and the Problem of Adaptation." In *Organization and Pathology of Thought,* edited by D. Rapaport. New York: Columbia University Press, 1951.

Karpman, Stephen B. "Fingograms." *Transactional Analysis Journal* III,4 (1973):30–33.

——. "Script Drama Analysis." *Transactional Analysis Bulletin* 7,26 (1968):39–43.

Kerr, Carmen. "Teaching Psychology to High School Misfits." *Issues in Radical Therapy* I,3 (1973): 24–25.

Laing, Ronald D. *The Divided Self.* New York: Pantheon, 1969.

——. *Knots.* New York: Vintage Books, 1970.

——. *The Politics of the Family and Other Essays.* New York: Pantheon Books, 1971.

Lucas, F. L. *Tragedy, Serious Drama in Relation to Aristotle's Poetics.* London: Hogarth Press, 1971.

Marcus, Joy. "Intimacy." *Issues in Radical Therapy* I,3 (1973): 18–19.

Marcuse, Herbert. *Eros and Civilization.* New York: Vintage Books, 1962.

Mariner, Allen S. "A Critical Look at Professional Education in the Mental Health Field." *American Psychologist* 22:4 (1967):271–80.

Menninger, Karl. *Theory of Psychoanalytic Technique.* New York: Basic Books, 1958.

Merton, Robert K., *Social Theory and Social Structure.* Glencoe, Illinois: The Free Press, 1957.

Nelson, Linden L., and Kagan, Spencer. "Competition: The Star-Spangled Scramble." *Psychology Today* 6,4 (1972): 53–57.

Perls, Fritz S. *Gestalt Therapy Verbatim.* Lafayette, California: Real People Press, 1969.

Piaget, Jean. *Logic and Psychology.* New York: Basic Books, 1957.

Reich, Wilhelm. *The Function of the Orgasm.* New York: Farrar Straus and Giroux, 1961.

——. *The Sexual Revolution.* New York: Noonday Press, 1962.

Samuels, Solon D. "Stroke Strategy: I. The Basis of Therapy." *Transactional Analysis Journal* I,3 (1971):23–24.

Schiff, Aaron Wolfe, and Schiff, Jacqui Lee. "Passivity." *Transactional Analysis Journal* I,1 (1971):71–78.

Sophocles. *The Oedipus Cycle.* New York: Harcourt Brace and World, 1949.

Spitz, Rene. "Hospitalism, Genesis of Psychiatric Conditions in Early Childhood." Psychoanalytic Study of the Child 1 (1945): 53–74.

Staines, Graham; Jayaratne, Toby Epstein; and Tavris, Carol. "The Queen Bee Syndrome." *Psychology Today* 7,8 (1974): 55–60.

Stedman, Thomas L. *Stedman's Medical Dictionary,* 20th ed. Baltimore: Williams and Wilkins, 1962.

Steiner, Claude M. *Games Alcoholics Play.* New York: Grove Press, 1971.

——. "Inside TA." *Issues in Radical Therapy* I,2 (1973):3–4.

——. "Radical Psychiatry." In *Going Crazy,* edited by Hendrik M. Ruitenbeek, New York: Bantam Books, 1972.

——. "Radical Psychiatry: Principles." *The Radical Therapist* 2,3 (1971):3. Reprinted in *Readings in Radical Psychotherapy,* edited by Joy Marcus, Claude Steiner, and Hogie Wyckoff. New York: Grove Press, 1974.

——. "A Script Checklist." *Transactional Analysis Bulletin,* 6,22 (1964):38–39.

——. *TA Made Simple.* Berkeley, California: TA/Simple, 1973.

—— and Steiner, Ursula. "Permission Classes." *Transactional Analysis Bulletin* 7,28 (1968):89.

Szasz, Thomas S. *The Myth of Mental Illness: Foundations of a Theory of Personal Conduct.* New York: Hoeber-Harper, 1961.

Vance, Dot. "Reclaiming Our Birthright." *The Radical Therapist* 2,3 (1971):21.

White, Jerome D., and White, Terri. *Self-Fulfilling Prophecies in the Inner City.* Chicago: Illinois Institute of Applied Psychology, 1970.

Wise, David. *The Politics of Lying: Government, Deception, Secrecy and Power.* New York: Random House, 1973.

Wyckoff, Hogie. "Amazon Power Workshop." *Issues in Radical Therapy* I,4 (1973):14–15.

——. "Between Women and Men." *Issues in Radical Therapy* I,2 (1973):11–15.

——. "Permission." *The Radical Therapist* 2,3 (1971):8–10. Reprinted in *Readings in Radical Psychotherapy,* edited by Joy Marcus, Claude Steiner, and Hogie Wyckoff. New York: Grove Press, 1974.

——. "Problem-Solving Groups for Women." *Issues in Radical Therapy* I, 1 (1973): 6–12.

——. "The Stroke Economy in Women's Scripts," *Transactional Analysis Journal* I,3 (1971):16–20.

Zechnick, Robert. "Social Rapo—Description and Cure." *Transactional Analysis Journal* III,4 (1973):18–21.

Index

Games, Scripts and Archetypes

Subject Index

Authors and Therapists

ABOUT THE AUTHOR

CLAUDE M. STEINER, a West Coast clinical psychologist, was a close collaborator of Eric Berne in the development of transactional analysis. His previous book, *Games Alcoholics Play*, was published in 1971. He is at present associated with a group of Radical Therapists in Berkeley who publish the journal, *Issues in Radical Therapy*.

Bantam
On Psychology